Modelling the World

For my parents

Modelling the World

The Social Constructions of
Systems Analysts

BRIAN P. BLOOMFIELD

Basil Blackwell

First published 1986

Basil Blackwell Ltd
108 Cowley Road, Oxford OX4 1JF, UK

Basil Blackwell Inc.
432 Park Avenue South, Suite 1503,
New York, NY 10016, USA

British Library Cataloguing in Publication Data
Bloomfield, Brian P.
　　Modelling the world: the social constructions
　　of systems analysts.
　　1. system analysis
　　I. Title
　　003　　　QA402
　　ISBN 0–631–14163–4

Library of Congress Cataloging in Publication Data
Bloomfield, Brian P.
　　Modelling the world.

　　Bibliography: p.
　　Includes index.
　　1. Social systems — Mathematical models.
2. System analysis.　I. Title.
HM131.B595　　　1986　　　301'.028'51　　　86–1047
ISBN 0–631–14163–4

Typeset by Oxford Publishing Services, Oxford
Printed in Great Britain by T J Press Ltd., Padstow, Cornwall

Contents

Preface

Throughout history different groups of savants have come forward to announce a special message to the world, to prophesy some form of imminent disaster or calamity. Claiming unique insights into the nature of things, they have not only proffered explanations of how the world works, and therefore the reasons for impending doom, but have, at the same time, offered redemption in the shape of an alternative society which would bring certainty and order. These alternatives have ranged from millenarian utopias – including divine interventions accompanied by fire and brimstone – to totalitarian dystopias.

In modern times too we have our prophets – the world modellers. Unlike those of earlier periods, these do not 'cast runes' or perform calculations with astrological charts, nor do they examine the entrails of animals: rather, their predictions stem from the use of computers. Employing the tools and techniques of systems analysis and computer simulation, they have sought to model the world – and in one form or another they have attempted to forecast the future. In other words, although the world modellers share – along with forecasters of earlier times – a similar curiosity about revealing the course of future events, their methods could not be more dissimilar, and their endeavours – in certain quarters at least – appear to be legitimated by their very association with the traditions, successes, and tools of science and technology.

This book is devoted to a case study of one particular group of such world modellers – namely, the System Dynamics Group at the Massachusetts Institute of Technology (MIT) in the United States. The members of this group are among one of the foremost scientific/ technological elites in the world. Indeed, their founder – Jay W. Forrester – has a considerable reputation for achievement and invention in the fields of systems engineering and digital computers. The System Dynamics Group is most famous (some would say infamous) for the world models

(WORLD 2 and WORLD 3) which were built in the early 1970s; these looked at the Earth as a closed global ecosystem and from the computer simulations it was concluded that the world was facing a catastrophic collapse in its life-support systems. Depicting scenarios of mass starvation, the exhaustion of natural resources, global asphyxiation, and over population, the simulations opened a window on a nightmarish future. As an alternative to catastrophe the MIT modellers offered a global equilibrium society where growth in population and industrialization would be halted; a world of harmony between man and nature. The ensuing message was broadcast throughout the world and captured much attention, particularly within Western societies, and the debate which it stimulated still continues in many circles.

These world models were only two among a family of models which had been built upon the principles of *system dynamics*. Basically, the system dynamics approach involves the building of a computer simulation model to describe the behaviour of any particular system under study, followed by experimentation with the model in order to derive suitable policy options for modifying the behaviour of the 'real' system. Rather than viewing the system dynamics method narrowly, as a mere *technique*, here I will consider it in the same spirit as its chief exponents – i.e. as a systems philosophy: for system dynamics embodies a theory about the nature of complex feedback systems. This theory suggests that people live in a network of feedback structures (incorporating economic, political, and ecological subsystems) whose properties determine many of the problems – from famine to overcrowding, from inflation and unemployment to ecological collapse – which have caused much public concern over the past two decades. System dynamicists claim to be able to explain the causes of these problems and provide policies to remedy them.

System dynamics was originally developed within the Sloan School of Management at MIT during the 1950s, and its intellectual roots stem from systems engineering, feedback control, and the design of technological systems. Having achieved considerable success with such applications, systems engineering was later generalized to become a tool for the design and control of social systems, i.e. social engineering. It was thought that it could bring a more rigorous and objective approach to policy formation. Through successive phases – from industrial and then urban systems, through to the global system – it was expanded to become a *general systems theory* for the management and control of all complex feedback systems. As a general systems theory, it was assumed that the properties of any system, whether technical or social, could be explained on the basis of the same fundamental principles common to all feedback structures.

The justification for analysing system dynamics lies not only in its alleged efficacy in understanding societal problems which are of considerable importance in themselves, but also in the fact that its proponents claim that it offers a new and better approach to studying such problems. The system dynamicists actually envisage a reorientation of the social sciences towards a concentration on the feedback structures of social systems – which are argued to be a necessary basis for comprehending the behaviour modes of such systems. Further, they suggest that the human brain is not adapted to understanding the properties of complex systems – where many variables interact through time – and conclude that computers should be employed to aid in this task. Though the human brain may correctly perceive the structure of a complex system, they contend that it cannot predict how that structure will behave dynamically. The system dynamicists therefore envisage the spread of system dynamics into all levels of education. They also advocate the education of the electorate in order that people might better appreciate the dynamic properties of social systems and thereby make more 'informed' choices when voting for policies.

This background underscores the desirability of developing a comprehensive understanding of the origins and development of system dynamics; but how should such an investigation proceed? To answer this question it is worth referring to previous studies of system dynamics and pointing out how this inquiry must improve on them. In fact, many of the previous studies have been technical ones, in the sense that they have tended to address the mathematical aspects of system dynamics models, or the problems associated with the empirical data which have been used in their construction.[1] In contrast, as already indicated, it is my contention that system dynamics is not merely a modelling tool or technique, but is – as the system dynamicists themselves claim – a theory of the behaviour of social systems. It is really better viewed as a type of social theory (not in the mode traditionally found in, say, sociology – stemming as it does from an engineering tradition) which is explicitly designed for large-scale social engineering.

Other critics have concentrated on the ideological content of specific models which some have seen as a reflection of the interests of multinational corporations or of the 'bourgeois' social class.[2] Further, to a number of writers systems analysis appears as a symbol of the technocratic consciousness which is often identified with modern bureaucratic capitalism. Technocratic rationality reduces social and political problems to technical and administrative ones. With system dynamics I will show that while it too has tended towards the apolitical or suprapolitical conception of social problems, it has sometimes perceived them as moral ones and has not narrowly sought recourse to technical or administrative solutions. Quite the contrary, in fact, for we can discern an emphasis upon individual morality and the necessity for preserving long-term value structures. These elements can neither be explained in relation to the engineering origins of system dynamics, nor solely in terms of technocratic rationality, and indicate the need for more comprehensive tools for understanding its relationship to the prevailing cultural context in which it evolved.

My intention, therefore, is not to repeat previous lines of criticism but to take a lead from recent research in the sociological study of scientific knowledge and seek to throw some new light on system dynamics. I am not primarily interested in the truth or falsity of the propositions of system dynamics but rather in its status as a socially constructed body of knowledge. I aim to unravel the interconnections between this construction and the culture which nurtured it in order to seek some insights into how this systems view of the world has been generated. The thrust of the argument will employ anthropological and sociological ideas as tools to this end. For instance, some anthropologists tell us that reality is always a social construction, that our conceptions of the social and natural worlds are mediated by social relations. However, in contrast to the position adopted by those scholars who argue that the intrusion of social factors into the production of knowledge leads to error or falsity, the notion that reality is socially constructed does not imply judgements about the validity of our socially produced knowledge. Rather, it aims to make explicit the existential conditions which underpin the ways in which we think about the world, and indeed, which make knowledge possible.

This investigation actually falls between two intellectual camps or communities. On the one hand there is the sociology of scientific knowledge, and on the other the systems movement: it draws upon the former in order to provide an interpretation of the development of one specific branch of the latter. While aiming to adhere to the standards of the sociology of science, I will none the less attempt to pursue the investigation with a broad vision – broader than the confines suggested by any single approach or discipline – and seek to offer multiple perspectives on the subject matter. This will require that I tread in speculative areas but is justified by the complexity of the phenomena involved.

I do not propose, therefore, to examine specific models in isolation, but will endeavour to view system dynamics in much broader terms, to understand its cultural origins and the social influences which have shaped it as it has developed through application to different problems. In addition to this line of inquiry, I also wish to investigate the cultural or social role of system dynamics. More specifically, I will consider how system dynamics reacts back on to society; this will require that I address questions as to the social ramifications of the policy recommendations, and – in the case of the world models – the social and psychological impact on their audience.

My objectives are as follows. First, to elucidate the cultural tradition from which system dynamics emerged and the macro-social factors which shaped its extension into different domains. Second, to uncover the relationship between the micro-social environment which united the system dynamicists as a social group (that is, their shared social experience), and the intellectual style and content of system dynamics. Third, I want to understand the exoteric role of system dynamics in mediating and reinforcing external social structures – ranging from the legitimation of social policies in urban systems, to the assimilation of the ideas underpinning the system dynamics world models within a plethora of alternative visions of future society (e.g. from technocratic ideas of world government to utopian ideas of small-scale alternative communities).

The body of this book consists of three parts. Part One discusses the historical background to system dynamics, including the career of its inventor – J. W. Forrester. I will refer to the intellectual and practical foundations from which system dynamics developed, as well as the main features in the expansion of its domain of applications and theoretical core. It will also provide the theoretical groundwork for the approach adopted in this investigation, and more specifically, for the structure of the argument which is pursued in the subsequent parts.

In Part Two I will begin the analysis by looking at a dynamic general model of the relationship between worldviews and social structures. The aim will be to locate system dynamics within a cultural tradition; I will concentrate on Forrester in order to understand the relationship between his cultural background and his outlook, values, and theoretical beliefs. As part of this task I will draw an analogy between system dynamics and the social theory of Talcott Parsons – namely, structural-functionalism. This will establish that – as with Parsons – Forrester's worldview was oriented towards a traditional middle-class concern (social interest) with the preservation of social order, and was similarly committed to society's dominant institutions and values. The analysis will be conducted in dynamic rather than in static terms, leading to the consideration of the evolution of system dynamics in respect of social developments – particularly the urban and environmental crises – within American society. I will argue that it was originally devised in the spirit of furthering American dominance – both economic and political – in the world system, but was later expanded to address the issues of urban decline and environmental degradation. I will show that – in the face of such problems – the aim was primarily to maintain social order, and to do so without challenging society's dominant institutions such as capitalism, and the distribution of wealth. The expansion to each new domain entailed various theoretical shifts and extensions of the theoretical content of system dynamics, and I will examine these in relation to the specific threats to social order to which they were a response. Although I will trace the relationship between the development of system dynamics and Forrester's social interests, the dynamic orientation will also allow consideration of changes in interpretation of his interests. This is particularly important in view of Forrester's shifting perspective on capitalism – wherein he (and the other system dynamicists) came to expound the thesis that industrial growth must be halted.

Having looked at the broader cultural tradition from which system dynamics has emerged and developed, attention will then turn to the pattern of social relations which united the system dynamicists within the System Dynamics Group at MIT during the late 1960s and early 1970s. I will employ the anthropological concept of cosmology in order to obtain a more specific picture of the system dynamicists' view of the world and style of thought. In particular, I will employ Mary Douglas's grid/group theory which offers a typology of social structures and the corresponding cosmologies that mediate and reinforce them. In operationalizing these concepts I will undertake a comparative analysis between the System Dynamics Group and a selected control group – namely, the Science Policy Research Unit, at the University of Sussex. The comparison will include their respective social experiences, thought styles (considered in terms of methodological orientation, including the response to theoretical anomalies), and beliefs about knowledge, nature, man and society, and time.

In Part Three the task will be to examine the cultural roles of system dynamics and its exponents. For not only were policies put forward for the control and management of social systems, but the system dynamicists also sought to carve out a special niche for themselves as experts needed to build and interpret the requisite computer models. I will investigate the ways in which the system dynamicists aimed to re-structure social relations within the particular systems to which the theory has been applied, and the means by which they claimed legitimacy in their proposed task. This discussion will centre mainly upon the urban-modelling work but its implications are pertinent to system dynamics as a whole, and perhaps even to other uses of expertise in policymaking. The main questions I focus on concern the type of urban structure which was advocated in Forrester's urban policies; the role of system dynamicists in relation to politicians and the electorate; and the way in which system dynamics provided an explanatory resource for structuring the problems of urban decline.

The use of system dynamics for the design of social policy raises the question of the negotiation of social consensus and the reasons why it may be seen as legitimate – both to the electorate and to the politicians and administrators who would be responsible for implementing the policies. Given the predominantly technological orientation of its cultural setting – the United States – its legitimacy might seem unproblematical. For example, one cultural observer has described American society as a 'culture centering its interests upon purposive technical mastery of its physical environment (and to some degree, of its social problems also) . . . [in which] emphasis upon efficiency is obviously related to the high place accorded science (especially as translated into technology) and to the overwhelming importance attributed to practicality' (Williams, 1960: 401). While this has certainly been one dimension of the appeal of system dynamics, it must also be noted that when the system dynamicists addressed the problems of potential environmental collapse they eschewed technological fixes and talked of harmony with nature. This indicates that its sources of legitimacy were not solely rooted in images of technical rationality and I will discuss the cosmological elements – the symbols and metaphors pertaining to the ultimate nature of the world or cosmos – which permeated the system dynamics policy recommendations and gave them moral import.

Then I will turn my attention to focus on the apocalyptic message of the world models and will construct an argument about the personal effects on its audience. This will include the role of the models in explaining the world and endowing it with meaning and coherence, as well as the way in which they symbolized the social context of the time – a period which included the blossoming of the environmental movement. Dominant themes during this period centred upon the relationship of man to the natural environment, and projections of alternative futures in which different groups sought respite from the material, social, and spiritual decay that they saw as pervading Western society. The policy recommendations to emerge from the world models included an image of a global equilibrium society – a stable state which would last indefinitely and where man would live in harmony with nature. Here, religious and ethical concerns would supposedly help to reorientate people away from material desires and values towards long-term values centred on the stability of the global ecosystem and the perpetuation of the human species.

The world models emerged on to a social landscape where many people were looking for an alternative belief system, and I will consider the millenarian aspects of the period. But the message of the world models also countenanced another form of reaction; pitched in curiously suprapolitical terms the message demanded individual moral restraint and self-discipline. In this regard, I will argue that – like a computerized form of astrology – system dynamics offered to bring structure and certainty into a world that appeared to be rent by contrarieties and mounting global problems. In this sense it held out an ideology which could enable people to adjust to and accept the conditions on 'Spaceship Earth'. However, some groups saw no basis for the belief in disaster: in short, there was a variation in the beliefs and disbeliefs which met the message. To tackle this variation I will employ Douglas's grid/group theory of cosmologies in order to distinguish the reactions of different audiences.

Acknowledgements

I would like to express my appreciation to John Naughton (Systems Group, The Open University) and Gerard de Vries (Filosofisch Instituut, Rijksuniversiteit Groningen, The Netherlands) for their constructive criticisms of earlier drafts of this book. Any errors are of course solely mine. Thanks are also due to colleagues and friends in Milton Keynes and Groningen who provided both intellectual and moral support. Part of the research described herein appeared as 'Anomalies and Social Experience: Backcasting with Simulation Models', *Social Studies of Science*, 15 (1985), 631–75.

Brian Bloomfield

PART ONE
Introduction

1 The History of System Dynamics

In this chapter my aim is to provide an introduction to system dynamics and its history as seen in relation to the application of the theory to different domains. For the purposes of exposition and clarity it will be useful to distinguish between various stages in the development of system dynamics, such as industrial dynamics, and the books which bear the same name – e.g. *Industrial Dynamics*. Thus, 'urban dynamics' should be taken to refer to the stage in the development of the theory when urban systems were tackled, while *Urban Dynamics* refers to the specific book discussing Forrester's urban model. I will begin with a brief description of the career of the founder and chief exponent of system dynamics – J. W. Forrester – because it is important to grasp the application-oriented engineering context which nurtured the systems ideas that later became embodied in the theory of system dynamics.

Forrester's career is best understood by dividing it into two phases: first his education, training, and experience in electrical engineering – chiefly in connection with military/technological systems; and second, his movement into management science and the study of non-technical systems. Born in 1918, the son of a Nebraska cattle-ranching family, Forrester studied electrical engineering at the University of Nebraska. Then he moved to MIT and between 1940 and 1946 worked at the Servomechanisms Laboratory – where feedback control theory was being used in the design of military equipment. Feedback control centres on the idea of monitoring the output of a particular piece of equipment and feeding back – electrically – selected information about the behaviour of the device, comparing actual behaviour with some reference point and effecting action to eliminate any detected discrepancy between the two. One early application was in fire-control devices for weapons systems and Forrester's work proved a notable contribution to the field.

At the time MIT was a major centre for research into feedback control;

in addition, significant developments in analog computers were achieved in furtherance of the study of control systems. Eventually, however, technical difficulties constrained the practical use of analog computers in researching control systems, but the concept of a digital computer held out the prospect for further advances. In fact, MIT had become a focus for intensive research into the development of digital computers. A move into this new area was therefore a logical progression and in 1947 Forrester took up the directorship of the MIT Digital Computer Laboratory. The work at this laboratory was still tied to military funding and directed toward applications in military systems; but Forrester came to realize that the emergence of digital computation would be of much greater significance than his military sponsors could imagine. Despite conflicts with his paymasters (e.g. concerning cost-overruns) Forrester oversaw the successful construction of *Whirlwind I* which was one of the world's first high-speed digital computers (Redmond and Smith, 1980). In fact, while engaged upon this work Forrester invented (and indeed, holds the basic patents on) random-access magnetic core storage memory devices – for many years the standard memory units in digital computers.

The next stage in Forrester's career took him to MIT's Lincoln Laboratory where between 1952 and 1956 he was head of the Digital Computers Division. During this period he directed the military and operational planning and technical design of the Air Force SAGE system for continental air defence – this being one of the first applications for the *Whirlwind* computer.

The second phase of Forrester's career began in 1956 when he decided to move into the field of management science. He accepted a position as a professor at MIT's Sloan School of Management where he sought to bring his experience and knowledge of engineering systems, military decision-making structures and computers into the domain of corporate management. The concept of feedback control had proved a formidable tool in the analysis of physical and technical systems and he believed that it might also be applicable to non-technical systems like business organizations. The Sloan School has a long engineering orientation, its origins stemming from the School of Engineering at MIT (Noble, 1977). It was established in 1952 at the bequest of Alfred P. Sloan, the former head of General Motors, who believed that a management school within a technical environment such as MIT would develop in promising new directions. While at the Sloan School Forrester undertook a survey of the operational research and scientific management techniques that were current practice among corporate analysts. He thought that these techniques were quite restricted and low-level, leading him to devise the forerunner of system dynamics – industrial dynamics: a feedback theory of the behaviour of industrial systems.

Industrial dynamics grew out of an interest in finding and developing connections between engineering and management; it was based on four foundations – namely, information-feedback control theory, knowledge of decision-making processes, the experimental approach to systems analysis, and the digital computer (Forrester, 1961, 1975b). Having been at the forefront of research into feedback systems and digital computation, Forrester was in a unique position to see the potential application of these techniques in non-technical systems. For some time, operations research – incorporating mathematics and scientific method – had been used to tackle various industrial problems. However, Forrester saw these efforts as being flawed in two important respects. First, they were restricted to individual low-level problems and decisions containing only a few variables, characterized as 'open-loop' processes where the policy output was seen as unconnected to the information input used in deciding upon the policy. That is, when decision-makers (or managers) assembled information about the operation of a system they did not consider how their policy decisions would modify the information that might be gathered at a later point in time. Second, the mathematical approach of operations research was restricted to linear relationships between variables. This was because equations for non-linear relationships could not be solved analytically.

In contrast, Forrester advocated a 'closed-loop' approach in which a feedback loop is established between policy output and information input, and he contended that because non-linear relationships were an important characteristic of non-technical systems these too would have to be included in any realistic analysis of corporate systems. The impetus for his new perspective grew out of his experience at the Servomechanisms Laboratory and the use of *information-feedback control theory* (control theory is a branch of mathematics which is applied to the engineering problems involved in the design of feedback control devices). As stated earlier, Forrester's work in this field was connected with military projects, but a simple example of a closed–loop system is that of a heating system and thermostat. (The thermostat receives information about the temperature in a given room and 'decides' whether or not to start up the boiler; if it does so, it monitors the increasing temperature of the room before eventually shutting off the boiler at some pre-selected temperature.) Forrester contended that the feedback approach was more representative of real–world situations than the open-loop approach: it was therefore better suited to the complex problems of corporate management.

Forrester's knowledge of control theory was complemented by his experience of *decision-making processes* while at the Lincoln Laboratory, where he had developed systems for automating military tactical operations: this was the second foundation.

As in military decisions, we shall see that there is an orderly basis that prescribes much of our present managerial decision making. Decisions are not entirely 'free will' but are strongly conditioned by the environment. This being true, we can set down the policies governing such decisions and determine how the policies are affecting industrial and economic behavior. (Forrester, 1961: 17)

Thus, he believed that the analysis and design of systems for automating decision structures in a military setting provided a basis to pursue the analysis and control of policy within a business environment. Like operations research, control theory was also limited to the analysis of linear relationships. This constraint led to the third foundation – that is, the belief that the *experimental approach to systems analysis* offered the technique of simulating a system using a mathematical model and did not require analytical solutions for the equations involved in describing a non-linear system. The fourth foundation – the *digital computer* – provided the means whereby large simulation models could be programmed and run relatively cheaply at a high speed. This was facilitated by the formulation of a specialised computer language, called *Dynamo*, to handle the model simulations. With funding being provided by the Ford Foundation these four elements – which had all largely been spurred by military and commercial interests – fused into the development of industrial dynamics (Forrester, 1961).

In formulating the concepts of industrial dynamics Forrester drew upon the state variable approach of engineering. He saw this as a distinct part of many fields, including economics and psychology – for example, the idea of a psychological field (Lewin, 1951). It is worth explaining this approach in some detail because it underpins the basis of all system dynamics models. At any given moment in time, the state of a system can be described by the values of its variables – the state variables (which in system dynamics terminology are called *levels*). Given knowledge of the present state of the system, together with information about its present and future inputs, the future states and future outputs can be calculated. Thus, the state of the system at the time $(t+1)$ is only dependent upon the state of the system at time (t) and the inputs between (t) and $(t+1)$. Let me illustrate this by returning to the example of a heating system. Figure 1.1 shows a system dynamics flow chart (a systems description) for such a system – composed of a room with a thermostatically controlled heater. The temperature in the room is represented by (T) a state, or level variable; (R) represents the rate of temperature increase (e.g. degrees Celsius per minute) which of course is related to the difference between (T) and the temperature corresponding to the setting of the thermostat

(C). The connection between (T) and (R) represents a feedback loop and is controlled by the thermostat. The equation for (T) at time (t + dt), where (dt) is a small time increment, is given by the following difference equation:

$$T_{t+dt} = T_t + R_t \; dt$$

And, the equation for (R), the rate of temperature increase is some function of (T) – e.g. $R_t = C - T_t$.

Although in more complex system dynamics models there are often many auxiliary equations which are used to calculate various parameters within the rate equations, nevertheless system dynamicists contend that all complex systems can be ultimately conceived as being composed of just levels and rates. The levels in a system actually represent integrations through time and completely describe its state; they are also used to calculate the rates. These represent policy decisions which cause the levels to change; in the example just given, I have discussed a physical flow (heat), but rate variables may refer to other 'flows' such as births and deaths etc. Simple though the example is, it illustrates the fundamental building blocks from which industrial dynamics models of a corporate system were constructed.

The first step in model construction was to identify the goals and

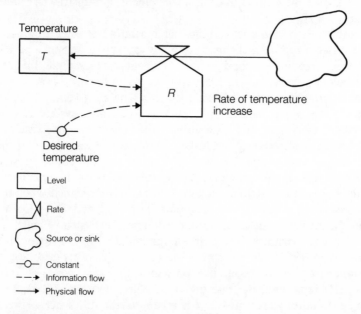

Figure 1.1 Flow diagram for a heating system

problems of the organization or system under scrutiny, followed by a description of the problem situation which was to capture the significant interrelationships between the factors involved. An important tenet of the method was that it was better to include a parameter which was known to have an influence on a system, but which might be poorly quantified, rather than to omit it. This stage would lead to the identification of the system's feedback loops and substructures. The resulting verbal description – which largely depended on the analyst's skill, expertise, and intuition – was then translated into a system dynamics flow chart. When the analyst had checked this systems description for internal consistency and plausibility, it would be implemented in a mathematical model. This would be composed of equations for the levels, rates, and any auxiliaries, encrypted in the *Dynamo* simulation language. The resultant model was then used for simulation experiments on a computer.

Obviously, the properties of large aggregates of feedback loops can become quite complex. In fact, Forrester stated that the behaviour of an information feedback system was derived from three factors: structure, delays, and amplification. The structure of a system is given by the interlocking feedback loops which interrelate the system levels and rates; delays may occur in a material or information flow and introduce transient responses into the behaviour of a system; and amplification is the property whereby a small change in one part of a system may produce a large variation in another part. These three factors may also interact with each other to produce further complex patterns of behaviour.

The period from 1956 to 1961 saw the application of industrial dynamics to the steady-state dynamics of corporate policies (i.e. fluctuations about an equilibrium state). Later, effort was devoted to the consolidation and clarification of the concepts of industrial dynamics and experimental courses were devised for teaching them to management students. Industrial dynamics was also extended to cover situations where non-linearities were important and positive feedback processes were investigated. The example of a heating system contains a *negative feedback* loop where the system maintains a temperature equilibrium – i.e. it is goal-directed. In contrast, *positive feedback* loops move away from a goal; a good example is the exponential growth of a bacterial population (until it exhausts the carrying capacity of its environment, at which point negative feedback checks the growth rate). In an industrial context the processes studied involved stock–control problems, growth in products and companies.

By 1968, Forrester claimed that over 200 undergraduate and postgraduate students were being instructed in industrial dynamics every year. The basic lecture notes for the tuition were published in book form as *Principles of Systems* (Forrester, 1968). Apart from its successful growth as a discipline, it is difficult to assess the practical efficacy of industrial dynamics because much of the applications work undertaken by Forrester and his colleagues was carried out on a consultancy basis. An early appraisal by Schall (1962) was quite favourable; however, a larger survey of industrial dynamics by Ansoff and Slevin (1968), which was published in *Management Science*, was markedly sceptical in tone.

Although forged to tackle the problems of corporate organizations, the horizons of industrial dynamics came to be seen in much more extensive terms.

> During this period the view of industrial dynamics was enlarged not only to include the application to enterprise design but also to become a general systems theory to serve as a unifying framework capable of organizing behavior and relationships in areas as diverse as engineering, medicine, management, psychology, and economics. (Forrester, 1975b: 135)

What this indicates is that Forrester had come to see the theory of industrial dynamics as being of much greater importance than corporate systems – i.e. it was a 'general systems theory'. This provides a key to the next phase of the development of system dynamics – namely, the movement into the modelling of other types of social systems such as cities.

Urban dynamics

In 1968 Forrester extended the domain of industrial dynamics to encompass the processes involved in the growth and decline of cities. He believed that industrial dynamics could shed new light on the problems of urban stagnation and again obtained funding from the Ford Foundation. Forrester examined policies for urban revival and also sought to explain the failure of past policies which he thought had often merely exacerbated the very problems they were devised to tackle.

The cornerstone of Forrester's urban-modelling project was the alleged behavioural properties of complex systems; these were formulated as follows: the counterintuitive nature of complex systems; insensitivity to parameter changes; resistance to policy changes; the existence of sensitive influence points; the tendency for corrective programmes to be counter-acted by the system; the difference between long-term and short-term responses; the drift to low performance.

In *Industrial Dynamics* Forrester had stated that at the time of writing it was not possible to generalize about the nature of complex non-linear systems. *Urban Dynamics* (Forrester, 1969) represented a departure from this position, since in it these general properties were spelled out. They are therefore worth brief discussion but I will leave the detailed examination of the assumptions underlying them for later analysis.

In his earlier work Forrester had suggested that intuition was unreliable in inferring the behaviour of a complex system; now he stated more firmly that complex systems were actually *counterintuitive* – that is 'they give indications that suggest corrective action which will often be ineffective or even adverse in its results' (Forrester, 1969: 9). He argued that human intuitions are formed by exposure to relatively simple systems and are not capable of inferring the behaviour of a complex system with many non-linearities and feedback loops. Though the human brain could correctly perceive the structure of a complex system, evolution had not equipped it with the skills to interpret how feedback structurers behaved dynamically – a task which required the use of a computer simulation model. 'Here lies much of the explanation for the problems of faltering companies, disappointments in developing nations, foreign-exchange crises, and troubles of urban areas' (Forrester, 1969: 110).

A complex system was alleged to be *insensitive* to changes in its parameters; in other words, changes in the value of a parameter do not appreciably alter the behaviour of the system. This led to the argument that the structure of a system is more important than the data specifying the values of its parameters, an argument which underscored the system dynamicists' general systems approach – i.e. irrespective of differences in parameters, systems with similar structures tend to have similar behavioural properties, whether those systems be an electronic circuit, a stock-control system, or a city.

Complex systems were said to *resist* policy changes; the system reacts to any change so as to defeat it and preserve its initial state. This property is analogous to homeostasis in living organisms (e.g. maintenance of body temperature), and the equilibrium states in systems of chemical reactions. Conversely, although systems are largely insensitive to parameter changes, they are said to have a few sensitive influence points where the change in a parameter may greatly affect the system's behaviour. This idea of sensitive influence points was a development of the notion of amplification in a system which had first appeared in industrial dynamics.

While complex systems resist all policy changes, it was contended that typical corrective programmes, based on intuitive, short-term considerations, were even more disadvantaged because of the fact that they tended to displace or perturb corresponding internal processes within a system – thus having less effect than anticipated. 'Probably no active, externally imposed program is superior to a system modification that changes internal incentives and leaves the burden of system improvement to internal processes' (Forrester, 1969: 111).

This idea was then coupled with the supposition that realistic programmes had to mobilize the 'negative forces' of a system (i.e. the negative feedback loops); it was suggested that these might initially cause apparent bad effects but that in the long run they would be beneficial. Conversely, a programme which had initial short-term benefits might have disastrous consequences in the long run. The latter point goes back to industrial dynamics and centres on the idea that the behaviour of a system in response to policy changes may be very different in the long term than the short term.

Finally, there was the idea that complex systems tend to move into a condition of *low performance*; this was thought to be mainly due to the interplay of the other properties and the intuitive, short-term solutions which are usually designed to alter system performance. Forrester contended that effective programmes required a full consideration of these properties of complex systems – of which an urban system was but one example – and should be tested out beforehand on a computer which, unlike the human mind, was alleged to have the ability to map out the behaviour of a complex system.

The number of levels (or state variables) in Forrester's urban model was twenty; it included different economic classes, housing categories and business enterprises. These formed three subsystems which were thought to govern the central processes involved in urban growth and stagnation. The aim was to focus attention on the entire life cycle of an urban area, and the model simulations were run for a 250 year period. The model did not correspond to any real city and Forrester relied largely on guesswork to calibrate the dozens of relationships and parameters which were used to describe the interconnections between the levels and rates. In fact, *Urban Dynamics* contained only six references, five of which were to other publications by Forrester. But his lack of reference to the literature on urban planning, and the absence of any discussion about the statistical estimation of parameter values used in the model – almost a benchmark of other work in the area – were not the only factors to draw the attention of critics. The most vehement reactions were formulated in response to the policies Forrester recommended for urban revival. For example, Forrester argued that low-rent housing encouraged an 'excessive' influx of underemployed people into cities, with the consequent erosion of the tax base and the fuelling of urban stagnation. The suggested remedy was to constrain this inward migration by demolishing the slums and not replacing them with alternative housing. As one critic put it, many might conclude that Forrester's assumptions were evidence of 'violent elitist prejudices and a manifest contempt for poor people' (Rochberg, 1971: 154).

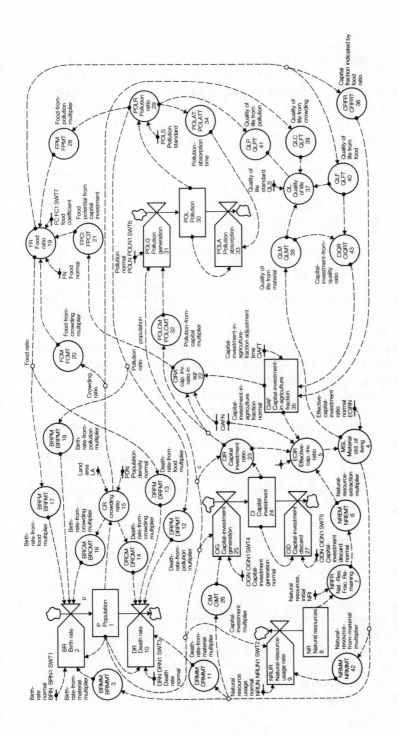

Figure 1.2 The flow diagram of WORLD 2

Reprinted, with permission, J. W. Forrester © *World Dynamics* (Cambridge, Mass.: MIT Press, 1971).

World dynamics

The next major extension of system dynamics was the global model WORLD 2 which is described in *World Dynamics* (Forrester, 1971). This project grew out of a meeting between Forrester and members of the Club of Rome in 1970. This organization is an international group of scientists, businessmen, and policymakers; it was founded by Aurelio Peccei in order to draw attention to and study various world problems.[1]

> The members act as private citizens. They are not in governmental decision-making positions. Their orientation is activist – that is, they wish to do more than study and understand. They wish to clarify the course of human events in a way that can be transmitted to governments and peoples to influence the trends of rising population, increasing pollution, greater crowding, and growing social strife. (Forrester, 1971: viii)

Forrester believed that system dynamics offered a powerful method of formulating the problems which concerned the Club, and after the initial meeting in Bern, Forrester invited Club members to MIT for a two week meeting for which the world model was prepared. 'The meeting included the general theory and behavior of complex systems and talks on the behavior of specific social systems, ranging from corporations through commodity markets to biological systems, drug addiction in the community, and the growth and decline of a city' (Forrester, 1975b: 221).

The model addressed the global interactions between population, agriculture, industry, resources, and pollution. Being aggregated at a global level it did not differentiate between international and intranational differences and only contained five levels. The model contained just two empirical data points – the population levels for 1900 and 1970 – all remaining values and relationships again being guessed by Forrester. The simulation began in 1900 and ran until the year 2100. Although the WORLD 2 model contains only five levels, the total number of variables is an order of magnitude larger, as can be seen from the system dynamics flow diagram for the model which appears in figure 1.2. The model is actually quite complex in appearance, even though its behaviour is crucially linked to certain key assumptions concerning the nature of the world system – for example, that the world is undergoing exponential growth in population and capitalization. The standard run of the model is shown in figure 1.3; population and capital investment grow exponentially while natural resources become increasingly scarce. Eventually – indeed inevitably, given that it is assumed that resources are fixed – the exhaustion of natural resources precipitates the collapse of population and

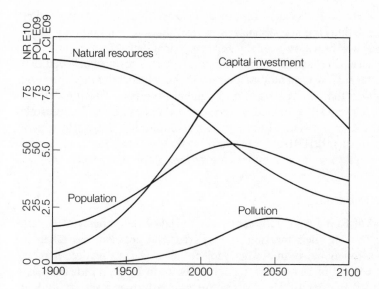

Figure 1.3   Standard run of WORLD 2

capital investment. Forrester ran WORLD 2 under several different sets of 'optimistic' assumptions – such as a drastic reduction in the usage of natural resources, or the introduction of implicit technological improvements in agricultural production – but in each case catastrophe was not averted; it was at best merely postponed for a few decades. His aim was to show that while the particular parameter values he had used for the model might be in error, the feedback properties of the world system were such that any discrepancies were irrelevant.

Forrester actually began to talk of the fundamental laws of nature and social systems; natural resources were finite and therefore the world could only support a certain number of people at any given standard of living; further, it could only absorb so much pollution. Forrester argued that the world must move towards an equilibrium society where the growth in population and industrialization would be permanently halted. He suggested that one way to achieve this would be to reduce world food production, the birth rate, capital investment, the generation of pollution, and natural resource usage. Perhaps the most surprising aspect of these suggestions was the idea of reducing food production; for this could greatly increase the death rate amongst the world's population. However, Forrester argued that increasing food production (an intuitive solution to rising population levels) would only stimulate still further population growth and thereby lead to an even greater collapse in the future. The model sparked off a very heated debate in academic circles and in other forums – not only because of the controversial nature of the policy recommendations but also because of the assumptions built into it and the fact that it was based on virtually zero empirical data.

While accepting that his model was not perfect, Forrester believed that it was better than the 'mental' models which he considered to be operating in relation to the received wisdom on global problems. 'Having defined with care the model contained herein, and having examined its dynamic behavior and implications, I have greater confidence in this world system model than in others that I now have available. Therefore, this is the model I should use for recommending actions' (Forrester, 1971: ix).

The limits to growth

The Club of Rome were sufficiently convinced of the potency of system dynamics during their meeting at MIT that the decision was taken to sponsor a much more ambitious project. This was to involve a more complex version of Forrester's model, to be built by a multidisciplinary team headed by Dennis Meadows – Forrester's former research student who had previously built system dynamics models of commodity production cycles. The new model was to take account of the criticisms levelled against WORLD 2, and in particular there was a concerted effort to calibrate the model parameters. Financing was obtained from the Volkswagen Foundation and the new model was named WORLD 3. Forrester did not actively participate on the project because he was committed to further urban modelling work. The findings of the team were published in *The Limits to Growth* (Meadows et al., 1972) and largely reiterated those of *World Dynamics*.

The Limits to Growth was a 'popular' report and as such contained no detailed technical information. It sparked off a tremendous controversy – receiving a great deal of media coverage, particularly in the United States. In fact, this can be partly attributed to the manner in which the book was launched. The WORLD 3 project was the subject of a public presentation given in the Great Hall of the Smithsonian Institution in Washington, D.C.; several hundred persons, including US government officials, the diplomatic corps, members of the business and academic communities, and the military, were invited along with the press and television. Moreover, 10,000 complimentary copies of the book were distributed throughout the world. By 1976 the book had sold nearly three million copies worldwide, with almost half a million in The Netherlands alone.

From their scientific audience the project team drew some scathing criticisms; this was partly because they had not gone through the normal channels of scientific publication, but had instead launched the results of the model amidst a publicity campaign without first submitting their work for detailed critical evaluation. The full technical report – *Dynamics of Growth in a Finite World* (Meadows et al., 1974) – followed only 2 years later. In an interview with (Gillette, 1972: 1091) in the journal *Science*, Meadows claimed that the 'packaging' of *The Limits to Growth* was mostly due to Peccei, the head of the Club of Rome. He continued: 'This isn't our mode of doing things. We want to sink back out of sight – we're not letting TV cameras in our laboratory.' As for Peccei, his view of the whole affair demonstrated a conviction about the enormity of the challenge facing mankind, coupled with a recognition of the powerful means of communication afforded by the computer. Speaking about the Club's reaction to the global predicament, he stated:

[The Club's] immediate response was . . . the search for a device capable of opening a breach in the hearts and minds of people, of arousing their awareness to the complexity and seriousness of the world problematique. After long consideration, a commando operation was decided upon, in the hope that its rapid tactical success might have strategic consequences' (Peccei, 1973: 205).

The system dynamics national model

For the last several years Forrester and his colleagues have been engaged upon modelling the economy of the United States – though Forrester has argued that in principle the model is applicable to any national economy. This model is the most ambitious to date, both in terms of size and complexity, and is addressed to the problems of inflation and long-term unemployment. It has been financially supported by the Rockefeller Brothers Fund and contains some 1500 levels. Unlike earlier system dynamics models it contains processes which are said to generate three distinct cycles of behaviour; these are the business cycle (3 to 7 years), the Kuznets cycle (*c.* 20 years) which arises from factor replacement between capital and labour, and the Kondratieff long wave cycle (*c.* 50 years) which stems from the growth and collapse of capital sectors. (Full details of this model are not yet available and consequently only brief references will be made to it in this book. For preliminary details see: Forrester, 1976b, 1976c, 1981.)

Overview

It would be useful to have an easily visualized means of summarizing the main features in the development of system dynamics. To achieve this I propose to adapt a view of theories derived from the philosophy of science

ENGINEERING SYSTEMS	INDUSTRIAL SYSTEMS	URBAN SYSTEMS	GLOBAL SYSTEMS	NATIONAL ECONOMIC SYSTEMS
One or two loops linear	Multi-loop non-linear	⟶	⟶	⟶
Time scale c. secs – mins	5–10 years	250 years	200 years	200 years
State variables c. 5	Up to 25	20	5	1500
	Delays	⟶	⟶	⟶
	Structure	⟶	⟶	⟶
	Amplification	Sensitive influence points	⟶	⟶
	Better for worse sequences	Short-term long-term goal conflict	⟶	⟶
	Intuition unreliable	Counterintuitive	⟶	⟶
	Can improve performance without a trade-off	Limited good – improving one factor worsens another	⟶	⟶
	Steady-state dynamics	Growth and stagnation	Exponential growth transition to equilibrium	Long-term growth cycles
	Stable equilibrium	Unstable equilibrium	⟶	⟶
		System modes have corresponding pressures	⟶	⟶
		Insensitive to parameter changes	⟶	⟶
		Insensitive to policy changes	⟶	⟶
		Corrective programmes counteracted by system	⟶	⟶
		Drift to low performance	⟶	⟶
		Realistic goals must include negative forces	⟶	⟶
			Fundamental laws of nature and social systems	⟶
			Need for long-term value structures	⟶
				Multiple behaviour modes – business cycle, Kuznets cycle, Kondratieff long-wave

Figure 1.4 The development of Forrester's work

THE HISTORY OF SYSTEM DYNAMICS 17

– namely, the structuralist or 'non-statement' view (Kuhn, 1976; Stegmuller, 1976). According to the structuralist view, one can consider a scientific theory to consist of two components – first a theoretical core, and second a domain of applications. Further, the two parts are indissolubly linked together: the development of the theoretical core takes place with a given domain in mind; conversely, the choice of each new application is guided by the success of previous applications and is also bounded by the theory. For example, the theory of classical particle mechanics comprises Newton's Second Law of Motion (the core) and applications such as the solar system and falling bodies (the domain). By extending this scheme to system dynamics, we can consider its core in relation to the different major domains to which Forrester and his colleagues have applied it. To be sure, it must be acknowledged that the core of system dynamics cannot be formulated in the same rigorous terms usually employed by philosophers who adopt the structuralist view, wherein theories are expressed in the set-theoretic terms of a predicate calculus. But this problem also applies to many well-established scientific theories (e.g. the theory of evolution); this is because the structuralist view has been developed in close connection with theories in mathematical physics. However, I can cite those features of system dynamics which constitute specific clusters of theoretical assumptions and chart them in relation to the different applications.

The result is depicted in figure 1.4 where it can be seen that a consistent change and expansion of the theoretical core has occurred as each new domain has been tackled. The shift from technical to non-technical systems saw the inclusion of non-linear relationships and the formulation of multi-loop feedback structures. The timescale involved in the transient responses found in technical systems could typically vary from a fraction of a second to, say, a few minutes; but with industrial systems the time horizon was expanded up to 15 years. At this point the properties of complex feedback systems began to emerge. With the move to urban systems the time horizon was stretched to 250 years; the feedback properties of complex systems became refined and expanded, and the behaviour of interest was long-term growth and stagnation rather than the equilibrium states of business organizations. Ironically, the WORLD 2 model was much simpler in structure than the urban model, though the behaviour of interest was arguably more complex – the dynamics of exponential growth and the policies for managing a transition toward global equilibrium. And again the assumptions implicit in the core were expanded. The study of national economic systems has brought the most complex system dynamics model to date and has been augmented by the claim that it can provide a unifying theory to explain different cycles of economic behaviour.

Viewing system dynamics in terms of a core and a domain raises interesting questions as to the possible explanations for the particular pattern of development and this will be a theme of central importance in chapter 3. The system dynamicists have tended to present each new domain as yet another technical application of system dynamics – rather than a development of the theory itself; but this account is not sustainable if one considers the importance of the changes which can be documented. Moreover, it doesn't give due consideration to the other background assumptions which have infused the different modelling projects.

In this chapter I have dealt with the main features in the development of system dynamics, but other system dynamicists have applied the theory to an extraordinarily diverse range of domains. These include the following: real estate economics, US energy systems, the search for a policy on heroin, occupational programme planning, economic development, the cultural structure of pre-christian Rome, the world cocoa market, terrestrial ecosystems, retirement policies within the military, gypsy moth populations, dynamics of world peace, education, crime, urban traffic, regional employment (Greenberger et al., 1976; Randers, 1980).

Within the Sloan School, Forrester set up the System Dynamics Group with its own laboratory. This group has been a major source of system dynamics research but there are now a number of different system-dynamics modelling groups in several countries. In Britain, for example, there is one group at the University of Bradford, and another at the London Business School. There are international conferences on system dynamics; an international society has been formed; and a Forrester Prize for achievement in system dynamics has now been instituted.

2 System Dynamics – a Cultural Artefact

The aim of this investigation is to gain a comprehensive understanding of the relationship between system dynamics and the cultural contexts, both inside and outside the laboratory, within which it evolved. Specifically, I want to analyse the ways in which system dynamics has co-developed in relation to its cultural background and the social experience of the System Dynamics Group, and to determine the nature of the cultural role, if any, that it might play. The general problem that confronts us, therefore, is the relationship between knowledge and social structures.

The method of analysis represents a synthesis of various elements drawn principally from sociology and anthropology – the greatest debt being to Douglas (1966, 1973, 1975, 1978, 1982). The overall perspective of the approach will be to consider system dynamics as a cultural artefact – a product of culture – produced by, in, and for culture. The term culture is used here in Douglas's sense; that is, to encompass the traditions, standards, and values which are produced by the transactions – negotiations and interactions – of individuals. In other words, culture is actively produced. Social structure is a more precise theoretical concept which is used to describe different patterns of cultural transactions.

The form of the relationship between knowledge and social structure can, my perspective argues, be interpreted only in terms of some specific theoretical model since both social structure and knowledge are theoretical constructs. Accordingly, the inquiry will be based upon a specific model of the relationship which will be outlined shortly. First, however, it would seem relevant to consider some other ways of conceptualizing this relationship because some of the problems that they engender are instructive and lead to the approach adopted here. The exposition of these approaches will be brief and inevitably somewhat crude; rather than attempting a detailed critical evaluation of each, I will point out some specific problems associated with them and thus set the scene for the approach which is taken here. In any case similar arguments have been much rehearsed elsewhere (Barnes, 1974, 1976; Bloor, 1976, 1982; Knorr-Cetina and Mulkay, 1983; Mulkay, 1980; Shapin, 1982).

Different solutions to the problem of tackling the connection between knowledge and social structure have often been predicated on various epistemological and methodological dichotomies – such as those between science and ideology, internal history and external history, base and superstructure, or cognitive and social. For example, the inquiry might begin by trying to establish whether or not system dynamics meets some particular demarcation criterion for science such as that proposed by, say, Popper.[1] Explicitly underpinned by the notion of a dichotomy between science and pseudoscience, or between science and ideology, in this perspective scientific knowledge is seen as being objective and true, justified belief; the process of science is the continuous accumulation of facts. Belief in true knowledge is regarded as unproblematic, it is due to rationality: scientists believe what they believe because it is rational to do so. The methodological implication of this view is that the scientific status of knowledge determines how it is to be investigated sociologically. If system dynamics were scientific, then from a constitutive point its social origins would be considered relatively unimportant, and we would be reduced to the once all too familiar histories and biographies of science; conversely, if it were judged to be false knowledge, it might be regarded as constitutively social.

However, such an approach is sterile for it reduces the sociology of knowledge to the sociology of error, and if applied to the subject here would prevent us from pursuing a full-blooded sociological investigation and thereby apprehending system dynamics in a proper cultural context. For science (or scientific activity), however one tries to define it, is also a cultural product; an ever-growing body of empirically oriented work in the sociology of science has demonstrated that traditional explanations of scientific belief – based on the force of logic, rationality or reason – do not constitute sufficient explanations for why true knowledge is believed.[2] It is also worth noting that system dynamics is addressed to the analysis of both physical systems and social systems. It may be that it could meet some criterion for science when applied to the domain of physical systems, but this of course would not imply validity in application to social systems. (Unless, that is, one adopted a positivistic view founded on the alleged unity of method in natural and social sciences.)

Of course this is not to say that differences between some particular conception of science and system dynamics do not exist or are unimportant; the point is that my focus is deeper in the sense that I wish to draw attention to the cultural factors and conditions which may influence the production of both true and false knowledge. Put another way, I will be concerned with the reasons why knowledge is believed – whether it is true or false. And in any case if, for the sake of argument, the sociologist of science were to accept some scheme for assessing the scientific status of knowledge, he or she could put the question as to how such differences in status arise and could still justifiably pursue a sociological explanation for how 'scientific' beliefs come about.

The second dichotomy rests on the idea that the growth of scientific knowledge can be differentiated according to distinct internal and external histories: wherein a cleavage is posited between internal factors – such as cognition, knowledge, rationality, and scientific institutions – and external factors such as social and political interests, science policy, and financing structures. This view allows that social factors are present in the internal history of science but often, following Mertonian style sociology of science, it has been predicated on a functionalist model (M. D. King, 1971). Thus science, like any other social institution, is seen as a social system; as long as it functions in line with the canons and norms of scientific method, such that each scientist is committed to the norm of rationality, all is well and the knowledge produced will be true. Questions of legitimacy – the context of justification – are thereby restricted solely to the internal sphere; and so while external factors may influence the direction or pace of development of true knowledge, they have no bearing upon its actual validity. But if knowledge turns out to be false, then it follows from functionalist premises that either the social system of science must have been perturbed by external factors – these are only considered to be constitutive of knowledge when it is false; or particular scientists deviated from the norm of rationality. So arguments in this mould also rely upon notions of rationality to explain scientific beliefs and therefore run into the same problems discussed in connection with the first dichotomy.

The third dichotomy centres on a distinction between the realm of thought, or ideas, and that of material existence. One sphere is considered to determine the other, with a different view of the direction of influence being taken by idealism on the one hand, and economic determinism on the other. In a number of critiques of system dynamics one can find an idealistic bias in which the development of this body of knowledge is explained in terms of ideas – for instance, as a fusion of systems engineering and management science. Indeed, this sort of account is conveyed by the system dynamicists themselves. To be sure, they make reference to the tradition out of which their theory emerged, but this is presented as a source of legitimation, a mark of intellectual ancestry. Their aim is to establish the connection between system dynamics and ideas which have been successful in the domain of technical systems, rather than to raise the issue of that tradition as a topic for investigation in its own right. In these accounts, then, system dynamics has tended to be represented as a solely intellectual entity which appears to have only a tenuous link with the social experience of the system dynamicists and the wider societal culture which enveloped them. Discussion is devoted to the assumptions governing specific system dynamics models, but no serious consideration is given to the possible reasons why the model builders believed in their utility or value.

At the opposite extreme from idealism we find economic determinism; this is a form of *reflection theory*, being a crude version of Marxist materialism. Put in simple terms, Marx posited the idea of a material base (the economic infrastructure) which gave rise to a superstructure of knowledge that reflected the base. 'The mode of production of material life determines the general character of the social, political, and spiritual processes of life. It is not the consciousness of men that determines their being, but, on the contrary, their social being determines their consciousness' (Marx, 1979: 67). In economic determinism this formulation has been overextended to cover all levels and forms of consciousness and all levels of social reality. Every product of culture is then reduced to a mere *reflection* of the underlying economic base. Such a position cannot account for the relative autonomy of thought as evidenced in certain branches of knowledge, modern physics or mathematics for example. While not wishing to suggest that these areas of knowledge are unaffected by material or economic interests, the point must be made that they are not reducible to such interests.

Some other critiques of system dynamics have implicitly operated upon the premises of the base–superstructure model. For example, certain critics have tied the world models to the interests of multinational corporations (Enzensberger, 1974; Golub and Townsend, 1977). Although such studies can sometimes provide useful insights into the background of world modelling, they too often sound like conspiracy theories of history, or articulations of economic determinism. As such, they fail to capture the breadth and depth of the relationship between knowledge and social structures. For instance, they tend to equate system dynamics with the content of a particular model (say, WORLD 2), along with certain economic interests which they associate with it. However, a model may be built with the *intention* of supporting specific interests or, it may have the *effect* of supporting them. The distinction between these two possibilities cannot be ignored, for in so doing one neglects the fact that system dynamics is related to other areas of culture, such as the movement towards the technocratic control of social systems. This strand of technocratic rationality within the development of system dynamics is not of course divorced from economic interests, but it cannot be reduced to them either, any more than the wider development of culture itself can be explained in economic terms alone.

Finally, the fourth dichotomy involves a separation of cognitive and social factors. One example of this is evident in the interest model suggested by Barnes and Bloor (the so-called 'strong programme of the sociology of knowledge') in which reasons for scientists' adherence to knowledge are sought in relation to their goals and interests – which may be social or political in nature (Barnes, 1977; Bloor, 1976). Research conducted in accordance with this model has aimed to cut across the science/ideology and internal/external dichotomies, and has shown empirically that accepted scientific knowledge requires just as much sociological explanation as false knowledge. However, the interests model is susceptible to the charge that it relies on a mechanistic causality to account for the relationship between knowledge and social interests. Indeed, Bloor has made causal explanation a tenet of his 'strong programme' (for philosophical and other critiques of the strong programme see Note 3).

Further, other critics of the interest model have drawn attention to its neglect of the important role played by scientists' interpretative procedures. Informed by the tenets of ethnomethodology, they contend that scientific knowledge is a social construction, the result of a process in which scientists bargain and negotiate about interpretations – e.g. of experimental results or of nature. This view has been adopted in a number of so-called 'laboratory studies' in which sociologists of science have sought to enter the culture of the laboratory in the same spirit as anthropologists seeking to study exotic tribes. These observers of the micro-social world of laboratory practices have pointed out that scientists not only interpret the world in terms of their social interests, but that these social interests too are the subject of scientists' interpretative procedures (Latour and Woolgar, 1979; Mulkay et al., 1983). Hence, social goals and interests cannot be put forward as simple causes of knowledge but must themselves be the subject of sociological inquiry. But the over-emphasis on the role of interpretation leads to its own problems: for interpretations – whether about experimental findings, the goals of a research programme, or the contribution of research to the wider good of society – are socially constituted; they are shaped during the course of social interaction, among scientists themselves, and between them and their environment (Dynamics of Science 1982).

Knowledge and Social Structures – a Different View

I will now outline an alternative approach which will form the framework for this inquiry. The fundamental premises of this derive from the foregoing arguments in which various problems arising from other approaches were identified and discussed. In particular, it must seek to avoid the pitfalls inherent in the various dichotomies – science/ideology; internal/external; base/superstructure; cognitive/social – upon which they are founded. Not that dichotomies are problematic in any *a priori* sense; the point is that hard-and-fast distinctions are best avoided. In this respect the works of Elias (1971a,b) and Fleck (1979) provide theoretical guidelines which are useful for the purpose. Only the skeleton of the alternative approach is described here but the details will be fleshed out as different parts are deployed in the forthcoming chapters.

The first premise is that the relationship between knowledge and social structures is bi-directional. Knowledge is produced in society and bears the scars of its birth. It is not just a mere epiphenomenon – e.g. a reflection of economic interests – but something which may reinforce the society or social group from which it is derived, serving as a form of 'binding agent' that 'cements' people together. Knowledge and cognitions are actually part of the social bonds between people – including those in scientific communities and laboratories. The approach taken here will therefore assume a holistic view of the relationship between knowledge and social structures.

The second premise is that bi-directionality does not necessarily mean that knowledge is an isomorphic reflection of particular economic or material interests, nor is it to be seen as a mere reflection of social and political interests conceived in static terms. Rather, knowledge can have a degree of relative autonomy such that it may prescribe new patterns of social relations or radical changes to existing ones. It is a power resource by which groups may seek to further their interests or, more strictly speaking, their interpretations of their interests. Changes in social interests will lead to changes in knowledge; or, alternatively, changing interpretations of interests will lead to changes in knowledge. The possibility of relative autonomy does not of course mean that knowledge can be 'neutral' or 'objective'. Indeed, while one particular body of knowledge may be more detached than some other, it will still impose its own constraints upon human thought and action.

Following Elias (1971a: 158) we can think of a continuum, without absolute end states, wherein knowledge can be more or less autonomous in relation to social structure. Thus, for example, the development from the geocentric cosmology to the heliocentric cosmology represented a change in knowledge in which the socially accepted model of the universe became more independent of people's self-image and began to move away from its role of reinforcing the prevailing social order. It signalled a movement away from man's suject-centredness, anthropomorphism, and egocentricity. Even so, the heliocentric cosmology was constrained by its theoretical framework, which was still – though to a lesser extent – tied to the surrounding social structure. Though the Earth was no longer conceived to be at the centre of the universe, the sun and the solar system were. The heliocentric cosmology was later displaced by Einstein's model of the universe – we can see a form of progress in the development of each model, each becoming more detached, but none representing an ideal end state or ultimate truth.

The third premise, again taken from Elias, is that we must take a dynamic view of the relationship between knowledge and social structure. Elias argued for – and demonstrated empirically (Elias, 1978b, 1982) – the utility of an approach in which the development of knowledge is located within the context of the wider development of ideas and society. In other words, instead of just relating knowledge to the immediate social context of the group which embraces it – e.g. the social experience within a scientific laboratory – we should also be aware of the longer-term changes (including those in ideas) in the society of which the group and its knowledge are but a part.

It is contended that ideas are not the sole property of individuals, but are the collective products of parts of societies – 'our colonisation of each other's minds is the price we pay for thought' (Douglas, 1973: xx). The focus here, therefore, will eschew any concentration on individualistic explanations of the growth of knowledge and will instead look to the social contexts, including the development of ideas and society, in which individuals reside. In so doing it will concentrate upon the social roots of knowledge and beliefs, and thus avoid the pitfalls of the more familiar biographies and histories of ideas.

One immediate consequence of the first premise is that the investigation is bifurcated according to the two possible directions of the relationship between knowledge and social structure. Accordingly, in Part Two the discussion will be concerned with the social construction of knowledge, while Part Three will focus upon the potential impact of knowledge on social structures, and specifically on its role as a resource to establish, or reinforce, or to change, particular patterns of social relations.

This model of investigation also finds a predicate in the work of Fleck and the recent revival of his ideas amongst Dutch sociologists and philosophers of science (Dynamics of Science, 1982; de Vries and Harbers, 1985). In the 1930s Fleck developed a theory of science which posited a central role for the collective nature of scientific activity. He suggested that the genesis and development of scientific knowledge occurred within a scientific collective; this was thought to consist of two circles or subgroups – namely, an esoteric circle of experts and an exoteric circle of laypeople. Together these interdependent groups share a thought style. Further, Fleck contended that the development of scientific knowledge was marked by two forms of connections: those imposed 'actively' through the thought style of the collective and those imposed 'passively' through the resistance of nature and experienced as objective reality. For example, the choice of 16 for the atomic weight of oxygen constitutes an 'active' connection, it is a social convention. But further, nature imposes a 'passive' connection between the ratio of the atomic weights of oxygen and, say, hydrogen: if oxygen is 16, then hydrogen must be 1.008. And moreover, the active connections are not freely chosen, but rather are part of a cultural tradition.

On Fleck's view, the growth of scientific knowledge within the collective is characterized by two complementary processes – namely, the esoteric translation of popular knowledge within the esoteric circle, and the popularization of scientific knowledge within the exoteric circle (de Vries and Harbers, 1985).

A traditional view of the dissemination of scientific knowledge sees it as a process of diffusion in which the products of science remain valid and essentially unchanged – facts speak for themselves – as they are embodied in increasingly less abstract and more popular versions. In contrast, Fleck's notion of popularization allows that scientific knowledge is interpreted in accordance with commonsense, everyday intuitions within exoteric circles. In short, the cultural impact of scientific knowledge does not consist of a simple displacement of old ideas by new ones; rather, new ideas reshape existing notions and practices (de Vries and Harbers, 1985). This view will be particularly useful when we come to deal with the cultural impact of the world models.

Fleck's work foreshadowed much of Kuhn's (1970) work on paradigms; however, Kuhn only dealt with the equivalent of the esoteric circle, thus omitting the role of the exoteric circle and the diffusion of scientific knowledge – which in relation to system dynamics is of particular importance here because of its policy orientation. Indeed, many of the articles and books crafted by the system dynamicists were for popular consumption. In the terms to be employed here, the esoteric translation of popular exoteric knowledge corresponds to the social construction of knowledge in the System Dynamics Laboratory; while the popularization of esoteric knowledge corresponds to the social role of system dynamics outside the laboratory. Now let us consider the main features of the investigation in greater detail.

The social construction of knowledge

The relationship between social structure and the specific kind of knowledge represented by system dynamics will be examined from two different perspectives. The first will seek to present a dynamic view of the relationship between system dynamics and the developments in ideas and society from which it has sprung. Such a general perspective is provided by Elias who takes a dynamic view of the origin and development of ideas. Rather than viewing knowledge as a mere epiphenomenon, he treats it as a necessary part of the social bonds between people. Further, he sees it as a power resource by which people can influence the development of social relations within the societies in which they live.

Elias posits the notion of social development which refers to the processes by which social structures (or the social relations between people) change – e.g. through the rising and falling of classes, or the division of labour, or social crises etc. I will consider this notion in relation to Forrester's worldview – which is taken to be a pre-theoretical construct encompassing theoretical beliefs, values and outlook. I regard worldviews as part of a cultural tradition shared with other people. (As noted earlier, in Fleck's terms the active connections constructed by scientists to describe nature are not independent, freely chosen objects, but are part of a cultural tradition.)

The reasons for taking a dynamic view are not only theoretical but also empirical: for system dynamics is not a static theory which has been applied uniformly to different domains at different times. On the contrary, as we have seen, it has been expanded and revised during the course of its development and an explanation of these changes will be sought in relation to various social developments which have impinged upon Forrester during his career. It will be argued that these developments influenced not only the choice of applications (the domain extensions) but the specificities of the core expansions as well.

The second perspective will address the micro-social environment within which system dynamics evolved – the System Dynamics Group and the System Dynamics Laboratory at MIT. It will draw mainly upon the work of Douglas and will focus on the concept of cosmology, which is a more precise theoretical construct within her theory. Cosmology is used to denote the systems of knowledge through which the universe is construed – including people's place in the nature of things and their relationship to society, their views of knowledge, theoretical anomalies, and time.

Douglas's thesis is that cosmologies are related to the type of social bonds in society, that they are correlated with the prevailing pattern of social relations – i.e. with social experience. Utilizing this theory I will undertake an analysis of the social experience and cosmology of the System Dynamics Group in order to understand how these have influenced the style and content of the knowledge embraced by the system dynamicists. Thus, in Part Two I will concentrate on the social bonds which unite the people who have produced the cultural artefact system dynamics.

The cultural effect of knowledge

Once this artefact has been created, it may itself serve as a binding agent between people – knowledge and cognitions are part of the social bonds that people share; Part Three will concentrate on how knowledge may be used to maintain or promote various patterns of social relations. Or in terminology derived from Fleck, I will consider the popularization and exoteric role of esoteric knowledge; this will include both the use of system dynamics as a resource for promoting the social and professional interests of its adherents, and its use in the management and control of social systems.

I will not endeavour to prove that system dynamics has actually played an active role in forcing or legitimating any particular policy decisions by politicians or social administrators. Rather, the point of interest is the fact that the policies which its practitioners have advocated carry blueprints for social systems; although these plans may never be put into operation, they are certainly a valid focus of analysis. System dynamics is aimed at large-scale social engineering and we can distinguish between its character as a resource for management and control, and the separate questions of whether it has been implemented, or would be likely to succeed. Although this implies that my argument will enter speculative areas, this will be necessary in order to do justice to the subject matter.

For this part of the analysis I will employ Douglas's view that cosmologies legitimate social relations; the focus of interest will be on how various cosmological elements within system dynamics models serve to legitimate the policies inferred from them. Douglas's position on this is derived from Durkheim (1964), the basic tenet being that cosmologies reflect an interest in social management and control. This idea stems from the postulated connection between the social and natural orders: the classification of the natural environment being seen as an extension of the system of social classifications. The social order provides a model for structuring the natural order, but it is the context of usage which is deemed to be most important. In constructing arguments about what they desire, people often couch their appeals in terms of the alleged natural order of things; these appeals tend to have a compulsive force – because they stem from a collective moral consciousness – and thereby have the effect of legitimating social relations. To understand the moral force of such appeals we must also note Douglas's use of Durkheim's theory of the sacred. This theory was based upon an epistemology which – according to Douglas – can be developed to apply to all systems of knowledge, including science. It does not relate to the validity of knowledge, but to the reasons for which it is held to be true.

For Durkheim, sacred and profane are the two poles of religious life on which the relation between individual and society is worked out. The sacred is that which the individual recognises as having ultimate authority, as being other than himself and greater than himself . . . Sacredness inheres in the moral law erected by consensus to which each individual himself subscribes. (Douglas, 1975: xiii)

Douglas argues that Durkheim's theory is about socially constructed knowledge of the universe and that it is pertinent to fundamentalist religious doctrines as well as fundamentalist theories of knowledge. (This is actually a more radical version of Durkheim's sociology of knowledge, for he had held that the sciences of his day were special and outside its domain.)

The sacred has two essential features. First, it is dangerous and hedged by protective rules; second, its boundaries are inexplicable because the reasons for any particular delineation of them are embedded in the social consensus which protects it. 'The ultimate explanation of the sacred is that this is how the universe is constituted; it is dangerous because this is what reality is like. The only person who holds nothing is sacred is the one who has not internalised the norms of any community' (Douglas, 1975: xv).

Returning to the notion of cosmologies, it is possible to suggest that conceptions of the natural order have the same quality of the sacred and any demands which are couched in such terms can be similarly difficult to evade. The idea of the sacred is therefore one root of the argument concerning the force of appeals to nature; it also pertains to the beliefs that will be uncovered in system dynamics policy recommendations – e.g. policies inferred from the natural properties of feedback systems – and is one instance of the social effect of knowledge.

The emphasis on the social interests underlying cosmologies is not the only position on the subject. For example, other anthropologists have drawn attention to the importance of contemplative and expressive interests (Horton, 1971; Shapin, 1979). However, because of the explicit policy-oriented nature of system dynamics, I do not consider that these other positions are relevant here. (The problems in Douglas's position will be discussed in chapter 4.)

In chapter 8 attention will be focused on the urban dynamics model. In addition to examining the nature of the urban structure implicit in the policy recommendations, I will also examine the implied role of system dynamics experts in urban management and planning. I will want to ask how the knowledge contained in the policies could secure social consensus and thereby cement social structures, and how it would be legitimated in this task.

Chapter 9 will be concerned with the debate that surrounded the world-modelling projects. Of particular interest to the investigation will be the different ways in which people responded to the apocalyptical message of the models. I will argue that the message was in fact interpreted in a number of disparate ways – i.e. there were several exoteric interpretations of the esoteric message – and was built into a variety of correspondingly divergent social cosmologies. These ranged from ideas of world government to small-scale alternative communities.

Throughout these two chapters I will be seeking to understand how the corpus of knowledge encapsulated in system dynamics has different, though related, social ramifications. Taking the view that knowledge is an inextricable part of the social bonds between people, I will endeavour to show that system dynamics played a more complex role in social relations than the various approaches referred to earlier might allow.

Reflexivity and the Interpretation of Texts

Before beginning the analysis, it is necessary to deal briefly with two further points. The first concerns the notion of reflexivity, the second centres on the problem of textual interpretation. Given the nature of the task and the theoretical framework that has been laid out, questions must inevitably arise about the social construction of this book. For example, the reader might wish to consider what bearing the perspective adopted here has on the status of the investigation itself. Of course the answer must be that my adopted theoretical position applies similarly to this book. But this does not mean that the arguments outlined here are merely another articulation of sociological relativism. The reason for this rebuttal is that it is possible to distinguish between the explanation of the growth of knowledge (the context of discovery) on the one hand, and the justification of knowledge (the context of legitimation) on the other. The first centres on the origin and development of ideas and is therefore the proper concern of the sociology of knowledge; it is the position taken here. The second, in contrast, centres on the validity or truthfulness of knowledge and is the concern of philosophers. The statement that knowledge is a social construction has no implication for its ultimate validity; it merely informs us about how it was produced. Similarly, the fact that this book is a social construction has no bearing upon the final validity of the arguments put forward.

The question of the perspective of the investigation raises a related question concerning textual interpretation – for much of the evidence which will be employed here to substantiate the arguments will take the form of textual extracts. I am not concerned with the history of science as such, and will therefore confine the analysis to the development of system dynamics as given by evidence in the formal record – i.e. the books and articles published by Forrester and his colleagues – and will not draw upon informal sources such as letters or personal meetings. The use of textual extracts begs many questions concerning the problem of interpretation. For example, how does the reader know that extracts selected from a text are a genuine representation of the text as a whole? And, further, what standing or meaning does a text have in relation to the sort of topics pursued here – for instance, the worldview and cosmology of the system dynamicists?

In reading a text one does so from a particular perspective or interpretative framework – whether implicitly or explicitly. Some exegetes, or interpreters, may place an emphasis on style, authorial peculiarities of terminology, or the grammatical rules governing the language of a text. (A comprehensive discussion is given by Mazzeo, 1978.) Another position – derived from hermeneutic theory – is represented by Mannheim who argued that a satisfactory understanding of a text can only be arrived at if the interpreter can assimilate the framework of meanings from within which the text was written (Mannheim, 1968). In opposition to those who advocate the semantic autonomy of a text, Mannheim held that understanding required consideration of the *weltanschauung* or worldview of the writer. (Here I will use the term worldview but it is worth stating that it does not entirely capture the meaning of its German counterpart.) Understanding requires not only that a text be analysed with a view to characterizing the worldview of the writer; but also, understanding of the text is itself informed by knowledge of that worldview. This notion of the circuitous route of interpretation is known as the 'hermeneutic circle of understanding'.

Now all this may seem to present us with a paradox: because on the one hand we need to know about the worldview of the system dynamicists in order to interpret their textual output, and yet on the other hand we need the texts to understand their worldview. However, the point about the hermeneutic circle is that understanding proceeds step by step – from text to worldview, back and forth – until the picture gradually becomes clearer.

In seeking to comprehend the context of meanings from within which a text was produced, we do not necessarily have to make any evaluative statements with regard to the truth or falsity of the text. Although the identification and characterization of a worldview logically implies the particularity of a viewpoint, and is therefore evaluative, this is not the purpose of the exercise in comprehension. In characterizing the worldview of a group or person we inevitably particularize and delimit the extent of validity of the knowledge of that group or person. However, the mere imputation of a statement to say Marxism or Liberalism does not imply the truth or falsity of that statement per se.

Having drawn attention to some of the more obvious problems involved in textual interpretation, there is another and deeper problem which centres on the status of texts. Earlier it was stated that the analysis would concentrate on the formal record of the system dynamicists but I have not discussed the standing of the texts in relation to the aims of the analysis or indeed to the system dynamicists themselves. To address this issue it is useful to describe Mannheim's ideas a little further.

Mannheim discussed textual interpretation in relation to three levels of meaning. These levels are denoted by the terms 'objective', 'expressive', and 'documentary' (Mannheim, 1968; Simonds, 1978). A text has an objective meaning in that it describes, or states, or argues for, or against, some state of affairs. It also has expressive meaning in that its author wished to express or communicate something. Further, a text has a documentary meaning which is not the intentional object of the author. Although the author controls the expressive meaning of a work, he or she cannot inform the reader as to how the work is to be interpreted. Documentary meaning appears as the context of communication; it is not available to the author; he or she is part of their own socio-historical location and this is reflected in the documentary evidence accompanying the text. Documentary evidence is concerned with the socio-historical context of meaning that is established alongside intentional acts of expression. 'The context of meaning relations which makes communication possible is thus a construct which (like any metalanguage) can only be considered from outside – by a reflexive or retrospective act of consciousness' (Simonds, 1978: 83). To arrive at documentary meaning, Mannheim set forward certain traits which he used to characterize a worldview. These included the meaning of concepts; the absence of concepts; the structure of the categorical apparatus which is used; dominant models of thought; the level of abstraction; and the ontology that is presupposed (Mannheim, 1936).

A very different approach was taken by Foucault (1972) who argued that texts could only be viewed in relation to certain 'discursive practices' and 'rules of formation': these govern the articulation of specific classes of statements and thereby make texts intelligible. (See also Guedon, 1977; another view of the nature of discourse is adopted by Mulkay et al., 1983.) While I cannot pursue these matters here, nor those raised by other writers on interpretation, I must at least acknowledge that like any interpreter I start from a theoretical position. For the purposes of this investigation it is given by the concepts of worldview and social development, cosmology and social structure. From these I seek to understand the shared knowledge of the system dynamicists via the texts of their formal output. It is perhaps fair to say that the validity of the interpretations is rooted more in the validity of the adopted theoretical position rather than in the problems and contingencies of textual extraction itself.

While not following Mannheim, there are some parallels in the approach taken here. For example, during the course of the analysis of the worldview and cosmology implicit in system dynamics, I will draw upon elements similar to the traits listed earlier. Moreover, the discussion in Part Two will, in seeking to locate the development of system dynamics within a cultural tradition and social context, indirectly address the documentary level of meaning. Of course this does not provide any final solution to the problems outlined earlier: one can always pose the question as to the representativeness of textual extracts. However, by giving clear references to the sources, I can provide the opportunity for the falsification of my assertions. In other words, although I cannot prove the validity of my interpretations, it is possible – by indicating the source of the extracts – to allow them to be refuted.

PART TWO
The Social Construction of
System Dynamics

3 Social Engineering: From Corporate Power to Crises of Social Order

In this chapter I will construct an argument about the relationship between the evolution of system dynamics and the social structure which nurtured it. At the end of chapter 1 we saw that the theory of system dynamics was marked by changes and expansions of its theoretical core during the course of its application to successive domains. The task here is to interpret this pattern of growth and I will do so by relating it to the social development of the society in which system dynamics evolved.

In order to set out the problem which confronts us, let me first reiterate the major flaw of the 'reflection theory' posited by economic determinism. While accepting the basic premise of such theories – i.e. that ideas do not exist in a social vacuum – nevertheless, it is contended that they cannot be reduced to a mere reflection of the economic base of the social structure. Thus, in the case of Forrester, the position adopted here is that it is simplistic to see him solely as some 'puppet' of capitalism. While certainly not denying the possibility that his models may be used to promote or justify specific features of the social structure – for example, the interests of capitalism – such interests are not in themselves sufficient to explain the development of his work. For instance, although Forrester remains committed to capitalism per se – a commitment which represents a social interest – we shall see that his changing interpretation of his interests has led him to move from the idea of American-style capitalist expansion throughout the world, to the idea that industrial growth must stop. We therefore need a more sophisticated model than can be provided by a reflection theory.

The writings of Elias (1971a,b, 1978a,b, 1982) are relevant in this context because he argues that the relationship between knowledge and social structures is neither simple nor static, and in fact contends that they are inextricably *intertwined* in their development. Thus, rather than employing a reflection theory or the various other dichotomies to be found in the philosophy and sociology of science – for example, those which differentiate between cognitive and social factors, or internal and external histories – Elias's formulation suggests that such artificial distinctions must be transcended, and requires us to understand ideas in the context of the social development of the society in which they originate and evolve.

Before elucidating this notion of social development, it is first necessary to discuss Elias's concept of a 'figuration'. He uses this term to denote the different networks of interdependencies which link people together – both within and between societies. This concept does not readily map on to class boundaries alone; rather, classes are but one type of figuration. The linkages between classes (e.g. through the mode of production) are another type. But a family too is a specific figuration, as is the network of families which make up a small community, or the the members of a research laboratory etc. Elias's concept of social development centres on the processes by which the interweavings of different figurations change: for example, through the division of labour; political integration into nation states; or the changing power differentials between different groups or classes. Defined in this way, it should be obvious that the concept of development does not have any *a priori* positive or negative connotation.

The processes of social development do not just denote material changes in society, but also point to developments in knowledge and ideas. In fact, shared knowledge binds people together and is a power–resource which may cause some people to have more influence on the development of the social relations within the figurations in which they live. To take an example, it was only at a certain period in history that people came to think that the world contained an economic sphere which was distinctly separate from the realm of politics (Elias, 1978a). This occurred during the rise to power of the entrepreneurial bourgeoisie; they wished to avoid political interference by governments – which at that time were largely made up of the pre-industrial aristocracy – and demanded that the 'separate' economic sphere should be allowed to follow its own 'natural' laws. Such a view contrasts with that sustainable by a reflection theory. For although the new ideas about the economy are seen as representing the interests of the rising class, they are not seen solely as a reflection of those interests. Rather, they are seen as a product of the social development of the wider society and in particular of the figurational interrelationship between the aristocracy and the bourgeoisie. It was this that helped to shape the bourgeoisie's perceptions of the world – including their notions about the economy – which metamorphosed from the idea that economy *ought* to be autonomous, to the idea that it actually *was* autonomous and was subsequently perceived as such. Further, as a power-resource these ideas contributed to social development – such as the transformation of political economy and the subsequent birth of economics as a distinct discipline – and were therefore not insignificant epiphenomena as economic reductionism often suggests (Elias, 1978a: 140).

At that time the bourgeoisie had a generally optimistic outlook on the world and embraced ideas of progress and development 'for the better'; they were in the ascendant, and so to them the future looked bright. In contrast, the pre-industrial aristocracy represented a power that belonged to the past. For Elias, this link between a figuration's social situation, its outlook, and the knowledge to which it adheres, is an important one – it transcends any *a priori* distinction between thought and feeling. He argues that not only must we desist from a strict distinction between cognitive and social, but the cognitive element itself should not be rigidly construed so as to exclude feeling. For the separation of thought and feeling is not a trans-historical given, but depends upon social development (Elias, 1978b, 1982). He thus allows an important role for feeling and outlook, for wishes and fears, in the development of society and knowledge.

Later, Elias argues, the social situation of the bourgeoisie changed and so too did their knowledge and outlook. Interstate and intrastate developments – such as the First World War and the Great Depression – helped to blunt the idea of progress. The bourgeoisie became more pessimistic in their outlook and the future appeared less bright. Moreover, it appeared to contain forces – such as communism – which threatened to undermine the whole bourgeois world order. The knowledge they adhered to subsequently changed as well, and theories about progress became replaced by theories which focused on the present social order and were directed at conserving and defending it (Elias, 1978b: 242).

These ideas concerning the relationship between knowledge, outlook, and social development, suggest the basis for an argument which is useful to the study of Forrester and system dynamics. In Simmons's (1973) review of the emergence of system dynamics he draws an analogy with the 'Technocracy' movement of the 1930s. At that time, during the Great Depression, a group of engineers led by H. Scott put themselves forward as saviours of US society – adumbrating the thesis that only the rational and scientific methods of engineering could solve the crisis. However, in my investigation of the modern social engineers of MIT, I will show that their work embodied an important difference in the form of a conservative moral outlook which cannot be explained by reference to the goals of technocratic elites. In order to execute the task I propose to draw an analogy between Forrester's work and a particular development within academic sociology. This is the emergence of Talcott Parsons's social theory (structural–functionalism) which is of interest here for two reasons: first, it too was based upon a systems-theoretic view of society (Parsons,

1951); and second, the history of structural-functionalism provides an illustrative example of the relationship between knowledge and social development. In fact, Gouldner (1971) has provided a detailed critique of Parsons which attempts to demonstrate the relationship between his social theory and the social contexts in which it evolved – that is, the period between the 1930s and 1950s. I propose to consider this critique as a case study of the type of approach advocated by Elias, who in fact has also drawn attention to the development of functionalist sociology, and has singled out Parsons's work as an example of social developments which have impinged upon the middle–classes during the past century (Elias, 1978b: 222–63). Like Elias, Gouldner focuses upon the changing fortunes and outlook of the middle classes and uses this to chart the evolution of Parsons's social theory. For instance, he argues that the problem of social order – e.g. during the Great Depression of the 1930s – played an important role in shaping Parsons's particular systems view of society.

Given that the plausibility of the analogy can be established, I will be in a position to use Gouldner's conclusions to make inferences concerning Forrester's own work – the threat to social order posed by the urban and environmental crises of the 1960s and 1970s being particularly relevant in this respect. The comparison with Parsons will enable us to go into detail concerning Forrester's theoretical position (and its evolution) and relate it to social developments and his changing outlook. In order to structure the comparison, I will consider the worldviews of both theorists – which are taken to consist of theoretical beliefs, values, and general outlook. The argument will not be limited to showing how social developments helped influence the successive choice of domains to which system dynamics was applied (external history): rather, it will also demonstrate their constitutive role in the expansion and changes in the theoretical core.

At this point I should note that the analogy may appear open to the charge that it seeks to establish some form of guilt by association. However, the argument developed here is both more subtle and more complex than the charge allows. For the parallels between Parsons and Forrester are not drawn to uncover any form of shared guilt – rather, the purpose is to justify the extension of Gouldner's critique to explain the development of system dynamics, and to establish that elements in the worldview which encompasses it are not isolated to systems engineers but are part of a specific cultural tradition. (For other comparisons between functionalism and systems theory see: Buckley, 1967; Checkland, 1982; Lilienfeld, 1978; Sullivan, 1976.)

The Worldviews of Parsons and Forrester

In order to establish the similarities between the worldviews of Parsons and Forrester I will consider several important background (domain) assumptions and themes which are discernible in their respective systems theories – namely, process-reduction, the oneness of the world, conflict, common interests, system interdependence, system requisites. These features not only illustrate their theoretical beliefs, but will also be used to yield information with regard to their value orientations and outlook.

Process-reduction

The models of social systems which are postulated by structural–functionalism and system dynamics can readily be seen as examples of process-reduction – that is, they reduce the processual nature of society, its long-term social fluxes, to a *state* (Elias, 1978a: 115). For example, Parsons drew upon an organic analogy for describing social systems; he thought of society as a living organism in which social processes corresponded to organic processes (Buckley, 1967). Despite its obvious attraction, this analogy has the drawback that it forced him to refer social processes back to some static framework which corresponded to the organism itself. This turned out to be the dominant institutional infrastructure of society at the time. Further, though processes were indeed present in Parsons's model, they were seen as intrinsic to the system. In contrast, social change was perceived as a perturbing force which was extrinsic to the system. 'Social change thus appears as a phenomenon resulting from the accidental, externally activated malfunction of a normally well-balanced social system. Moreover, the society thus disturbed strives, in Parsons's view, to regain its state of rest' (Elias, 1978b: 230).

The organic analogy has surfaced in Forrester's work too (Forrester, 1969: 129), and he accordingly perceived the dynamics of systems in relation to an unchanging structure which again largely reflected dominant values and institutions. System dynamics models were purported to simulate past and future time, but their structural features remained fixed. The present was therefore projected into the future and the ensemble of processes that pervade the fabric of societies – and which in fact make them societies – were frozen into an unchanging concrete structure.

Parsons and Forrester regarded social systems as 'real world' entities which existed above and beyond the individuals within them. In other words, systems had an ontological status in their respective frameworks. Systems theory was not just seen as a way of gaining knowledge about the world (a matter of epistemology): for Parsons and Forrester it was a way of revealing the properties of a world that is actually systemic. This helped to reinforce the important role played by process-reduction, for if society was a system and – through the organic analogy – had an institutional core which was unchangeable in its essentials, then long-term social processes would be ignored as extraneous to the system as it was construed at the time.

The oneness of the world

System dynamics and structural-functionalism share a similar metaphysical conviction about the 'oneness' of the world. Thus, a social system is not merely a unity of elements – an integration of separate parts – it is a *whole*, and its elements express this oneness. 'Its oneness, Parsons believes, is the world's most vital character. Its parts, therefore, take on meaning and significance only in relation to this wholeness' (Gouldner, 1971: 199).

This conviction can be seen in system dynamics by the way in which analysis has proceeded: whether it was a corporation, a city, a nation, or the whole world that was being studied, each was seen as a totality and it was the total system which provided the point of departure and the frame of reference for analysis. With Forrester, one immediate consequence was that the causes of social problems – as well as prescriptions for their solution – were sought solely in terms of system properties. For example, some problems were attributed to the pursuit of short-term goals, or to the counterintuitive nature of complex systems. The upshot of this approach was that theories based upon the notion of class conflicts or contradictions (for instance, Marxist theories) were excluded from any debate concerning the nature and origin of social problems.

This exclusion-tendency can be seen also in structural-functionalism. In fact, Gouldner argues that Parsons was motivated to counter the model of society posited by Marxism. Marx too had conceived of society as a system; yet for him the divisions in the social world – its conflicts and contradictions – were its deepest reality. In contrast, Gouldner suggests that for Parsons it was not the cleavages in the social world that were real, but rather, its *unbroken oneness*.

The vision that the world is one contributed to a distinct view of subsystems. Simply stated, Parsons's approach entailed the study of social relations in terms of the functions they had or performed for some larger structure – hence the name 'structural-functionalism'. For example, an organization was conceived as a cluster of functional relationships which were ordered so as to produce a self-maintaining entity. Further, the organization was seen to have a common pattern of values and norms which integrated its separate elements or subsystems into the organizational whole. This idea of the functional integration of system elements underpinned industrial dynamics; the term 'functional' being used to describe organizational activities, which were looked upon as a contribution to the working of the total system.

Conflict

Given that they were committed to the notion that the world was one, Parsons and Forrester – not surprisingly – discussed conflict in a distinctive way. Anything which was functional was thought to be implicitly good; with structural-functionalism this bias was derived from its positivist heritage. The 'positive' orientation of that philosophy meant that social phenomena were to be explained in terms of some functional operation in a larger system; they were therefore seen as something positive, something which contributed to the integration and maintenance of the system. This connected with the idea that conflict was bad, for it was seen to be 'dysfunctional' – it threatened the disintegration and breakdown of the system. Forrester adhered to a corresponding view and his consequent commitment to social order (i.e. the absence of conflicts) is clearly seen, for example, in the following extract.

> Our most challenging intellectual frontier of the next three decades probably lies in the dynamics of organizations, ranging from the growth of the small corporation to development of national economies. As organizations become more complex, the need for skilled leadership becomes greater. Labor turmoil, bankruptcy, inflation, economic collapse, political unrest, revolution, and war, testify that we are not yet expert enough in the design and management of social systems. (Forrester, 1961: 1)

Though Forrester did perceive the possibility of goal conflicts between different subsystems, he did not believe that conflict was a structurally inherent feature of social systems. Much the same can be said of Parsons, and in fact his neglect of conflict has frequently been cited as an important flaw in his social systems model. 'By no feat of the imagination, not even by the residual category of 'dysfunction', can the integrated and equilibrated social system be made to produce serious and patterned conflicts in its structure.' (Dahrendorf, 1967: 471) Neither theorist could accept that conflict might be part and parcel of the social world. Moreover, it has been suggested that Parsons's concern with social order was basically a moral one (Gouldner, 1971). In connection with this we may usefully note that Forrester has advocated an important role for religion in maintaining a future global equilibrium society – thus evincing a similar moral dimension in social order.

Common interests

The belief about the world's oneness, coupled with the functional perception of subsystems, led both men to embrace the idea of common interests or common system goals. The argument seems to have been that if the world was one, there must be certain goals which unite all of the subsystems within the system. Parsons was concerned with the import-ance of value consensus – which he saw as vital for the integration of the system; this was only possible if common goals existed. In Forrester's case we find an argument that (in the long run) only the pursuit of system goals (for instance, common interests) could benefit the system as a whole. He therefore called for the subordination of subsystem goals to the system goals which alone serve the common interest of all. His view of conflict surfaces again here: conflicts of interests were seen not only as threats to system stability, but also as blocks preventing subsystems from achieving long-term benefits through the integration and stability of the total system.

Interdependence

The concept of system interdependence is a central feature in many systems theories. Basically, the idea is that a system's elements are in reciprocal interdependence with each other and there are therefore no single-factor deterministic elements – no simple causes and effects. The concept of interdependence has a number of problems associated with it: for instance, the issue of the measurement or quantification of inter-dependence; or the perception of the system *vis-à-vis* system elements. By examining these problems we can see the conceptual overlap between structural-functionalism and system dynamics and the contrast between them and other systems theories.

In Parsons's work the problem of the varying degrees of interdepend-ence was not raised. In part, Gouldner tells us, this was due to the lack of a body of mathematics which would be required to address the problem. A measure of interdependence implies quantification and therefore calls for a mathematical approach. Turning to Forrester, we can see that although he used mathematical modelling techniques and computer simulations, the model variables were enclosed in feedback loops – where everything influenced everything else – and he did not raise the question of the differential degrees of interdependence between the variables.

The lack of attention paid to the measurement of interdependence was rooted in the form of the relationship posited between a system and its elements. In contrast to conceiving of systems in terms of interdependence, Gouldner (1971) outlined an alternative model based upon the idea of the functional autonomy of system elements. According to his model, systems can be seen as an assembly of elements which have a varying degree of functional autonomy with regard to each other. Thus, some elements may be highly autonomous – meeting most of their own needs – while certain other elements may have a low degree of functional autonomy and therefore depend upon interchanges with the other elements for the satisfaction of their needs. In this model, a system is seen as a group of elements whose interchanges restrict their functional autonomy.

Conceptualizing in terms of interdependence – as Parsons and Forrester did – focuses on the whole and the close-connectedness of its parts. This therefore emphasized the oneness of the whole and the parts were seen in relation to their systems character. Conversely, conceptualizing – as Gouldner did – in terms of functional autonomy, sharpens focus upon the parts themselves. In this alternative model the system elements are not seen merely as 'parts' but have an existence on their own; and their connectedness actually becomes problematic because it restricts their autonomy. And whereas the positions of Parsons and Forrester led them to concentrate upon the mechanisms that protected the system in its totality, Gouldner's approach leads to a consideration of the mechanisms that protect the autonomy of the parts.

System requisites

The Parsonsian theoretical framework included the idea of four system requisites (or system problems) which were all involved in the protection of the system and its persistence. These system 'needs' were: adaptation, goal attainment, pattern-maintenance, and integration (Gouldner, 1971: 207).

The idea of *adaptation* was concerned with the manner in which a system responds to changes in its environment. Given a situation of scarcity and contingency, it is necessary for a system to adapt to environmental conditions by allocating personnel and resources in the best possible configuration to pursue its goals. Related to this, *goal attainment* was the problem of ensuring that a system is actually directed towards its goals. The notion of *pattern-maintenance* was used to describe the way in which a system tends to maintain its equilibrium state through homeostasis. As suggested earlier, the steady state was seen as the normal condition of a system and change was perceived as being extrinsic – a transient phenomenon as the system moved from one equilibrium state to another.

The patterns which a system maintains were thought to be constituted by shared norms and values, which in turn obtained various 'patterns of action' – the pattern variables. With reference to this, Dahrendorf (1967: 471) employed the metaphor of a 'village pond' to encapsulate the basis of Parsons's social systems model. 'Homeostasis is maintained by the regular occurrence of certain patterned processes which, far from disturbing the tranquility of the village pond, in fact are the village pond.' Lastly, *integration* was the problem of maintaining value consensus, or a shared value system, which was seen to facilitate goal attainment and pattern-maintenance.

In system dynamics we can find ideas which are analogous to these four system requisites, though they are not given the same formal role. For example, in *World Dynamics* it was suggested that physical limits to growth were being encountered by the world system and that continued growth in population and industrialization represented a threat to the system's viability. This pointed to a problem in the relationship between the world system and its environment and was therefore a problem concerning adaptation. The proposed solution to the problem was said to lie in a global equilibrium society where growth in industry and population would cease. Forrester discussed the problem of maintaining long-term operating goals (which were thought necessary to achieve and preserve equilibrium) in the face of short-term desires – this paralleled the Parsonsian problem of goal attainment (Forrester, 1975b: 262).

Forrester believed that systems were purposive, by which he meant that they were goal-seeking. Further, that goal was conceived of as an equilibrium state where any growth tendencies in a system's positive feedback loops were arrested (or checked) by its negative feedback loops. In fact, we can actually consider negative feedback to be a type of protective mechanism for a system; indeed, positive loops move away from a goal while negative loops move towards a goal. Parsons viewed equilibrium in more sociological terms – through the operation of the pattern variables – but despite this difference in the exact phenomena implicated in equilibrium, the central core of each conception was the same, that is, order and the absence of structural change were considered to be the normal or preferred conditions of a system.

Negative feedback is not the only protective mechanism to be found in system dynamics; in fact, as with structural-functionalism, other mechanisms turn out to be rooted in the role of value structures, and so the problem of integration also surfaced in Forrester's theory. Forrester's ideas on values were primarily confined to his later work, from the period of urban dynamics onwards. This marked a very interesting change in his theoretical position for, in addition to the cybernetic feedback properties of systems, he then began to re-focus his theory to include the role played by individual value commitments in securing system equilibrium and stability. For instance, Forrester (1975b: 266) asserted that long-term value structures determine what society may be like up to 1000 years ahead, so these structures were obviously perceived to play an important role in system stability. 'The long-term value component in an operating goal is an enduring standard that transcends adversity and short-term pressures. It is deeply embedded in the collective character of the system' (Forrester, 1975b: 262). This compares with the Parsonian perspective, where value structures contributed to goal attainment by ensuring system integration.

Forrester contended that many of contemporary society's values, such as humanitarianism, were only oriented towards short-term interests. In contrast, he believed that there were certain long-term values which were oriented towards long-term interests, such as the viability of the system as a whole. 'Morality and ethics must focus on how we are to make the choice between that which is favourable to us in the present and that which is right for humanity in the future' (Forrester, 1975b: 252). Not only did Parsons and Forrester share a similar concern about value consensus, they also treated some values – namely order and stability – as transcendental. With Forrester, these values would presumably have been judged to be 'right for humanity'. The notion that some values are transcendental and not culturally specific, was really another extension of their conviction of the world's oneness and underscored their fixation on the present order of things – they could see no alternative to it because it rested on immutable values.

This brief survey of Parsons and Forrester has demonstrated a cluster of common theoretical beliefs and has provided a useful picture of their systemic view of the world. Throughout the discussion I have endeavoured to establish the similarities between them by reference to alternative theoretical beliefs and views of social systems. Interwoven with their beliefs we can discern a number of value orientations and can begin to obtain an insight into their outlook. Thus, for example, both placed a similar value on the moral basis of social order – in contrast to non-moral bases of social order (e.g. material gratifications); they were both committed to society's dominant institutions. Of course this account of both worldviews is not exhaustive and needless to say one could point out many differences between Parsons and Forrester; nevertheless, the theoretical beliefs discussed here played a central role within structural-functionalism and system dynamics. It suggests that the beliefs upon which system dynamics were founded were not confined to the aspiring social engineers from MIT but have also played an important role in a branch of sociology. A fundamental question of interest thus arises as to the reasons for these important similarities.

My contention is that the root of the parallels between Parsons and Forrester does not just lie in their adherence to similar forms of systems theory – as if these could exist in a social vacuum – but more importantly, in the cultural traditions and social developments which have moulded their respective formulation and use of systems ideas. The application of a concept is not determined by the concept itself but depends upon the judgement of human agency (Barnes, 1983); so too with systems theory. I contend that Parsons and Forrester both drew upon systems theory and shaped it as a knowledge resource to promote their interpretations of their interests – these being related to their class position and the tradition in which they stood. The next task therefore, is to discuss Gouldner's thesis that Parsons's work was a product of the changing fortunes of the American middle classes. This will help to further exemplify the model of the relationship between worldviews and social development to which I referred at the beginning of the chapter. I will then be in a position to make inferences concerning Forrester's work and in the final section will discuss the development of his theoretical framework in relation to these inferences. This will actually consolidate the analogy because it will demonstrate the similarity between the separate evolutions of system dynamics and structural-functionalism in relation to social development. In other words, it will establish the fact that Parsons and Forrester not only shared similar beliefs, values and social interests (e.g. a desire to preserve society's dominant institutions), but that in addition, their theories have evolved in connection with similar pressures and constraints – namely, threats to social order.

Parsons's Work as a Product of Social Development

Structural-functionalism has roots which can be traced back to the sociological positivism of Comte; but while the latter had an evolutionary perspective the former has been more oriented towards the present. In Comte's time the middle classes had embraced a forward–looking utopian vision that sought to sweep away the power of the old elites who opposed the rising tide of industrialization. In contrast, the middle classes of Parsons's society upheld a very different outlook; for them, the future appeared far from bright.

> [U]nlike the Positivists, the middle class of Parsons's society was not threatened by an *old* elite which was identified with and drew attention to the past, and thus did not need to look forward to a future in which it would be rid of that incubus. The forces threatening the modern middle class are themselves very future-

oriented and look forward to a radically different society. Parsonsian Functionalism, therefore, is grounded in a class experience that has no stimulus to focus upon the past and little desire that its future be radically different. Its impulses are fundamentally conservative: they want more, but more of the *same*. (Gouldner, 1971: 199)

Thus, on this view, Parsons's theory is to be seen as part of a long–term change in the outlook of the middle classes; its sentiments were focused upon the present while the future was seen to contain potential dangers to the social order. Gouldner viewed Parsons's early work as a theoretical response to the Great Depression of the 1930s. He also notes that it had developed at a time when the world had witnessed the growth of communism after the Bolshevik Revolution; the rise of fascism in Germany and Italy; and the shattering, by the First World War, of middle-class confidence in the idea of progress. In connection with this it is pertinent to note that Parsons (1970) himself referred to some of these international developments, and in fact stated that his first book – *The Structure of Social Action* (Parsons, 1937) – which emerged against this background, marked a major turning point in his professional career and clarified the development of his thought concerning the problems of the state in Western society.

Gouldner's thesis was that Parsons's work reflected the international concern of the world's middle classes with the problem of maintaining social order. 'The empirical emptiness and abstractness of the Parsonsian analysis of social order reflected an effort to respond to the existence of an international crisis that simultaneously threatened the middle class in capitalist countries on different levels of industrialisation and within different political traditions' (Gouldner, 1971: 145). He argued that Parsons had evinced a conservative optimism in the status quo and in society's institutions; realizing the extent and depth of the crisis, he had focused on the problem of social order rather than the contemporary social problems of the everyday world at that time. During the Great Depression the economic system had broken down with catastrophic consequences, it could no longer provide the things which had held American middle-class society together. Thus, Gouldner asserted, because Parsons dearly wished for society to be held together, he was forced to find a non-economic source of social integration.

In the time-worn manner of the conservative, Parsons looked to individual moral commitment to cement society. Parsons' voluntaristic sociology did not consider the crisis soluble in terms of the New Deal's welfare efforts, so, in effect, it concerned itself with what was necessary to integrate society *despite* mass deprivation. (Gouldner, 1971: 141)

Parsons thought that society could be held together by morality and that it would require neither changes in its economic institutions, nor redistributions of income or power. Also, he was suspicious of the New Deal and it was only during the post-war expansion of the welfare state that he came to accommodate his theory to the idea of the need for the state to take an active interventionist role in society.

Parsons's later work took on a more sophisticated systems-theoretic perspective in the 1950s. Since the Second World War the state had acted in the name of national security; war-induced solidarity was complemented by the integration of the unions and the working class into mainstream society and the threat of social disorder receded (Gouldner, 1971: 141). 'To see society in terms of firm, clearly defined structures, as Parsons' new theory did, was not now dissonant with the collective experience, the shared personal reality, of daily life' (Gouldner, 1971: 142). It was at this time that he came to perceive society as a self-maintaining homeostatic system; going beyond the integrative function of shared values he came to focus on the mechanisms which internally contribute to the stability of the social system. Parsons's work at this time also developed in the context of what he believed to be a dangerous threat imposed by the Soviet Union: Gouldner argues that this concern, particularly in light of the Marxist prophecy that capitalism contained the seeds of its own destruction, acted as another important influence upon his theoretical output.

> At the very source of Parsons' whole intellectual effort, then, was an effort to combat this death prophecy; to seek or formulate a social system so general in character that it need never die; to endow it richly with a perpetual, self-maintaining character; to remove or iron out all hint of internal disruption and decay. (Gouldner, 1971: 434)

His work subsequently changed its emphasis from the central problem of order, and its solution in voluntarism (spontaneous individual value commitments), to the complex mechanisms of pattern-maintenance and self-regulation.

Finally, Gouldner argued that although Parsons did move some way towards the welfare state, functionalism still adopted a characteristic moral attitude towards social problems.

> Sociological Functionalism's emphasis on the role of moral values and on the significance of morality more generally, often leads it to locate contemporary social problems in the breakdown of the moral system; for example, as due to defects in the systems of socialization and as due to their failure to train people to behave in conformity with the moral norms. (Gouldner, 1971: 343)

Functionalism, therefore, did not advocate the kind of technocratic rationality – and the technocratic conception of social problems – that came to play a predominant role within the welfare state (Gouldner, 1971: 342-4).

It must be noted that Gouldner's thesis is rather controversial within sociological circles and I do not wish to imply that the matter is cut and dried. However, I do not propose to evaluate Gouldner's position *vis-à-vis* his critics. The justification is twofold. First, much of the controversy arguably does not address any substantive issues bearing upon whether or not Parsons's thought was influenced by social development; instead, it tends to revolve around semantic differences – for example, discussions of whether Parsons was a 'conservative' or a 'liberal' thinker.[1] This criticism misses Gouldner's point for it ignores his definition of 'conservatism'. Though he allowed that Parsons may indeed have been liberal in a narrow political sense, he was 'conservative' in that in the face of the threat to social order his overriding concern was the conservation of society's dominant institutions. A second – though weaker – reason is that the very existence of controversy is of no value in reflecting upon the worth or merit of any particular thesis. Indeed, the history of science provides us with numerous examples of why this is so (Kuhn, 1970).

Gouldner's critique of Parsons suggests inferences which could be applied to Forrester. In fact, there are a number of plausible reasons for viewing Forrester in the same light as Gouldner views Parsons. First, Parsons was a member of an elite educational establishment – Harvard – while Forrester worked at the exclusive MIT – both strongholds of middle-class institutions and values (Riesman, 1980). Secondly, Forrester developed his early ideas on social systems during the 1950s when Parsons was working on his more sophisticated systems model; though working on very different applications of systems theory – one military/technological, the other sociological – both worked within the tense climate created by the ideological confrontation between the US and the Soviet Union. Thirdly, each of Forrester's later modelling efforts were addressed to some form of crisis in society; thus – as with Parsons – he faced the problem of social order. Thus, we might conjecture that the successive domains and core expansions of system dynamics were constrained by a wish to preserve social order in the face of social crises. Further, we can infer that whatever policies were to emerge from Forrester's models, they would be bounded by his worldview and the goals and interests enmeshed within it.

In the next section I will examine the extension of system dynamics to different domains and the theoretical shifts which characterized that expansion. If the analogy with Parsons is reasonable, then it should be possible to explain these shifts – as well as the overall direction of Forrester's work – in relation to these inferences.

Theoretical Shifts and Social Context

Forrester developed industrial dynamics during the late 1950s and early 1960s; one of his justifications for the approach was that it would contribute towards the American challenge for world leadership. 'We see already that the international struggle of the 1950s that was based on military technological competition is changing to a struggle to achieve economic strength and sufficient understanding of economic change to form a new basis for world leadership' (Forrester, 1961: 7). Forrester's earlier work on military systems had directly supported the 'military technological competition' to which he refers, and his work on industrial dynamics was intended as a basis for improving the strength of American corporations – something which would presumably aid the US in its struggle for global leadership. He did not believe that this would be won by the space race under way at the time but rather thought that success lay in the control of economic systems. In a paper which first appeared in 1959 in the *Harvard Business Review* and is reprinted in Forrester's *Collected Papers* (1975b: 44) he stated

> The challenge and new frontier in our capitalist society during the next three decades is not space flight but the science of management and economics. It is in management and economics, not on the moon or Mars, that the current international competition will be won. The American corporation is the heart of the American economic system. How well we fare will depend on how well American corporate management understands its job.

And in another paper, from 1960, we find the following:

> For the last twenty years, international competition has been in the area of force supported by scientific advances. The rules of the contest are now changing. The test is now of leadership in showing the way to economic development and political stability. (Forrester, 1975b: 45)

Thus, Forrester held up American economic development and political stability as a model for the rest of the world to follow. Though he did not specifically refer to the Russians by name, it was of course the Soviet Union which was the other main contender in the competition to which he refers. In other words, we can conjecture that the Cold War ideological confrontation with the Soviets left its imprint on his work, for its aim was to help the United States win the international competition.

Turning now to the urban-modelling project, this took place against a background of urban decay and poverty on a vast scale; rioting and arson in cities such as Detroit; and mass protest by American Blacks. Forrester's view of the emergence of this stage of his work focused on biographical details. For example, he has referred to his contact with the ex-Mayor of Boston, Collins, who after leaving public office occupied the room next to him at MIT (Forrester, 1969). He also stressed the fact that the ideas upon which the model was based did not come from the academic literature but largely from top men in urban management and his own knowledge: he provided the model structure while they gave insights into the detailed relationships. On this reading, only the model was new but the underlying systems theory remained the same.

But of course this view is only one possible interpretation, or description, of the emergence of the urban model, and it contrasts with the inferences made earlier. For example, it notably does not take into account any of the various theoretical shifts that can be unearthed within urban dynamics *vis-à-vis* industrial dynamics. Another interpretation is that we should not see urban dynamics merely as a theoretical elaboration of industrial dynamics – i.e. a technical adjustment of the theory to fit a new domain – but as a *new* theory which, in part, was forged beneath the hammer of the threat to social order. In other words, after his consultations with urban managers, Forrester withdrew to his computer terminal and produced a model which encompassed an esoteric variant of the exoteric knowledge he had accumulated. Moreover, this knowledge was constrained by the social interests of the parties involved. It is this second interpretation which will be pursued here, and I will substantiate it by reference to the relevant theoretical changes.

Forrester had definite views on government intervention in the urban crisis and the responsibilities of local administrations. He was, for example, opposed to massive influxes of government money to tackle urban problems for he believed that they could only be solved by changed internal practices, that only programmes of intrinsic low cost were feasible. He took the view that a city should be a master of its own destiny – that, in other words, it should be a self-regulating system. Of course, the idea that systems could be self-regulating was not new; the point of interest is in the way Forrester drew his system boundary around his hypothetical city. His choice was in fact resonant with a common feature of American culture – namely the notion of individual freedom which has evolved amid suspicion of the Federal Government. (This parallels Parsons's hostility towards the New Deal during the Great Depression. Then and now proposals for government intervention to solve social crises were often perceived by the middle classes as a further destabilising threat to social order and were debarred from the agenda of possible solutions.)

In other words, he offered a systems-theoretic justification for a long held middle class conviction; this illustrates an important point – namely, the rationale in drawing a system boundary depends upon the worldview and social interests of the systems analyst.

In *Urban Dynamics* we find that Forrester makes the assumption that underemployed Negroes (his term) should be integrated into the economic framework of the city. 'This study assumes that extreme concentration of economic and social groups is detrimental and that success will be more easily achieved in a single economic system than in two separate and parallel systems' (Forrester, 1969: 115). Interestingly enough, he provided no systems-theoretic justification for this assumption although it represented an expansion of his theory of social systems and one which apparently contradicted his thesis that a city should be master of its own destiny. For, if a city can be a self-regulating economic entity, then why not part of a city?

There is, however, a way of understanding this contradiction, for in fact it exemplifies an argument made earlier when discussing Forrester's view of system interdependence and the alternative idea of functional autonomy. Forrester ignored the fact that the social and economic integration of Blacks (into the mainstream social and economic system) would restrict their ability to build a functionally autonomous system of their own. Although there is the possibility that Forrester was only expressing some humanitarian desire for racial harmony, another plausible explanation lies in the prevailing threat to social order. We might suggest that he was merely expressing a concern for order and stability – factors which were deemed to be more important than functional autonomy for Blacks. His aim was to protect the social order of the whole rather than the autonomy of the parts.

At the time there was great concern over the urban problem, and in particular its racial dimensions. For example, Conant warned of 'social dynamite' in the cities. 'The building up of a mass of unemployed and frustrated Negro youths in congested areas of a city is a social phenomenon that may be compared to the piling up of inflammable material in an empty building' (Connant, 1961: 18). Harwood (1979) argues that local strategies for social control centred on the police, schools, and welfare agencies, but that at a national level poverty programmes, such the Ford Foundation's community action programme, aimed to integrate Blacks into the political machinery and thus restore order. These programmes were never intended to eliminate American poverty; rather, Harwood contends, they were designed to try and re-establish the social order that had been disturbed by the effects of economic change upon Blacks after the Second World War. Though Forrester's emphasis lay in economic rather than political integration, this is also a possible implication of his position. Moreover, Forrester's objection to the extreme concentration of social groups can be seen as expressive of Conant's concern about the 'piling up of inflammable material' – Forrester was responding to the threat posed by the urban problem and his abiding priority was the restoration of social stability.

But if Forrester sided with the local autonomy of city administrators rather than with the exponents of national programmes, he did not advocate their traditional methods of social control. Instead, he looked to housing policy as a means of controlling the numbers and political influence of the poor: the slums were to be demolished but not replaced with low-rent alternatives. Forrester urged the need to stop low-rent housing projects because of their allegedly detrimental economic and political effects on the city (Forrester, 1969). He suggested that because of their greater numbers the political power of the poor was too strong; the proposed housing policy would effectively serve to constrain that power because it was designed to deter the further influx of the 'underemployed'.

The theoretical changes under discussion are not the only ones that can be seen in the urban model; others centred upon the concept of limited good and the role of pressures and stresses in maintaining system stability. In *Industrial Dynamics* Forrester had been optimistic about being able to improve the performance of a system without a trade-off. 'Since most industrial systems seem to operate so far from a hypothetical ideal, it is reasonable to hope that system improvements can first be obtained without requiring any compromise. Improving one factor may not require a penalty elsewhere' (Forrester, 1961: 276). However, with the advent of urban dynamics his outlook had somewhat changed. Forrester now exhorted his readers to differentiate between the possible and the impossible (or the utopian) and he implied that there was only a limited or fixed amount of good that the urban system could provide for its subsystems. He took the view that the goals which may benefit one subsystem may cause another subsystem, or even the system as a whole, to decline. Ideas about value commitments began to surface and he talked of the 'responsibility' of urban residents (Forrester, 1969). Thus, he implied that order in cities could not be secured by economic incentives alone, but also required the allegiance to certain values. Moreover, he also implied that the urban crisis was partly caused by the breakdown of responsible values amongst the poor (Forrester, 1969). (These points will be discussed in detail in chapter 5.)

Forrester's concept of limited good was related to his belief that no sustainable system mode can be free from pressures and stresses. In fact, systems were said to actually need pressures as restraints to stop a system from drifting into undesirable behaviour modes, i.e. out of equilibrium.

So, pressures and limited good (scarcity) can be considered to be further types of protective mechanisms for a system. The new outlook reflected in these theoretical concerns was therefore sharply distinguished from his earlier work. The idea of limited good did not appear in *Industrial Dynamics* where he had been concerned to pave the way for American economic leadership in the world economy. In the political climate of the time, such a notion could conceivably have been construed as the statement of a fault or limitation inherent in the capitalist system. However, with the onset of the urban crisis the idea came to the fore, for if it hadn't, other goals – utopian goals which certain sections of American society firmly wished to resist – might have become predominant (Harwood, 1979).

The next phase in the development of Forrester's work was his world model; by this time the imputed generality of industrial dynamics led him to adopt the term system dynamics. The building of the model took place in cooperation with the Club of Rome, and the burgeoning environmentalist movement provided a backcloth to the project. The main points made by this study were that there were fixed limits to growth in the world system and that it was necessary to undergo a transition to an equilibrium society if the system were to avoid a catastrophe.

Implicit in Forrester's theoretical development was a changing emphasis on the role and importance of individual and collective values. Here again we find an interesting parallel to Parsons, who during the Great Depresssion had advocated the potency of individual effort in contrast to collective solutions. Similarly, the need for individual action was evoked by Forrester – in his case to avert world catastrophe – and he urged people to change their values so that they might derive satisfaction from an equilibrium society. 'To make the best of the future requires restraint, self-discipline, and intentionally increased pressures in the present' (Forrester, 1975b: 253).

Forrester's new theoretical emphasis and Parsons's early work both evolved amidst dangerous threats to social order; notably, both thought that such threats must be solved without changing the fundamental economic structure. With the urban crisis the challenge to order was already present in many cities; with the world modelling project the perceived threat of catastrophe was seen to be potentially more devastating. Although this threat lay in the future, Forrester considered that the world system had already begun to manifest symptomatic signs of the predicted calamity.

Forrester's idea of stopping industrial growth stood in stark contrast to his work in *Industrial Dynamics* where he had stated that '[c]apital formation, education, and the aspirations of the people must grow in synchronism if revolution and war are not to overtake economic development' (Forrester, 1961: 7). In *World Dynamics*, however, we find a rather different position:

> We may now be living in a 'golden age' when, in spite of a widely acknowledged feeling of malaise, the quality of life is, on the average, higher than ever before in history and higher now than the future offers . . . There may be no realistic hope of the present underdeveloped countries reaching the standard of living demonstrated by the present industrialized nations.' (Forrester, 1971: 11–12)

Forrester observed the fact that values were acquired through socialisation and he believed that man had not evolved fast enough to cope with a world system that had become so complex and was pressing against the limits of nature (Forrester, 1975b: 255–69). Growth oriented values were seen as transient phenomena that constituted an aberration in the contemporary context, while the values consistent with an equilibrium society were more basic. Thus, in functionalist style, Forrester continued to look for the root of social problems in the breakdown of the moral system.

In the mid-1970s Forrester and his colleagues became preoccupied with modelling the American national economy. This work began during a mounting concern with the problems of inflation and unemployment, when the social order once more faced crises and potential disorder. Forrester claimed that the system dynamics structure of the model could reproduce the inflation and unemployment crises which many capitalist countries had been experiencing. He viewed these crises rather as system properties which had hitherto been misunderstood and mismanaged, and he looked to the concept of long-wave economic cycles (e.g. the Kondratieff cycle) in order to explain them.

> I believe the System Dynamics National Model is beginning to provide the first coherent theory of how the long wave is generated, and to relate that theory to the historical evidence for the long wave, thus unifying many observations previously thought contradictory. We see these waves as the source of much of today's rising unemployment in industrial economies. (Forrester, 1982: 107)

This expansion of the domain of system dynamics was complemented by yet another addition to its theoretical core: the business, Kuznets, and Kondratieff cycles came to be seen as emergent properties of feedback structures. Once again we can see that the core expansion played a conservative role similar to the other theoretical developments. As we saw earlier, Forrester's thinking upheld the legitimacy of the social order; starting from the oneness and unity depicted by the model, it explained the problems troubling Western societies without resort to ideas of conflict or contradictions. The social and economic problems of inflation and mass unemployment thus emerged as system characteristics. The possibility that they were the product of a contradictory system, a system divided against itself, or – in the case of unemployment – deliberately fostered by government agency, was not entertained; rather, they were perceived more like 'natural' properties of the system and the implication was that they were to be accepted as such.

We have now looked at the general evolution of system dynamics through successive domains of application. Pointing out the inherent theoretical shifts, I have sought to explain them in relation to specific social developments. The discussion of these developments has mainly centred upon various social crises but of course other longer term processes were involved. For example, I noted the question of the political power of the urban poor and the autonomy of Blacks in relation to the urban crisis. These issues are connected to the changing power differentials between different groups and classes in American society and are therefore specific strands of social development in their own right. Forrester responded to each crisis with a modelling project which sought to derive policies to solve it. In each case the restoration of social order was paramount in his thinking.

We have seen that Forrester's worldview – like that of Parsons – represented a traditional middle-class concern with social order. Further, his allegiance to the American social system, to capitalism, and indeed to social order generally, was not just a conscious matter in the sense that he explicitly valued them. They were also rooted in the theoretical beliefs which structured his perceptions. And these beliefs were themselves grounded in his social background and, together with his values and general outlook, have shaped the development of his work in relation to the social problems he has sought to tackle.

Forrester's outlook became more pessimistic over the years and this too influenced his theoretical position. For example, not only did he come to look for a moral solution to the problems of social systems, but he also came to perceive such problems as being rooted in deficient value structures – that is, in failures of the moral system itself. Further, we have seen how the blunting of his optimism led him to advocate the necessity of 'pressures and stresses' in order for social systems to maintain their stability. Thus, what was once construed by some people as a social problem (or by technocrats as a technical problem) may now, according to Forrester's position, be seen either as a value problem, or as a system necessity.

Though we have seen that Forrester was committed to capitalism, his increasingly moral perspective cannot be explained in relation to capitalist interests alone – i.e. as a reflection of the economic base. Indeed, his position was noticeably different to the technocratic perception of social problems, which ironically, some critics see also as a reflection of capitalist interests.

The analysis of Forrester's worldview has shown that it has entailed a number of shifts in his theoretical position – in other words, his actual interpretations of the world have changed. Although it has been argued that he was committed to social order, the signs indicate that his interpretation of how that interest might be secured shifted. Indeed, this had ramifications for his other interests and I have shown that he moved from the promotion of the hegemony of American capitalism to the idea that industrial growth must end. If only a simple static model of the relationship between interests and the development of knowledge had been adopted, we could not have grasped these important changes – this bears out the utility of the developmental model posited by Elias. This model has begun to afford us an explanation of Forrester's shifting interpretations of his interests – in order to secure the goal of social order; it has illuminated the expansion of the domain of application of system dynamics; and it has enabled us to comprehend the various theoretical shifts which mark the expansion of its theoretical core.

In this chapter I have focused upon the general macro-social relationship between the knowledge formulated in the System Dynamics Laboratory and social developments in the wider society that has embraced it. In the following chapter I will consider the specific micro-social relationship between the cosmology of the members of the System Dynamics Group and the social bonds which unite them as a research group. The need is to understand how social relations shape their values, outlook, and theoretical beliefs – not just in times of perceived social crisis, but also during the ordinary mundane world of experience and, most importantly, in the context of their modelling practise. In other words, we need to know how beliefs are transmitted and constantly reinforced in the consciousness of individuals. To flesh out the bones that I have laid bare I now need tools of greater precision. Their provision will be the subject of the next chapter.

4 Cosmology, Knowledge, and Social Structure: Technical Issues

The aim of this chapter is to develop a picture of the co-development and interrelationship between system dynamics and the social environment of the System Dynamics Group (SDG). Using the anthropological concept of cosmology, I will endeavour to connect the shared knowledge and professional outlook of the system dynamicists with their social experience as a group. In addition to social experience and cosmology (with the focus on the content of knowledge) I will also consider the style of SDG's cosmology (or thought style). This will be interpreted in relation to evidence concerning their methodological orientation: including their approach to modelling and response to theoretical anomalies.

Beginning with the work of Bernstein (1971) and the relationship between cosmologies, linguistic codes and the social bond, I will consider two elaborations of his work. The first, Douglas's grid/group theory (1973, 1978), is directed towards the content of knowledge, to shared beliefs about man and the cosmos. The second, due to Bloor (1978), is a development of the first via the work of Lakatos (1976) in which the focus is on method and the form or style of knowledge (or thought style). It is of course not necessarily the case that the content of knowledge should be the same as style, particularly if one takes a methodological view of thought style. In Douglas's work it is argued that the style and content of knowledge are connected but for the purposes here they will be kept separate during the investigation. I shall undertake a comparative analysis and endeavour to show that on three different levels – social experience, the style of knowledge or thought, and the content of knowledge – the System Dynamics Group manifest a systematic difference in contrast to a chosen control group.

The anthropological concept of cosmology is of a system of knowledge encompassing shared beliefs about how the universe is construed. These include beliefs about the fundamental building blocks of the cosmos, such as the relationship between the self and society, or beliefs about nature and time. Douglas has developed some widely discussed ideas about cosmologies and how they are related to social structures. She views cosmology as being related to the type of social bond in a society – a line of reasoning related to that of Durkheim and Mauss (Durkheim, 1964; Durkheim and Mauss, 1963). The basic idea is that the social relationships in a society provide a prototype for the logical relationships between things. Thus our social boundaries are said to influence our cognitive boundaries and therefore how we make sense of the world and endow it with intellectual coherence. For example, Douglas suggests that the rigid set of animal classifications set out in the *Old Testament* complemented a strongly sustained social boundary between the Jewish people and other contemporary cultures (Douglas, 1975: 276–318). Put crudely, the wish to preserve the purity of Jewish culture resonated with the perceived purity of classifications in nature: the order of the natural world mirrored that of their social structure. 'The first logical categories were social categories; the first classes of things were classes of men into which these things were integrated. It was because men were grouped and thought of themselves in the form of groups that in their ideas they grouped other things' Douglas (1973: 12). Another influence on Douglas's thought derives from the work of Bernstein. In particular she incorporates his idea that social structures include various linguistic codes which mediate social relations and, most importantly, set constraints or limitations upon the medium of expression – that is, language. In order to develop the idea of such constraints it is necessary to elucidate the idea of linguistic codes; this will introduce ideas about the nature of the social bond and cosmologies that will underpin most of what is to follow later in the chapter.

Linguistic Codes

Bernstein's thought on linguistic codes is derived from Durkheim's sociology of knowledge and Sapir's work on the influence of language as a cultural control.[1] Bernstein's focus of interest is upon the role of speech forms in encoding the patterns of social relations, and in mediating and reinforcing those patterns. The basic idea is that during socialization a child learns a language that is encrypted in a linguistic code that reflects the social structure within which it resides. Linguistic codes not only define the concepts used by the child, they also set limits on what is perceived and on how perceptions are structured into meaningful patterns.

. . . different speech systems or codes create for their speakers different orders of relevance and relation. The experience of the speakers may then be transformed by what is made significant or relevant by different speech systems. As the child learns his speech, or, in the terms I shall use here, learns specific codes which regulate his verbal acts, he learns the requirements of his social structure. From this point of view, every time the child speaks or listens, the social structure is reinforced in him and his social identity shaped. (Bernstein, 1971: 144)

The 'different orders of relevance and relation' impose different constraints upon the child's perceptions and experiences, and these have their correlates at a linguistic level. Not surprisingly, there has actually been a great deal of debate on this matter, especially with regard to the precise mechanism of the codes – e.g. do they operate through syntax or semantics? Whilst wishing to acknowledge the controversy surrounding these points I do not intend to become bogged down with them here.[2] Indeed, their purpose here is to provide one way of thinking about the relationship between language and culture; they are not introduced as established concepts but stepping stones to Douglas's grid/group theory of cosmologies.

In order to illustrate the notion of linguistic codes it is sufficient to introduce the idea that language may have two distinct functions: one is to transmit information, and the other is to express the social structure from which it emerges and to reinforce it. Bernstein posits the idea of two distinct linguistic codes, one restricted and one elaborated. The restricted code is seen as having a narrow range of syntactic alternatives that are rigidly organized. Socially restricted speech conveys information, but also expresses and reinforces the social structure; the second function dominates the first. This code relies heavily upon the prevailing social context to convey meanings and therefore affirms the unchallenged metaphysical convictions upon which the social structure rests. In contrast, the elaborated code is more detached from its social role and is more of an independent tool of thought. It has a wide range of syntactic alternatives that are flexibly organized; it requires more complex planning and can be used to articulate generalized abstract principles; it organizes thought processes and distinguishes and combines ideas. This code carries a much smaller burden of implicit meanings for its aim is to make everything explicit – it elaborates meanings verbally.

Of course, this is not to suggest that the elaborated code is detached from a social role in an absolute sense. Indeed, each type of speech code is found in a different form of social structure, each is generated by a particular social matrix. Culture is actively produced and maintained by people in their daily interactions; for instance, social life is infused with coercive demands; people are constantly trying to get others to conform to their will, while evading the demands of others if they can. The codes underlying the speech acts used in these constant negotiations will reflect and reinforce the prevailing pattern of social relations. Put another way, the social bonds between people constitute a system of social control which interacts with the media of control – in this case speech. Bernstein has used the idea of family control systems (the way that adults control their children) as a way of characterizing the differences in social structure that generate different linguistic codes. He posits the idea of two opposite systems – one positional and one personal – corresponding to the restricted and elaborated codes. (In his empirical work, these concepts were operationalized in terms of working- and middle-class families.) With positional control, the restricted code reflects the statuses, roles, and hierarchy of the surrounding social context. 'The child in this family is controlled by the continual building-up of a sense of social pattern: of ascribed role categories . . . As he grows his experience flows into a grid of role categories; right and wrong are learnt in terms of the given structure; he himself is seen in relation to that structure' (Douglas 1973: 45). However, with personal control the value of the individual is celebrated rather than the fixed social pattern. The child here is sensitised towards the feelings of others and uses the elaborated code to articulate his own personal feelings and emotions. 'The curiosity of the child is used to increase his verbal control, to elucidate causal relations, to teach him to assess the consequences of his acts. Above all his behaviour is controlled by being made sensitive to the personal feelings of others, by inspecting his own feelings' (Douglas, 1973: 47).

These examples indicate how the speech between individuals, acting as a medium of control, is shaped by the nature of the social bond between them. The next step is to consider how these ideas tie in with the concept of cosmology. In fact, Bernstein's ideas show how cosmologies are part of the social bonds between people: for alongside the codes that structure speech lie implicit cosmologies. Whatever code is used, the communication of meaning by what is spoken does not reside entirely in the speech itself, but also requires a social context or shared culture between the conversants. Thus, each speech form transmits not only information, but also a concealed baggage of shared assumptions: for example, with restricted codes the individual is implicitly subordinated to the demands of the social structure; with elaborated codes the reverse is true. These assumptions are the 'taken-for-granted' beliefs about how the world is, they encapsulate ultimate principles about man and the cosmos: therefore what is left implicit may be just as important as what is explicitly articulated. The nature of the social environment is thereby perpetuated in speech forms and cosmology, and these in turn tend to reinforce that environment. The idea of linguistic codes can therefore be seen as a means of conceptualizing some different possible manifestations of that interaction.

In his later work Bernstein moved on from linguistic codes to develop the idea of educational codes which also carry implicit cosmologies – these too set constraints upon thought and persist beyond the school into the child's professional life. For example, syllabuses marked by a strict segregation, or purity of subjects, cultivate a different view of knowledge and the world than ones which integrate material from across traditionally disparate disciplinary boundaries. Codes, whether linguistic or educational, are qualities inherent in the social structure; the range of codes available to an individual in a particular location constrains his or her range of conceptualization. Thus, the experience of social relations – and the codes that are thereby acquired – sets limits on symbolic, or conceptual relations.

The Grid/Group Diagram

The notion of codes – whether linguistic or educational – and the idea that the control system and the media of control interact, provides the germ of a theory about how the social bond between individuals may be constituted in more general social contexts. 'For each distinct type of social environment . . . there is its necessary manner of justifying coercion. Through the classifications used, the furniture of the universe is turned into an armoury of control. In each social system human suffering is explained in a way that reinforces the controls' (Douglas, 1973: 136). In an elaboration of Bernstein's work, Douglas has sought to shift the focus from family control systems to the wider control systems of different cultures, and she has richly illustrated her emergent scheme – the grid/group theory of cosmologies – with empirical ethnographic material.

Within the grid/group scheme, social experience is captured by two variables which Douglas has named 'grid' and 'group'; these represent distinct dimensions of control within which individuals operate. 'Grid' refers to pressure wrought through classifications (for example, roles, rank, hierarchy), to the extent to which social interaction follows prescribed rules. A strong grid social context is equivalent to that of the family which relies on positional control, while weak grid – an environment unstructured by fixed principles – is equivalent to personal control. 'Group' refers to group commitments and responsibilities, it designates the extent to which an individual's life is constrained by membership in a group – thus indicating the strength of the boundary between a group and outsiders. Douglas's theory states that the different permutations of grid and group (given two variables there are four major possibilities) characterizes different social structures, to which there correspond specific cosmologies. A diagram depicting the scheme is shown in figure 4.1.

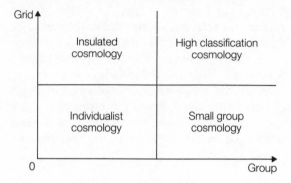

Figure 4.1 Douglas's grid/group diagram

Hierarchical groups where rank and classifications are very explicit are high grid – for instance, a military regiment or a bureaucracy. Moving down the grid dimension, at low grid there may be competing systems of classification describing different aspects of the social field. Hence overall coherence is low here. Alternatively, there may simply be an absence of classification. As for the group dimension, a large corporate entity, or an isolated group which is internally cohesive is high group; a fragmented group with unstable membership is located more towards zero on the horizontal line. At zero the individual is under no pressures from others at all.

Shifting from left to right, the view of the universe becomes progressively less benign. The world is less friendly; a more punishing, difficult place to survive in. . . . From top to bottom, false appearances begin to emerge as we move down. Diverse classifications compete. There is less coherence. A gap between reality and formal appearance is observed. In a tribal society, a man will worry whether his neighbours are what they seem, honest humans, or man-eating witches in disguise. Among ourselves, philosophers become dubious about the possibility of knowledge of the external world. . . . So there we are . . . our minds structured by the cosmologies which are generated by the ways we deal with one another, our categories reinforcing our social choices. (Douglas, 1975: 225–6)

The four different environments, and their respective cosmologies are known as: (1) high group/low grid (small group); (2) high group/high grid (high classification); (3) low group/high grid (insulated); (4) low group/low grid (individualist). Examples of these are as follows:

(1) *Social structure*: isolated groups without a clear distinction of roles, strong boundary between insiders and outsiders.
   Cosmology: dualism, preoccupied with the idea of good versus evil – pollution-conscious; nature and society are united but this relationship is negatively valued. Questions about knowledge or truth are black-and-white issues.

(2) *Social structure*: military, aristocratic, or bureaucratic systems; a strongly prescribed grid of rules governing social interaction.
   Cosmology: pious, ritualistic towards authority and its symbols, belief in a punishing moral universe; nature and society are considered to be isomorphic, united in their purpose. Knowledge is viewed as an all-embracing scheme; there is an emphasis on qualitative differences – either between people or objects – which are seen as real differences; there is a tendency toward systematizing or classifying procedures – 'a place for everything and everything in its place'.

(3) *Social structure*: sections of society where people are oppressed by a grid of impersonal rules – they have no choices and the wider society offers no rewards, they are insulated from other people.
   Cosmology: insulation limits social experience and therefore the theoretical elaboration of the concepts of nature and the self is impoverished. Intuitive, instant forms of knowledge; eclecticism.

(4) *Social structure*: highly competitive individualistic environments; no fixed cognitive or social boundaries, apart from the rules of fair competition.
   Cosmology: humans experienced as anonymous and merciless; time is an individual resource that is always in short supply; rules are abstractions which govern individual transactions; society separate from nature, and is an improvement on it. Knowledge is what people take it to be and is preferably quantitative.

The Response to Anomalies and Thought Style

A particularly interesting feature of cosmologies is the different characteristic ways in which people may respond to anomalies. Anomalies are objects or events that do not fit into our usual systems of classification;

transgressing the orderly boundaries of thought, they present a threat to our cognitive coherence and security. Anomalies may come in many forms; an animal that does not fit into the local taxonomy; pollution or dirt; a deviant who disregards the moral norms of some particular group.

> In a chaos of shifting impressions, each of us constructs a stable world in which objects have recognisable shapes, are located in depth, and have permanence. In perceiving we are building, taking some cues rejecting others. The most acceptable cues are those which fit most easily into the pattern that is being built up. Ambiguous ones tend to be treated as if they harmonised with the rest of the pattern. Discordant ones tend to be rejected. (Douglas, 1966: 36)

So far I have been concerned with the content of a cosmology but now I must consider its style. The style of a cosmology – thought style – is related to the system of boundaries and classifications by which our cognitive fields are put together and our views of the universe mapped out. Ultimately, Douglas argues, all knowledge rests upon principles of classification. Anomalies may threaten to transgress a classification system and hence it is the nature of the boundaries between categories that determines the range of response. More specifically, cosmologies are constructed with systems of classifications – for example, of natural objects, animals or moral actions – in which the nature of the boundaries (or divisions) between categories varies in accordance with the prevailing pattern of grid and group. This variation is an indicator of different thought styles: some cosmologies may have a strong tendency to maintain boundaries, while others may have a weak tendency.

If we return to the four cosmological types of the grid/group diagram, we find an interesting range of responses to anomalies. First, with small group, we find pollution-conscious tribes where people are constantly prone to fears of evil. The lack of structure in their social environment leads to a pervasive dread of anomalies, they are seen to be threatening; to use Lakatos's term for counterexamples (anomalies) in mathematics, they are perceived rather as 'monsters' – that is, they invoke revulsion and are abhorred. Thus, with small group we often observe strong notions of taboo; for example, according to the classifications set out in the *Old Testament* the pig was an animal that was to be abhorred. Douglas argues that this was because unlike other animals which have cloven hooves, the pig does not ruminate. In other words, the pig was seen as an anomalous creature, it straddled the boundary between ruminants and non-ruminants and as such was abominated. As noted earlier, at that time the Jewish people maintained rigid social (and therefore cognitive) boundaries –

hence the strong reaction towards the pig. Second, with high classification, the strong grid provides for a distinct category of rejects – those who
break the moral rules. The elaborate nature of the grid also allows the
redefining of boundaries, hence anomalies can be easily adjusted or
excluded so as not to disturb existing knowledge. Third, we have the
insulated cosmology – the realm of atomized individuals – where the high
degree of insulation means that anomalies pose no serious threat and are
embraced alongside of the public categories, with no attempt at synthesis.
Fourth, with the individualist cosmology, there are no stable social
categories because boundaries can be constantly made and broken. Hence,
there are no stable cognitive categories and so anomalies are the basis for
innovation and novelty; they can be used to revise existing categories.
Rather than the black-and-white dualism of small group cosmologies, we
could expect many shades of grey and a willingness to revise existing
classifications. The status of the pig would be seen as due to social
convention rather than some inherent evil in the animal itself.

Following Bloor (1978), I will consider thought style in a methodological perspective, and in the case of SDG I will refer to their approach to
modelling and response to theoretical anomalies. In Bloor's extension of
Douglas's theory he equated the different responses to anomaly with
distinct Lakatosian strategies for coping with mathematical counterexamples – see figure 4.2 – and thereby constructed an argument about how
social experience might influence the style and content of mathematical
knowledge. (*Note:* in fact, Lakatos did not provide any mathematical
examples of monster embracing.) These strategies are not confined solely

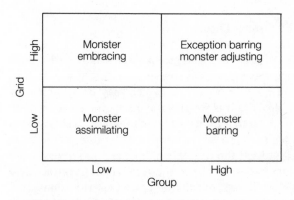

Figure 4.2   Bloor's extended grid/group scheme
Each of the four major areas of the diagram is characterized by a distinct strategy for coping
with anomalies. Except for the strategy of 'monster embracing', they are those described in
Lakatos's book *Proofs and Refutations* (1976) and will be defined below.

to mathematics but indicate general methodological styles; they therefore offer a prospect for identifying the thought style of SDG.

At this point it would seem appropriate to pull together the threads of the argument concerning the nature of cosmologies. A cosmology is a system of knowledge about how the universe is construed; it has a particular style of thought associated with it and this is governed by a system of classifications and the boundaries which delimit them. Its content includes beliefs about the relationship between the self and society, nature, knowledge and time etc. Corresponding to style of thought, each cosmology is characterized by a distinctive response towards anomalies – the objects or events which transgress our systems of classifications. Cosmologies are correlated with specific types of social structures, and their unspoken assumptions concerning the ultimate nature of the cosmos are the source of a legitimating ideology which justifies each pattern of social relations.

In the following section I will discuss some of the problems associated with the grid/group theory before going on to undertake a comparative analysis between the System Dynamics Group and a selected control group. A comparative approach is necessary because of course the four 'ideal types' of social environment and cosmology have a limited practical utility: it is not possible, for example, to state that a specific group is high classification per se, but only that it is high in comparison to some other group. Contrasting the differences in cosmological content and thought style between SDG and a control group, I will invoke the grid/group theory to explain them in terms of differences in their respective social experiences.

Problems with the Grid/Group Theory

It would seem fair to say that the grid/group theory is regarded as a promising but nevertheless controversial contribution to the sociology of knowledge. There are a number of reasons which may be suggested as contributory factors in this and it is worthwhile discussing some of them here because they are relevant to the analysis which follows. To begin, it is important to note that both Douglas and a number of her interpreters have apparently defined and utilised the concepts of grid and group in related but none the less divergent ways. In the exploratory *Natural Symbols*, grid is defined as the 'scope' or 'degree of rank' of shared classifications, it is the 'order' inherent in the symbolic system (Douglas, 1973: 81). However, in *Cultural Bias* we find that grid is described as a 'cross-hatch' of rules, and a set of insulations (Douglas, 1978: 8). Moving on to Caneva, we can observe that in his framework, grid 'measures the extent to which people classify themselves according to socially objectivated roles and are then controlled by an appeal to behavior appropriate to a given role' (Caneva, 1981: 104).

Parallel to this diversity in the interpretation of grid, we find a range of referents in the use of group. Douglas has argued against employing group to designate entire cultures when studying modern, highly differentiated societies. However, others have indeed stretched the concept of group to cover the social environment within particular national contexts. For instance, Bloor used university settings as the referents of social environment in which to locate the mathematicians he studied; but he also considered grid and group in terms of the wider societies in which they resided. Caneva followed Bloor along the same path; for example, in discussing certain nineteenth-century German physicists, such as Schweigger and Muncke, he states: '[the] society within which these individuals came to maturity was a relatively stable, highly differentiated society with the individual well integrated into the social fabric via his particular corporate identity' (Caneva, 1981: 114).

At times it is not clear whether the divergence represents theoretical extension; or alternatively, whether it has been due to the lack of evidence concerning a particular case where the theory has been applied, and consequently grid and group have been used only to designate previously known aspects of social context. Caneva (1980) and Rudwick (1982), for example, brought the theory to bear on materials with which they were already familiar.

Because of this range in the usage of concepts in the case studies within which grid/group theory has been applied it is difficult to construct an overall picture of either its development or status in terms of empirical corroboration. Thus, it is evident that the concepts of grid and group are not established; grid is not theory-dependent but, rather, is an intuitive construct. Therefore, given a reasoned position, one can choose an operationalization of these concepts which matches the requirements of one's analysis. In the case of the system dynamicists, I am interested in their professional cosmology and take group to be the System Dynamics Group within the institutional setting of MIT. As for grid, this will be considered as the degree of prescribed rules for social interaction – hierarchy, status, regimentation of time. Further, each of the particular conceivable referents of grid such as role differentiation, rule-governed behaviour, hierarchy etc., will be considered as dimensional variables which interrelate to set the overall value of grid (which is therefore considered to be a multidimensional construct). Such a designation of grid is useful because it would be a mistake to assume that it was some simple additive function of each referent – as implicitly assumed on occasion by Bloor (1982) and Hampton (1982).

This flexible view of grid has the advantage that it allows the specificity of each social location to remain in focus. Rather than blurring the 'individuality' and particularities of each social context beneath the rigidity of a single formula, it requires us to allow for the differential weighting that each dimension may take in any given social environment. The overall nature of an environment is what counts in the last instance (i.e. whether it is high or low grid) but a multidimensional construct prevents the prejudging of what is to be taken as the most important indicator of grid for any particular context. In other words, the weight to be attributed to, say, hierarchy as a measure of grid cannot be determined in advance.

It is also worth noting that support for this position can be found in Douglas's own comparative work: for example, she reports that the importance to be attached to the division between the sexes in an otherwise weak boundary culture (i.e. low grid/low group) – the Hadza – has important cultural ramifications. More specifically, this particularity of the Hadza, in contrast to another comparable culture such as that of Mbuti pygmies, requires a flexible approach to grid; the overall bias of Hadza culture is towards low grid but the importance of this specific social distinction between the sexes cannot be overlooked if one wants to understand their culture. This implies that the weighting one might ascribe to the symbolic division of the sexes – which is one possible referent of grid – will depend on the particular context in question.

The relevance of all this for the study here is that small differences in grid or group can have substantial significance for the comprehension of different cosmological systems. Compared to certain pre-literate peoples the cosmological differences between scientific groups in Western societies may appear quite small. However, here we are not concerned with a comparison between pre-literate and Western groups but rather one between different Western groups – SDG and a control group – and I shall try to explain divergences in their cosmologies by reference to (possibly) small differences in grid and group. Given the spirit of the comparative method set out by Douglas these intentions are not in dissonance – indeed they are in keeping with the professed subtlety of the whole approach.

For example, I want to understand how a slightly higher-gridded social context might sustain a different view of the universe than a context at lower grid. Similarly, in relation to group, I want to consider the possibility that small changes in group (a strengthening of the boundary between the established and the outsiders) can have the effect of enhancing the threat of anomalies or monsters – this will be particularly important when I come to consider how SDG responded to criticisms of their work. These points bring us to more fundamental problems; for in addition to the divergent – though related – uses of the conceptual terms of

Douglas's theory we must also consider the theoretical limitations which are inherent in the whole approach. Several criticisms have been articulated in *Essays in the Sociology of Perception* (Douglas, 1982) and elsewhere (Kearney, 1975; Rosaldo, 1976/7; Barnes and Shapin, 1977; Wuthnow et al., 1984) but I will focus only on those difficulties which are judged to have particular relevance to this study.

One significant problem would appear to be its rather static framework and the consequent lack of depth concerning the nature and causes of social change. Grid/group theory provides the basis for recognizing changes in cosmology in respect of changes in social context but does not directly address the mechanisms which, say, push a group towards higher grid or group. There are however certain clues or hints as to what is involved in such changes but a substantial theoretical omission remains. Of course the concept of social change itself is problematic, particularly with regard to class-based, stratified cultures. Indeed, very disparate processes may be involved depending upon the societal resolution and time scale in which we are interested. Here I am looking for any short-term changes such as might be implicated in the debate between SDG and its critics; particularly in view of the frosty, if not openly hostile reception meted out to system dynamics in various circles and organs of more established scientific disciplines. To pursue this line of inquiry it will be necessary to expand upon Douglas's clues and hypothesize about the nature of the processes involved.

Despite the difficulties of theory and interpretation arising from the problems concerned in conceptualizing these types of changes, certain advantages may accrue. For instance, it would constitute the addition of a longitudinal element to the analysis and would therefore buttress the case against those critics who might suggest that the differences between SDG and the control group might be located in factors not addressed by the theory. This is perhaps particularly advantageous in view of the fact that the theory is rather sensitive to charges that it lacks detailed empirical corroboration. It should however be clear that the contribution in this direction is more concerned with establishing the consistency of the analysis here and not with the substantiation of the grid/group theory itself.

But a more significant problem inherent in grid/group theory concerns the precise nature of the link between cosmology and social structure. More specifically, does cosmology *cause* social structure or does social structure determine cosmology? Alternatively, does each reinforce the other in a holistic fashion? Again one can find a variety of interpretations in the literature on grid/group analysis. A careful reading of Douglas's writings shows that her theory has shifted its theoretical locus. In her earlier work, particularly *Natural Symbols*, where the grid/group theory was enmeshed with the ideas of Bernstein, cosmologies appeared as collective phenomena which constrained thought – the constraints being generated by social relations and maintained by the codes thereby acquired. However, with the advent of *Cultural Bias* we find a preoccupation with the 'negotiating individual' in which cosmology is conceptualized in much more fluid terms: changing social experience is quickly followed by changing cosmology. Douglas (1982: 4) maintains that culture is actively produced: 'If they wish for change, they will adopt different justifications, if they wish for continuity, they will call upon those principles which uphold the present order.' In other words, there is always leeway and freedom of choice; but the credibility of arguments will rest upon the support of the surrounding social environment. That is, whatever individuals may believe, their social environment will be conducive only to particular forms of public knowledge. Thus a solitary voice calling for distribution according to need would be lost in the low grid/low group environment of individualistic competition. Likewise, justifications embroidered with notions about the survival of the fittest would fall on deaf ears in the communal life of low grid/high group.

The problems involved in this theoretical shift of grid/group theory are compounded by the fact that Douglas has not sought to reflect on it, nor has she set the development of her work in context. The earlier formulation allowed greater account to be taken of tradition, both at the social level of value orientations, allegiances and commitments, and at a cognitive level in terms of the persistance of codes – whether linguistic or educational. Bernstein's arguments about the coding and transmission of educational knowledge were earlier supported by Douglas herself when she contended that the patternings of relevances and relations which are learnt as part of the curriculum are carried beyond the classroom and through life (Douglas, 1973: 10). Now while not wishing to subscribe to a deterministic fixity which does not allow for, and indeed cannot accommodate social change, some compromise must be struck between Douglas's original and later positions. Certainly for those individuals who have had exposure to a variety of contrasting social environments, one can perceive the possibility of the almost instrumental manipulation of cosmological beliefs in the furtherance and legitimation of specific interests. For others this may not be the case; the socialization into a culture – or the learning of specific codes – represents a characteristic of cognitive structuring which may not change so easily. As an example to illustrate this argument, imagine how difficult it is for someone trained in, say, physics (especially within the highly specialized British educational system) to change directions as it were and become a historian, or for an artist to become a mathematician. Such transitions will have implications in terms of shifting cosmological perceptions but they will be accomplished only after much effort, unlearning and relearning. An example of a comparatively easier shift would be one from computing to, say, artificial intelligence or cognitive psychology.

Comparative Method: Choice of Control Group

Before the comparative method can be carried out I need to discuss the problems which are indigenous to the choice of a control group and the reasons for the particular selection made here. There are many possible groups with whom SDG could be compared and all would display both similarities and differences. Following the axiom that everything is both similar to and dissimilar to everything else, no *a priori* choice of control group can exist – there will be both advantages and disadvantages in whatever choice is actually made and the selection must therefore at least be based on a substantial argument.

If we took any two given groups it would be possible to compile a formidable inventory of factors – social, religious, political, economic and ecological – which could all have a bearing upon the beliefs held by them. However, the whole crux of Douglas's theory rests upon the claim that it is cross-cultural: that is, it purports to reveal how a specific range of patterns in social relations arises in different cultures and is justified by a similar range of beliefs about man and the cosmos. But, in order to argue that differences in intergroup beliefs are due to differences in grid and group, the groups in question should be comparable. For example, in one of Douglas's own test cases (Douglas, 1973) she selected neighbouring Nilotic tribes. This need for comparability is not a constraint of the theory, rather it is methodological requirement which pertains to all cases of comparative method. Comparative approaches are beset by the problem of many variables (i.e. sources of cultural variation) combined with only a small number of cases. Choosing comparable cases helps to filter out extraneous sources of variation but other possible strategies are to increase the number of cases; or reduce the property-space by means of combining similar categories; or by constraining the analysis to what are considered to be the key variables (Lijphart, 1971, 1975; Campbell, 1975).

I am interested in the professional cosmology of SDG and so the first requirement in the choice of control group is that it should be concerned with similar professional matters such as modelling socio-technical systems and policy formation. This requirement should circumvent any problems which might arise due to the glare of interprofessional differences and which would necessitate a task beyond the scope of this inquiry. Paradoxically, it may be that in seeking to choose a comparable control group one automatically restricts oneself to groups with relatively similar grid/group environments – relative, that is, to the variation that has been observed in the ethnographic record.

A second requirement is that one should compare sets of beliefs about the world as it is. This is because groups from different social locations might well support similar programmes for social change, all being drawn by the lure of a particular alternative cosmology. Therefore one must be careful when dealing with material that includes statements about how the world should be changed. Here, particular beliefs for analysis will include those pertaining to man and society.

A third constraint is that the control group must be a genuine group in the sense that the individual members give consensus to shared public knowledge – one cannot merely compare SDG with isolated individual utterances emanating from a source who are only a group in name. One can of course allow for intra-group variation but it is the overall style of public knowledge which is of concern here.

Choice of Comparative Elements

Douglas's programme for analysing cosmologies appears to have the potential for addressing an extremely diverse range of cultural elements; from attitudes to old-age and sickness, to millenarianism and gardening, it offers a kaleidoscopic picture of culture. However, this very diversity poses the question as to what particular cluster of cultural elements might be considered in comparative analysis – especially if one is to forestall the charge that the choice is too selective. To answer this question we may consider the following points.

First, with comparative analyses it is an accepted part of the method to select those variables which are considered to be important (Campbell, 1975; Lijphart, 1971, 1975). As I am interested in the professional cosmology of SDG it is valid to select those elements which form central features of their outlook. I will be comparing clusters of elements in which SDG and the control group will be closer together on some points and further apart on others – see figure 4.3. Second, the selected elements can themselves be regarded as clusters of sub-elements and I will therefore be grouping together similar variables and reducing the property-space. I will however seek to point out any non-uniformities within each cluster. Such disparities should be expected because any selection of elements – and thus the sets of sub-elements – must be an arbitrary one in that the clusters of sub-elements are not expected to reflect any real sub–divisions of culture. Third, the elements will have a certain degree of independence and therefore any systematic bias towards higher or lower grid/group will be all the more persuasive.

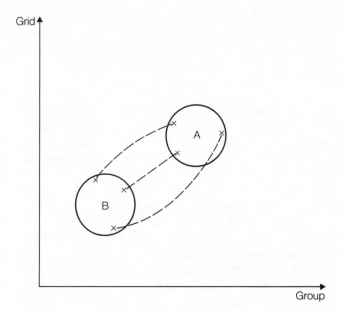

Figure 4.3   Clusters of comparative elements
Of course at the outset we do not know which group is group A and which is group B.

The chosen elements are (1) modelling methodology, (2) response to anomaly, (3) knowledge, (4) nature, (5) man and society, (6) time. The first two will be considered together as indicators of thought style, while the remaining four reflect the content of cosmologies. One reason for the choice of these six elements is that they pertain to the professional outlook of SDG. But there is a pragmatic reason too in that more citations are available concerning these elements than, say, for SDG's attitude to religion. In discussing *knowledge* I will refer to questions concerning ontology and epistemology, both the source and the justification for the knowledge which each group subscribes to. Second, the concept of *nature* is a fundamental element of all cosmologies, it provides the final justification in arguments about what is right and necessary in human affairs: it may be seen as part of, or separate to society, to be venerated or controlled. Third, beliefs about *man and society* represent another piece of the cosmological jigsaw. Is man changeable or static? Is he a modifier of the ecosystem or only one species along with all others? Fourth, *time* is perhaps one of the more difficult elements to get to grips with – uniformly immersed in 'clock-time' as we are in modern societies. Though I cannot endeavour to tackle the depths of inquiry undertaken by some anthropologists (Evans-Pritchard, 1940; Rayner, 1982) I can look at the conception of past, present, and future; the temporal extent of obligations; and the time-dependent character of the dynamics posited in system dynamics.

Possible Groups

Potential candidates for the control group could be institutions such as the Hudson Institute or the Rand Corporation, but these have been rejected for a number of reasons. The Hudson Institute is a private think-tank and is perhaps most notable for the work of Kahn, an ex–member of Rand and a futurologist whose books and articles included *The Next 200 Years* (Kahn, et al., 1976) and *Year 2000* (Kahn and Wiener, 1967). The work of the institute has been concerned with projections of likely technological developments and concomitant speculations about the potential social ramifications. It therefore does not meet the essential requirement of comparable professional interests or practices.

Although it is another private think-tank, the Rand Corporation is perhaps much closer to MIT (Checkland, 1982; Herzog, 1963; Smith, 1966). Born out of close collaboration between the military and civilian experts during the Second World War, it is famous for its pioneering work in systems analysis. Its earlier work in the field of systems engineering later gave way to the predominance of cost–benefit style systems analysis during the 1950s but largely remained tied to the study and planning of military systems. However, in the 1960s certain Corporation members did begin to look at planning in urban and governmental systems.

The aim of Rand systems analysis is to devise alternative techniques or instrumentalities by which specified objectives can be met. The selection of any particular alternative is related to criteria of economic efficiency and resource availability. The approach is not of the formal modelling type practised by SDG; rather, mathematical models are used only as a means for investigating the relationship between the objectives and the techniques or instrumentalities. Moreover, simulation modelling is viewed as being only one of a range of possible techniques for evaluating alternatives within the cost–benefit framework.

Arguably, the Rand Corporation's work has much more in common with Forrester's work in the 1950s than the later work on urban and global systems. In fact, it would appear fair to say that Rand's style of systems analysis remains essentially technocratic while system dynamics has developed the additional moral tinge discussed in the previous chapter. This difference apart, however, it may well be that both approaches do share other fundamental similarities. Indeed, a contrast between Rand and SDG would be an interesting history in itself – particularly when viewed as parallel strands of the systems movement which have developed from the common origin of systems engineering in a military context. Having said that, I am faced with the problem that there does not appear to be a clear articulation of beliefs concerning the cosmological elements in which I am interested; for instance, Rand have not been involved in any extensive model-based programme concerning population, resources and the environment. Also, I do not have any information concerning the style of response to anomalies which members of Rand might share. Because of these difficulties it is not feasible to develop an adequate account of the cosmological orientation which could be attributed to them.

The Science Policy Research Unit

The control group which has actually been selected is the Science Policy Research Unit (SPRU) based at the University of Sussex, England. Several reasons can be put forward for this choice. First, SPRU and SDG share a number of important professional interests centring on the nature and future developments of socio-technical systems and the problems they engender – they are part of the international scientific community who have focused upon similar societal and environmental issues. In parallel with this they share a commitment to the furtherance of policymaking. As a central feature of their work one finds that the definition of problems, and the formation of possible policy alternatives, are determined by their beliefs about the nature of society: in other words, their work explicitly reflects their view of the present. SPRU profess to take a systems approach in the study of problems and they are broadly interdisciplinary; they have a considered policy of bringing together natural and social scientists to work on shared projects (Science Policy Research Unit, 1977: 7).

Second, SPRU qualify as a group in so far as they issue joint papers, reports and books, and were also involved in the establishment and subsequent editing of the journal *Research Policy*. One can therefore speak of their shared professional outlook. Further, in their project work they are arranged into teams who – at least during their critique of world modelling – were in continuous close collaboration. 'In the early years of the programme all members of the team worked on their special assignments with one goal in mind: to contribute to a major common theme' (Science Policy Research Unit, 1977: 30). Both groups engage in the teaching of graduates and undergraduates, in addition to containing postgraduate research programmes. Like SDG, SPRU have also experienced an influx of international scholars.

Third, as with SDG, SPRU have been involved with outside consultancy work, including contracts with governmental agencies, corporations and international organizations. Indeed, their work on world modelling has been funded by similar bodies to those which sponsored SDG.

Fourth, SPRU entered into a professional dialogue with SDG. This stemmed from a contract in which they were requested to evaluate system dynamics as a technique, as well as the world models. This dialogue involved meetings and the exchange of letters but there were also formal interactions at international conferences and through the media of books and journal articles. It is out of this dialogue that one finds a clear expression of the beliefs held by SPRU and to a certain extent one also finds a clarification of those sustained by SDG – in other words, the exchanges made their beliefs explicit.

Moreover, this interaction contained not only technical issues but also focused on arguments concerning nature, man and society, and therefore highlighted the very types of belief necessary for comparative cosmological investigation. The fact that the dialogue occurred also lends force to the contention that, although SDG and SPRU are ostensibly located in different cultural settings (North America and Britain), they are part of an international scientific culture and I am therefore not in contravention of Douglas's methodological strictures.

Of course it could be objected that SPRU's criticisms of SDG did not really represent shared beliefs so much as opportunist responses. This challenge can be dealt with by reference to SPRU's earlier and later work. In fact, they shared some considerable expertise in the very areas (such as pollution and natural resources) which were addressed by SDG, and their criticism may therefore be considered as a fair reflection of their beliefs.

The threads spun through this dialogue also reflected the moves of each group in wishing to secure or enhance their status and credibility; I assume that each articulated beliefs which reflected the self-evident assumptions implicit within their style of thought, and therefore their social context, and used them to buttress their respective positions. Later I will endeavour to see how this dialogue can be analysed to illuminate the difference between SDG and SPRU: on the one hand, system dynamics modellers defending their intellectual products and sense of proper order; and on the other, hired critics who sought recourse to a different sense of intellectual order. This is particularly of interest in view of the fact that SDG subscribed to a shared philosophy and methodology – system dynamics – while in the case of SPRU no such single, concise, routinized approach is to be found. Within the dialogue between SPRU and SDG there arose arguments concerning certain anomalies in connection with the behaviour of the WORLD 2 model. This part of the interaction between the two groups – which will be referred to as the 'backcasting debate' – highlights the difference in style of thought of each group. Indeed, the short history of this debate will form a major part of the following comparative analysis.

5 The Social Experience of SDG and SPRU

In this chapter I aim to present some evidence concerning the relative grid/group characteristics of the social settings within which SDG and SPRU reside. Before embarking on the descriptions of each institutional location it is important to point out the relevance of the general liberalization in Western societies – and in particular the radical changes in university environments – during the late 1960s and early 1970s. In fact, most of the evidence that will be cited concerning SDG pre-dates this and so my remarks should not be construed as being in any way well-founded in relation to the later institutional setting of the group. The evidence I will present is also subject to the reservations discussed earlier in relation to the limitations inherent in operationalizing the concepts of grid and group. However, by referring to different sources I hope to gain an overall flavour of each institution and set the micro-social location of the groups in that context. Further, as the evidence is not based upon direct detailed observation of each group it will not constitute the basis for a stringent test of the grid/group theory but rather, is offered as auxiliary evidence on which to base the later comparison of cosmologies.

The major period of interest centres on the time of the world modelling debate (c.1973) but I shall also consider the broader time span associated with the tradition of each institution. With each group I am concerned with their location within a tradition. In the case of SDG, the period covers almost thirty years including the 1950s and 1960s, when Forrester and his colleagues moulded the ideas of systems engineering into system dynamics. In SPRU's case there is the very short period from 1966 when it was formed and the tradition built up mainly in the early 1970s. Moreover, the tradition behind system dynamics evolved within an institution which already had a distinguished reputation. These differences in historical extension and institutional setting of each tradition are reflected by the level of detail I can cite concerning each group.

System Dynamics Group

The System Dynamics Group reside within the Sloan School of Management at MIT which is a private, and one of the most prestigious institutions in the American education system; indeed it enjoys a world-wide reputation. Founded in 1865, MIT is a very large organization – in the academic year 1966/7 there were some 969 members of faculty (of which twenty six were women); 3857 undergraduates (200 women), and 3718 graduates (201 women). Further, there were 935 foreign students of whom some 201 were women (Singeltary, 1968).

MIT has a long tradition of contacts with military and industrial organizations – particularly through the design of military systems and co-ordination of private sub-contractors. Indeed much of the research at MIT is sponsored by the military (Nunn, 1979). And, as noted earlier, the Sloan School's chief benefactor was Alfred P. Sloan, the former head of General Motors; in fact it was originally named the School of Industrial Management. In 1960 some twelve persons were engaged on the programme in industrial dynamics but by 1968 some 120 graduates and postgraduates took industrial dynamics as a first-term subject; in addition some 100 men in the Sloan Fellow and Senior Executive Development Program also took the subject. Many of the graduates within the system dynamics programme were former engineering students – this being an approved route for the graduate study of the management of complex systems.

MIT is a very exclusive institution, and its entrants are restricted to those who are among the highest performers on various official verbal and mathematical tests – so much so that it has been said that students often stand in awe of each other (Riesman, 1980: 297). Largely vocational in orientation, MIT is permeated by the moral considerations appropriate to filling societal roles and meeting professional responsibilities (MIT, 1949: 9). '[A]ll members of the M.I.T. family, administration, faculty, and students, must be able to feel a sense of belonging to a great institution with a high moral purpose' (MIT, 1949: 135). The sense of vocation is coupled with that of social responsibility; particularly in engineering, from whence many Sloan School graduate students originate, we find much stress on these factors.

It is essential that the modern engineer be able to organize and direct men. His success depends as much upon his understanding of human relations and his skill in handling men as upon his technical competence. Full achievement in his profession requires that he be a man of broad culture with a deep sense of social responsibility. (MIT, 1949: 40)

This accent on the social responsibility of engineers would appear to be a general cultural characteristic and is not peculiar to MIT. Indeed, it is reported by several commentators (see Shepard, 1952; Soderberg, 1965). It is widely acknowledged that the student atmosphere at MIT is extremely competitive and demanding, with little time available or spent outside teaching and studying (MIT, 1949: 115; Parlett, 1969); for the professors too, student demands on their time would appear to carry a heavier burden than at other institutions.

> The Institute has a demanding curriculum which dominates a large part of the student's working hours. Its severe selectivity insures that it admits only highly able and, on the whole, highly motivated students . . . the demands it makes, and the rewards it offers, both in the present and in promise, have profound effects on the lives of students. (Snyder, 1970: 67)

With the vocational courses in particular, the curricula are marked by much routinized learning and practice – 'learning by doing' is a hallmark of MIT education. This often centres on laboratory practices and notably, system dynamics is taught in the System Dynamics Laboratory. The students are continually assessed and ranked, and it is the rewards of high grades – such as scholarships and graduate fellowships – which help to stimulate competition. 'At the centre, of course, are the grades. Not only do they certify accomplishment, but many future rewards are dependent on them' (Snyder, 1970: 15).

The heavy load of the curriculum, combined with a large student body (which therefore requires complex time-tabling) and regularity of testing all point to a high degree of punctuation and sequencing within the temporal dimension of social life. Following Zerubavel (1979), I would suggest that the complex time-tabling sets up a corresponding temporal structure within social life with consequent intricate patterns and rhythms. With greater organizational complexity, time becomes increasingly identifiable by one's particular location: the differentiation of time matches the division and integration of social practices such as lectures, laboratory work, seminars and study periods. The punctuation or differentiation of time is also evidenced in a historical sense. For instance, in Wylie's (1975) *MIT in Perspective*, the names of MIT staff are post-fixed by the year of their graduation (or receipt of their Masters) – e.g. Robert R. Everett '43. For some time this practice was observed in MIT's institutional journal *Technology Review* where one could also find frequent reference to specific classes – such as the class of '23. This convention was particularly in evidence in one section of the journal that was dedicated toward keeping the readership informed of notable achievements (honours, citations, medals), but also deaths, of MIT alumni.

Writing in 1970, in his study of MIT, Snyder observed that the longstanding strict regulations were beginning to be relaxed at elite colleges but that 'many universities still maintain close surveillance on the manners and mores of their coeds' (Snyder, 1970: 20). In other words, a rigid network of rules and regulations governed the social conduct of the students – 'the rules are spelled out so that the university can function in a parental role, particularly with respect to the conduct of women students' (Snyder, 1970: 119).

At a departmental level, social relations would appear to have been formal; in an interview, one professor is reported to have said that the individual departments operated in a 'traditional pattern, the format of which is too authoritarian to my way of thinking, although the individuals aren't' (Snyder, 1979: 71). This is not an isolated observation for several sources observe the conformity and subordination of MIT students (Riesman, 1980: 597). Indeed, Wylie notes that for a long time MIT had seemed 'immune' to the violent protests that occurred at Berkeley and elsewhere during the late 1960s and early 1970s. What is important in this respect is that although violence did erupt at MIT, it lagged behind that at other university institutions. In other words, taken as a whole these observations indicate that MIT was marked by higher grid and group (that is, a greater weight of rules, regulations, and general ordering of social life, coupled with a strong identity or sense of division between the 'established' members of MIT and 'outsiders') than the general social and academic scene (low grid/low group) in the USA. Moreover, in relation to SDG and the Sloan School we may usefully note that a number of investigations testify to the more conservative attitude of management and engineering students among the general student population (Ladd and Lipset, 1972, 1975; Meier, 1951). Snyder argues that competence rather than creativity had become the keynote of MIT education, which was arguably a contributory factor in the conservatism of the institution; for competence was a requirement of the vocational orientation of much of MIT's curricula and was ultimately assessed by others in the practising professions and industrial organizations. 'The concern for competence lies behind the work overload and expropriation of leisure that are the most immediately visible marks of difference between M.I.T. and liberal arts colleges' (Snyder, 1970: 68).

It would appear that the conformity, competition. and regulation of social life constitute an oppressive grid for the students at MIT. They are, however, a distinct elite and are trained to be leaders in their field – they therefore become socialized into the experience of the exercise of authority. Their sense of obligation is not only to MIT but also to the professional and social responsibilities which pervade the vocational orientation of the institution. Thus, it is within this culture that Forrester, his colleagues, and students, came to embrace system dynamics. With SDG itself the net of perceived duties was cast even wider for they considered themselves to have a responsibility for the future of mankind. Indeed, system dynamics is now an internationally embraced philosophy; there are international conferences, an international society has been formed, and an annual Forrester Prize has been instituted.

Other evidence concerning the group boundedness of SDG comes from their self-perceptions. We find a number of statements in which it is clear that they considered themselves to be cognitively set apart from others, and in particular social scientists whom they alleged lack a proper understanding of system dynamics (Forrester, 1975a,b, 1976a). In so far as system dynamics became a lens through which the system dynamicists orientated themselves in the world, we should expect that it gave them a common sense of identity. In fact, they tended to see themselves as pioneers standing at a new frontier in knowledge, and they perceived their abilities as something which set them apart from outsiders. For example, speaking with regard to those specialized in the profession of automatic feedback control, Forrester stated:

> The profession has been through a hundred years of developing appropriate theory and concepts. No one has a better professional background for understanding today's important social and economic forces. . . . Knowledge imposes responsibility. If no one is better able to deal with the important world and national issues, those with training and ability inherit an obligation to step into the void. (Forrester, 1975a: 3)

Bernstein conjectures that a restricted code will emerge amongst any group which shares a common identity. Thus, as the theoretical framework of system dynamics became more and more consolidated amongst SDG, so we should expect that communications among its members became 'shorter' – that is, less elaborated, carrying a greater burden of implicit meanings – becoming more like a restricted code. To a certain extent these points overlap with the questions raised by Kuhn (1970: 181–7) in relation to paradigms, and Fleck (1979) in respect of thought styles. In so far as system dynamicists knew each other and interacted as a social group, they did not just share common intellectual tools, for a restricted code affirms a set of common values and sense of identity as well. In reference to this we may note that many of the publications in system dynamics (between urban and world dynamics) became increasingly inward-looking – i.e. they came to rely more upon other works in system dynamics rather than drawing upon different intellectual sources. This reinforced both their commitment to system dynamics and the group boundary which increasingly set them apart from outsiders. This sense of apartness was of course rooted in the whole elitist ethos of MIT but it came particularly to the fore when SDG sought to defend themselves against the often vehement criticisms which stemmed from the physical and social science communities. Forrester, for example, even suggested that the nature of this criticism had educational implications for the teaching of social scientists.

I conjecture that group boundedness may not arise solely from internal social bonding (that is, cognitive bonding through a shared philosophy, group commitments and interests), but also from external pressure. Particularly with respect to the WORLD 3 project team, who had published a popular account of their work long before any detailed technical description was available, we can observe that the accepted procedures of scientific publication had been violated. The response of many in the scientific community was to denounce the MIT work and to reaffirm the grid of rules which conventionally govern publication; at the same time this also served to insolate SDG, to push them further towards higher group.

For example, one editorial in *Nature* (1972: 47) asserted that *World Dynamics* was 'a somewhat dangerously over-simple document'. Another in *The Economist* (1972: 20) argued that *The Limits to Growth* report:

> represents the highwater mark of an old-fashioned nonsense, because the MIT team has pumped into its computer so many dear, dead assumptions. It falls with both eyes open into the central trap before all futurologists, and is thus in danger of discrediting the germ of truth that should make more considered researches of this sort worth while.

Yet another editorial, this time in *Science* (1972: 1197), carried the following comment: 'Enthusiasts can easily lose sight of the limitations of computers.' Thus, it is conceivable that the grid/group rating of SDG actually shifted slightly during the period of intense criticism – I will return to these points in greater detail when discussing SDG's response to anomalies.

In the earlier discussion of problems concerning the grid/group theory I suggested that it was important to bear in mind the conservative bias of social experience (or of codes) – that is, it can constitute a form of resistance to changes in cosmology. In relation to this point it is possible to cite certain parallels between Forrester's early and later career. Forrester attributes his view of systems to his experiences when working with military systems, and indeed, I contend that there are important continuities between those experiences and the subsequent development of system dynamics. For example, in a history of the Whirlwind Project (Redmond and Smith, 1980: 17), it is reported that Forrester's investigative techniques were the product of his experiences since 1940 in the Servomechanisms Laboratory.

> They were not intuitive, unexamined procedures that he was unaware of and could not explain. On the contrary, he took it for granted that he should analyze and make explicit as possible the useful techniques that 'came naturally' from his experiences. He preferred to know where he stood and why, at all times and was committed in a very self-aware way to understanding and rationalizing and systematizing the procedures of his mind.

Now the relevance of this for the understanding of his work on system dynamics is that there too one can find similar ideas and concerns about explicitness; only in this case it was sought in the realm of formal computer models.

The Whirlwind Project was conducted in a building which was closed to outsiders because of military security measures; it was run as a tight, well-oiled machine. 'Drawing together as it did young men of ambition, ability, and spirit, and reinforced by a habit of daily operations that stressed, and for the most part obtained, intelligently planned and coordinated operations, this policy produced an unusually high esprit de corps' (Redmond and Smith, 1980: 38). In this social context, then, where a common purpose united all, the seeds were sown for the later ideas of the purposive nature of social systems, the need for sub-systems to subordinate their sub-goals to system goals etc. The social order which sustained a tightly organized research team, was mirrored by the material ordering of Whirlwind's components and the intellectual order that underpinned it. In other words, the social organization of the laboratory was a precondition for the eventual material organization of Whirlwind's components.

As leader of the project, Forrester was described as 'the Chief, cool, distant, and personally remote in a way that kept him in control without ever diminishing our loyalty and pride in the project' (Redmond and Smith, 1980: 135). In this regard he stood in contrast to his deputy – Everett – who was 'relaxed, friendly, understanding'. Thus, although Forrester was the 'Chief' his social interactions were more prescribed by a grid of rules than those of Everett. However, it would appear that Forrester was remote only in a personal sense – i.e. he maintained strict self-control – since in terms of technical issues he was continually involved in problems at a workbench level (Redmond and Smith, 1980: 131–5).

A second continuity between Forrester's earlier and later work is the fact that he continually found himself marching to a different beat. With Whirlwind he was under pressure from the military authorities because of his and Everett's unorthodox research practices – particularly as regards budget overspending (Redmond and Smith, 1980). Forrester was convinced that the experimental computer then being assembled was of much greater importance than his paymasters realized – he saw that a new threshold or frontier was being crossed – and he considered that he had to protect it from those who, not realizing its importance, could interrupt its progress. 'He saw himself as best carrying out his directorial function by shielding his men from potential outside interference' (Redmond and Smith, 1980: 47).

The project came under repeated criticism from different agencies as well as other groups who were also engaged on similar projects, and so the experience of being in a threatened group was not new to him. However, when his later work came under attack, it was not just an important project which was under threat: indeed, I shall argue that it was his sense of proper order which was at stake. There were also charges that Forrester's *Whirlwind* group did not cooperate fully with others in the field – though it must be accepted that certain groups avoided involvement because the project was classified – and again this arguably served to consolidate the sense of apartness. At a more symbolic level, one finds that the security regulations – which differentiated the insiders on the project from outsiders – were reinforced by the ordering of social space: 'Office walls were to be kept clean and bare of cartoons and frivolous pictures' (Redmond and Smith, 1980: 131). In other words, a strict sense of purity of categories prevented the contamination of the inside of the laboratory by the 'frivolous' objects from outside.

This information concerning Forrester's early career not only informs our understanding of the style of thinking which later manifested itself in system dynamics; it also helps to illustrate the deep cognitive commitment he had to it and the subsequent training of his students.

Science Policy Research Unit

The Science Policy Research Unit are based at the relatively new (1961) University of Sussex. This institution is rather small in comparison to MIT and only had 4500 students in 1977. The ratio of the sexes is much more equal at some 1.28:1 males to females (compared to 20:1 at MIT) and in 1982 contained some 425 foreign students – a somewhat smaller percentage than at MIT (University of Sussex, 1982). It is far less selective than MIT which in this regard is more strictly comparable to Oxford or Cambridge. In 1967 SPRU contained eight members of staff and one visiting fellow; by 1976 there were thirty-nine members of staff, eight visiting fellows, and fourteen postgraduates who were distributed amongst six project teams (SPRU, 1967, 1976). Notably, most of the staff members of SPRU came from other universities and institutions (SPRU, 1967, 1976) and they were drawn from a variety of disciplines.

One source of information concerning Sussex is David Riesman who spent some six months there (c.1965). He is a well-known social scientist with an international reputation and cannot therefore be regarded as a naive observer. In his comparison of American and British universities he notes that the planners of the university (among other new institutions) were 'insistent that institutions not grow too large, not beyond human scale, nor grow too fast to permit the induction of students and faculty into their own collegial and more or less experimental climates' (Riesman, 1966: 129).

In terms of university organization he observes that British universities are more decentralized, with faculty members being much involved in new appointments – a task which remains an administrative function in American institutions. He argues that British academics pay a price for their greater democracy through time spent in meetings; interestingly, he comments that this loss was 'excessive' at Sussex, partly because of its 'newness' and the 'belief in equality' (Riesman, 1966: 143).

As for the students, Riesman contrasts the 'playfulness', 'experimenta-tion', and 'joie de vivre' he found among those at Sussex with the 'intense meritocratic competition' often found in the United States. Moreover, he contends that the relatively smaller proportion of people who attend universities in Britain partly contributes to a greater sense of ease and the 'appearance of being relaxed and less bustling and busy than its American counterparts' (Riesman, 1966: 140).

The experimental nature of Sussex was manifest in the introduction of new ideas into curriculum planning and the interaction of disciplines.

What I found at Sussex was an exceptional energy of faculty members talking with each other about education, visiting each other's lectures, and bringing undergraduates into their discussions. One has to see in daily unfolding the details of the Sussex curriculum to realize the tenacious ingenuity: the framework of contextual courses, the grouping of people and topics into schools, the search for intellectual cement to relate the specialities in new and interpenetrating ways, and hence to alter them. (Riesman, 1966: 142)

Briggs (1964: 60), the former Vice-Chancellor at Sussex, also refers to the innovative nature of the Sussex experiment.

> From the start Sussex . . . has been thought of as a centre of innovation. . . . The freedom to work along new lines and the power to plan new combinations of subjects and new curricula have proved great attractions in recruiting academics from universities where curricula can be changed only with the greatest difficulty.

This experimental spirit was an important element in the foundation of SPRU in 1966: there was a deliberate attempt to bring together natural scientists and social scientists to work on shared projects. The aim was to develop cross-fertilization rather than the development of a single philosophy such as system dynamics. However, Freeman (SPRU, 1975: 14) noted that it is difficult to assess how far cross-fertilization – as opposed to mere juxtaposition of different views – was achieved.

The plurality of opinions among SPRU appears to be reflected in a comment in *Thinking About The Future* where Jahoda's guidance of the world-modelling project team is acknowledged: 'she made it possible for a diverse and sometimes unruly group to cooperate fruitfully' (Cole et al., 1973: editorial note). And later, Freeman (1973: 9-10) noted:

> It included people of very diverse political views ranging across the whole spectrum from Conservative to Marxist, and some of no identifiable political complexion. It included members from very different disciplines, and we were not united, as were the MIT group, by a common faith in system dynamics. But we were, and are, agreed on the urgency of many of the social and political problems raised by *The Limits to Growth*, and the belief that satisfactory solutions can only emerge as a result of a continuing process of research, political debate, and social experiment.

In comparison to what was stated about restricted codes, I can assert that this diversity prevented the consolidation of the kind of sense of identity that existed at SDG. Indeed, we may note that SPRU made many references to other works and bodies of knowledge and did not, therefore, maintain professional or disciplinary boundaries as rigidly as SDG (Cole et al., 1973).

The evidence I have presented concerning the social locations of SDG and SPRU suggests that the former should be regarded as further along the axes of grid and group. The greater level of conformity at MIT indicates stronger social control and this is complemented by the degree of ranking (including grading and historical age status), vocational orientation, the routinization of learning, complex punctuation and sequencing of institutional life, and the centrality of organizational power. To these points should be added the larger organizational size, much longer historical roots, and division of the sexes – with the virtual exclusion of women at MIT. All these factors indicate a higher grid position. As for group, we have seen that the vocational orientation of MIT is aimed at inducing a sensitivity to professional responsibilities, and therefore a sense of group identity. As a group within an institution which cultivates the sense of being part of an elite, SDG's group boundedness was further enhanced by their shared philosophy and position *vis-à-vis* the threat of criticism from large sections of the academic world. In Fleck's terms, SDG were more clearly bounded as a thought collective, an esoteric circle who shared a thought style. For in addition to shared interests, the social bonds among SDG were also constituted by the exchange of cognitions within the framework of their thought style (or, as I argued earlier, they shared a restricted code).

As for their reputation, SDG believed that they were marching to a different beat to others, having an insight into the workings of complex systems, and so academic standing was of little comparative importance – they knew that they were right. Indeed, this enabled the group to interpret hostile criticism as positive evidence for their own cause: outsiders objected to system dynamics because education had not equipped them to understand the nature of complex feedback systems. In contrast, SPRU did not have a shared theory of the world and so we can state that this lack of a strong cognitive bond further indicates the lower rating of group in their social experience. In addition, SDG were constituted by a core of members who had developed their professional outlook under the supervision of Forrester – the inventor of system dynamics, from whom they had learned – and had accepted his teachings on *authority*. SPRU, on the other hand, did not share a similar learning experience.

There is also an important international comparison to be drawn between SDG and SPRU. In *Risk and Culture*, Douglas and Wildavsky (1982) argue that the USA is a 'border' country – by which they mean a culture which provides fertile soil for the formation of sectarian groups (low grid/high group). Those in the 'centre', or mainstream of American society are closely tied to the rigours and concerns of the industrial system, while those on the border are more separated from it. Further, this difference in social location is marked by differences in the perceptions of risk – particularly of environmental dangers. More specifically, the centre has comparatively short time horizons as far as risk is concerned, whereas the groups on the border of the industrial system perceive distant dangers. (Similar arguments about the connection between environmental risks and social location have been advanced by Thompson, 1982). In connection with this it is worth noting an interesting difference between the formative years of system dynamics (which at the time was called industrial dynamics), during the early 1960s, and the later period of world modelling in the 1970s. During the earlier period, model building was tied to industrial applications and the time horizon of the models of industrial corporations was typically 10–15 years. During the later period, when SDG had been formed as a distinct group with its own laboratory and system dynamics had grown into a systems philosophy, the global models that were built had time horizons of up to 200 years – this was the time-scale over which the system dynamicists were concerned with environmental dangers. And, while their early industrial models were built to further the growth and efficiency of the capitalist system, SDG later became critics of industrial growth and advocated a zero-growth equilibrium society.

At the time of the world modelling exercises the social scene in the USA was characterized by apprehension about the future: within this context SDG provided some of the metaphors and cloak of scientific credibility through which that apprehension was articulated and legitimated. What this suggests is that not only did SDG become spokesmen for many border groups of environmentalists, but perhaps they themselves became a border group who saw themselves as defending nature and the global ecosystem against the dangerous forces of exponential growth. In contrast to the USA, Britain is not a border country; moreover, while SPRU also had criticisms of the industrial machine, it was not distant environmental dangers which concerned them but, rather, current economic and social problems (Cole et al., 1973).

The evidence presented here can not be construed as a definitive account of the social location of SDG and SPRU. Without direct observation I can not know the precise nature of the social relations behind the walls of the System Dynamics Laboratory or the Research Unit at Sussex, but by considering the different institutional traditions within which SDG and SPRU reside, as well as other information, I have offered an *interpretation* of their social experiences in terms of grid and group: SDG were marked by stronger grid and group than SPRU.

6 Dealing With Monsters: Methodology and Thought Styles

In this chapter I compare the thought styles of SDG and SPRU from a methodological point of view. To this end, a controversy known as the 'backcasting debate' provides a good opportunity to see how they reacted to the same kind of phenomena. I will employ Lakatos's ideas about how mathematicians deal with counterexamples in order to illuminate the different strategies by which SDG and SPRU responded to the anomalies which arose in the context of backcasting and thereby throw light on their thought styles. First, however, I will begin by considering the different views of modelling articulated by the two groups.

SDG's Approach to Modelling

The systems approach practised by SDG centred on the formal modelling of social systems – they defined a system as a set of elements which were united for some common purpose. They assumed that the 'true' purpose or goal of any social system can be represented in a model, and that policies to achieve it can thereby be tested. To them the general goal of modelling was to afford a better understanding of social systems in order to facilitate the objective of system management and control. In the specific context of world modelling, the goal was to aid the transition to a sustainable global equilibrium society some time in the near future. This orientation carried with it an instrumental, pragmatic view of modelling: it was asserted that a model should only be judged in accordance with the purposes for which it is built (Forrester, 1976a). Further, this outlook permeated the view that Forrester took of other research; for example, he argued that practical relevance should be accorded a higher place in judging research in the social sciences. 'Because the standards for judging publication and research originate in academia, criteria of excellence should be moved away from cleverness, mathematical skill, narrow precision, internal logical rigor, and data collection and analysis for their own sakes. Instead relevance to social policy should be expected along with a defense and explanation of the relevance' (Forrester, 1976a: 33).

As regards their methodological orientation, two main features which can be readily discerned are the use of a general systems theoretic framework and their position concerning the use of statistical – including time-series – data. They contended that the properties of all systems – whether physical or social – are governed by feedback structures whose behavioural characteristics are more fundamental than the particularities of individual systems. In other words, a knowledge of a system's structure rather than a precise knowledge of the values of the variables which describe its components, is sufficient to understand its behaviour – structure was therefore seen to more important than data. Forrester argued that models based on time-series data (as in the case of many econometric models) could replicate only behaviour modes that have been observed in the past. In contrast, he suggested that a system dynamics model could generate previously unseen modes and was therefore more pertinent for long-term modelling.

System dynamics models were not used to make predictions about system states at specific points in time; rather, they were used to predict 'behaviour characteristics' (stability, oscillation, growth etc.). In order to test a model's validity, it was required to be able to reproduce or predict the behaviour of the real system to which it was supposed to correspond – the behaviour was to be 'plausible', the model should show the same 'symptoms' and respond to extreme conditions and non-linearities in the same manner as the real system; any time phasing between variables or periodicities should also match those of the real system (Forrester, 1961: 54).

Aggregation is an important aspect of any modelling exercise and in the case of system dynamics it is useful to consider the aggregation of elements with similar behaviour; parallel elements; and aggregation in time. The system dynamicists argued that if two elements had similar underlying dynamic structures then – given the purposes of the model – they could be aggregated together. For example, in WORLD 2 capital and technology were aggregated together on the basis that the creation and depreciation of capital closely resembles that of technology. 'Much of scientific and technical knowledge resides in the heads and skills of people and disappears from the system through death and decay in a manner dynamically similar to the obsolescence and discard of physical capital' (Forrester, 1976: 29). Second, the world models were aggregated at a global level because individual countries were regarded as parallel elements. That is, world system behaviour was some additive sum of these separate elements – the feedback structure of the world system being regarded as identical to that which governs each individual nation. Third, short term responses such as price fluctuations were considered to be aggregated within long term dynamics; the world models had a long-range time horizon and the behavioural dynamics of the long term were considered to be more important than those of the short term.

In *Industrial Dynamics* (1961: 109) Forrester illustrated the essential principles of aggregation by considering an analogy between a water-supply system and industrial systems. He pointed out that in a model of a water system all individual drops of water can be considered to be aggregated together: it may be assumed that each drop flows through all the elements represented in the system description. In the case of an industrial system another example is that of the flow of an order item, and the aggregation of all order items within a particular flow channel – all items pass through the same decision points. Now, while these examples are fairly straightforward, the level of aggregation present in the world models was arguably of a qualitatively different kind. '[T]he models . . . were designed to examine the feasibility of continued growth in global population, capital and resource usage. These issues depend on the relationships between total world population, total food production, total resource consumption, and total capital, more than on the distribution of population or capital between nations' (Forrester, 1976: 30). Meadows's team took the same position on aggregation as Forrester: for them, global capital had 'real-world meaning' (Meadows et al., 1974: 24). The problem here is that although it is easy to see the relationship between a real water system, each drop of water in it, and a model of it, the same does not necessarily hold with the world models. For instance, to name but one difficulty, the concept of global capital assumes that all types of capital can be valued on the same basis. The point here is not to challenge the system dynamicists' use of aggregation but to understand it. By asking this question one does not refute the concept of global capital but draws attention to the fact that its meaning depends on a given perspective. The principles of aggregation are therefore context dependent because what one group may take as empirical may be regarded as fiction by another. (This will become clearer when considering SPRU's stance on aggregation.)

The system dynamicists contended that formal mathematical models were more open to inspection and criticism than mental models; however, this seeming openness to criticism was tempered by the fact that they believed that critics must put forward alternative models – criticism must take the form of a better formal model.

It is to be hoped that those who believe they already have some different model that is more valid will present it in the same explicit detail, so that its assumptions and consequences can be examined and compared. To reject this model because of its shortcomings without offering concrete and tangible alternatives would be equivalent to asking that time be stopped. (Forrester, 1971: ix)

Thus, it was implied that the way to improved models was through the construction of other formal models. While accepting that no model could ever be perfect, they argued that formal models were better than the intuitive models on which decisions about policy would otherwise be made. We can also note the argument that alternative formal models should be expected to be 'ready for use' (i.e. in social policy) – this being in keeping with an instrumental view of modelling (Forrester, 1976a: 32).

SPRU's Approach to Modelling

SPRU also favoured a systems approach to the task of understanding global problems; however, unlike the system dynamicists, they expressed more reservations about the practical difficulties of pursuing it. For them the concept of a system centred on the idea of interrelation between a group of elements but there was no assertion that a system necessarily has a common goal or purpose (Clark et al., 1975: 33). As for the aim of modelling, this they presumed lay in indicating the way to 'socially worthwhile futures' (Clark et al., 1975: 116).

Members of SPRU believed that suitable data were 'essential' to any modelling activity. This, they argued, was due to the fact that mathematical models require calibration and therefore 'complete and coherent data' are needed. This necessity to ground the theory which is represented in a model in suitable quantitative data was a recurrent theme in their critique of the system dynamics world models. Their concern indicates that they were somewhat *less* pragmatic than SDG as far as model utility and purpose were concerned; but it also represented a strong empirical flavour within their methodological orientation.

In terms of testing the validity of a model, they believed – along with the system dynamicists – that a model should have predictive power, it should be able to forecast. However, in contrast to SDG they required more precise predictions than mere behaviour modes; the degree of precision being sufficient if increased accuracy did not lead to different conclusions (Clark et al., 1975: 71). In their view, the world models fell short of the desired precision because they were rather sensitive to the assumptions on which they were based: plausible changes in parameters led to radically different policy inferences. 'What, then, remains of Forrester's and

Meadows' efforts? Nothing, it seems to us, that can be immediately used for policy formation by decision makers; a technique, one among several – system dynamics – of promise which needs improvement; but above all a challenge to all concerned with man's future to do better' (Jahoda, 1973: 215).

SPRU also advanced other strands of model testing such as simplicity criteria, linearization, and sensitivity analysis. Let us consider the notion of simplicity first. SPRU argued that a primary requirement for a model was that it should be as *simple* as possible. 'In view of the problems of construction, testing and communication, Ockham's razor should be used ruthlessly, no material being included simply "for the sake of it" as often seems to occur with simulation modelling' (Clark et al., 1975: 110). One way of simplifying a model is by linearization, which is the technique of replacing non-linear model relationships by linear ones; this not only reduces complexity and therefore aids understanding, it also permits the use of other testing techniques which have validity only in the domain of linear systems. As an example of the usefulness of linearization SPRU referred to the work of Cuypers (1973), in the Netherlands, which had shown that WORLD 2 could be totally linearized without affecting the standard run of the model.

Another major facet of model-testing which SPRU proposed was that of sensitivity analysis, the aim of which is to determine the relationship between a model's behaviour and the uncertainty in the knowledge of its parameter values. The system dynamicists also carried out a limited form of sensitivity analysis but – as we saw earlier – contended that complex systems were insensitive to parameter uncertainty. In contrast, SPRU argued that such analysis should not be carried out on one parameter at a time – as the SDG had done – but that one should seek to manipulate clusters of parameters. 'Both Forrester and Meadows, in their world models, employ one-parameter-at-a-time sensitivity testing, which is in general quite inappropriate to a highly-interacting model involving considerable nonlinearities' (Clark et al., 1975: 71). In fact, throughout their critique of the world models, SPRU endeavoured to test the effects of alternative assumptions, and for them this also constituted a form of sensitivity testing. They also suggested that sensitivity analysis should be used to locate redundant variables within a model – these were then to be excluded, and the model thereby simplified.

Although they regarded criticism as a necessary part of advancing the techniques of modelling, they did not equate criticism with refutation: 'One certainly should not reject a method because of intrinsic barriers, especially when they are not fatal. It seems to us not sensible, even dangerous, that only one method be prescribed or that any one method should be neglected' (Clark et al., 1975: 116). Thus, SPRU advocated the use of different models and modelling techniques when tackling a problem and indeed, much of their work on global modelling has taken the form of comparative analyses – in general they appeared to favour an eclectic approach. Another point worth making about SPRU's approach to modelling concerns aggregation. For instance, they pointed out that although WORLD 2 and WORLD 3 were policy-oriented, the high level of aggregation involved required a non-existent global decision maker – the policy utility of the world models was therefore seen to be questionable. Also, they objected to the global aggregation of pollution in the models because to them it did not have any empirical meaning (of course SDG would have contested this). For SPRU, an entity such as 'global pollution' simply did not exist. They supported their scepticism on this matter by asserting that almost no empirical data concerning pollution were available for periods of greater than 10 or 20 years – yet SDG had taken such short term data on specific pollutants and extrapolated global trends from them.

Thus, for SPRU, empirical validity in matters of aggregation was grounded in a criterion of quantifiability – in contrast to the rather intuitive criterion of SDG. Finally, SPRU discussed a test which required that if disaggregation at a specific point notably altered the behaviour of a model, or the conclusions drawn from it, then the model should indeed be disaggregated at that point. This test was connected to the suggestion that only independent parameters with similar properties (or numerous random processes), should be aggregated together (Clark et al., 1975: 62). They carried out the test with the WORLD 2 model by separating the world into two regions and it was found that the hybrid model gave different results to WORLD 2 (Cole and Curnow, 1973a). The argument that only independent parameters should be aggregated was also a factor in their criticism of the aggregation of capital and technology within the world models. Because the productivity of capital was seen to be intimately connected to the state of technological knowledge they were not considered to be independent. Indeed, SPRU found that the disaggregation of capital and technology – by the inclusion of incremental annual improvements in agricultural, resource and anti-pollution technologies – was capable of eliminating the collapse depicted by the models. In contrast, Forrester had only examined the effects of single discontinuous technical improvements – these only delayed the collapse for a few years.

Comments

There were substantial technical differences – but also some similarities – between the approach to modelling practised by each group. SDG embraced a universal framework and built models which were largely independent of formal empirical considerations. SPRU, on the other hand, repeatedly emphasized the need to calibrate models, to ground them in quantitative empirical data. This difference is partly explained by SDG's greater pragmatism concerning the question of model purpose. This pragmatism was essentially an instrumental attitude towards modelling: model purpose (the end) dictated the selection of model parameters (the means) and the degree of acceptable precision. In contrast, SPRU implied that the choice of purpose was constrained by the empirical validity and quantitative knowledge of the selected model parameters. On the point of model purpose, therefore, SDG appeared lower grid than SPRU.

Both groups considered it important that a model had surplus content, that it was able to predict. SDG provided theoretical justifications for their predictions – based upon the properties of feedback systems – while SPRU required more formal empirical verification. The former only claimed to predict behaviour modes but the latter preferred more precise predictions of system states. In terms of judging model predictions, then, SPRU's position (empirical) was lower grid than SDG's (formal).

As far as aggregation was concerned, both groups related it to empirical considerations but differed as to what could actually be taken as empirical; SPRU, for instance, did not accept the global aggregation of pollution. SDG accepted 'real-world' intuitive observations, while SPRU again required meaningful quantification. This disparity between intuitive and quantitative knowledge was one reflecting a difference between higher and lower grid.

SPRU discussed model testing to a greater extent; indeed, they proposed a battery of empirical and formal test procedures, together with other techniques for simplifying models. Moreover, while SDG's articulation of assumptions lay at the level of model structure – they enunciated concepts and justified them on formal grounds – SPRU aimed to challenge them (e.g. global pollution or global capital) and supplemented this with empirical arguments. Whether it was the degree of aggregation or implicit assumptions about technological change, SPRU manifested a curiosity in examining the underlying assumptions involved. This was complemented by their comparative approach to modelling.

Each group expounded a systems perspective but with a number of important disparities; for example, both stressed the interdependence of system elements, but SDG went further and assumed that system elements share a common purpose or goal. This rested on the further assumption that the goal could be decided relatively unproblematically, and it was a mark of higher grid: for at root it implied that the goals were real and not mere interpretations.

Monsters and the Backcasting Debate

Having outlined the respective approaches to modelling adopted by the two groups, let us now consider their engagement in the controversy surrounding the technique of backcasting. 'Backcasting' is the name given to the technique of running a simulation model backwards in time (retrodiction) in order to try and test its assumptions and parameter values. The proponents of backcasting contend that retrodiction is likely to drive a model's variables to unrealistic values and may thereby indicate implausible assumptions in its formulation. In a review of the world models of Forrester and Meadows at MIT, Cole and Curnow (SPRU) suggested the potential usefulness of the technique and demonstrated it with those models.[1]

Here I will concentrate on Forrester's model – WORLD 2, as described in *World Dynamics* (details of this model were discussed in chapter 1). The model contains a series of non-linear, non-probabilistic, first-order difference equations which are integrated by using the Euler rectangular method; in backcasting, the solution interval is assigned a negative value. The backcasters argued that a system dynamics model may (at least theoretically) be run either forwards or backwards in time. Of course some people may well object that backcasting is not a valid technique – that it requires a model to behave in a way that the real world does not. From such a perspective, backcasting would appear to be nonsensical. Now, to be sure the world cannot be run backwards – because of thermodynamic reasons for instance. However, models are mathematical objects and in backcasting one is attempting to explore the view of history which is indicated by the original starting values of a model. Thus, given the state variable conditions at time (t) one could ask what were the conditions at ($t-dt$) which preceded them, and so on. To take a simple example, consider the variable (P) representing population through time (T). Its trajectory can be described by the following difference equation:

$$P_{t+dt} = P_t + P_t (\text{BR} - \text{DR})dt$$

where BR is the birth rate, DR is the death rate, and dt is a small time interval (the solution interval). The retrodiction of the variable is given by:

$$P_{t-dt} = P_t - P_t (\text{BR} - \text{DR})dt$$

On the basis of such reasoning it can be argued that one should not reject the claims of the backcasters out of hand. Indeed, if something cuts across the grain of common sense then perhaps one should explore that grain – at the very least it may aid the understanding of one's position. There is another and stronger reason which lies in the fact that some (but not all) members of the MIT group later *accepted* that backcasting was a theoretical possibility, and different model improvements were proposed in the light of a certain model 'error' which was uncovered by the SPRU backcast of WORLD 2. In any case, I am not interested in judging who was 'right' or 'wrong' about backcasting in any absolute sense: it is no use attempting to understand the debate by asking what was the 'true' position to take. Rather, I assume that each group held its own beliefs on the matter rationally; therefore, what *they* each took to be the truth is the focus of attention here.

In fact, there are practical difficulties with backcasting. In particular, numerical errors affect the dynamic calculations and models may then generate spurious histories. However, Cole and Curnow argued that provided such errors are strictly controlled (through the use of a small – but not too small – solution interval), backcasting can yield useful information about a model.[2] For example, they found that WORLD 2 predicted anomalous population figures when backcast, and from this they concluded that the model was incorrectly formulated. Cole and Curnow clearly saw the errant population figures as an anomaly which challenged the system dynamicists' claim that the model adequately represented the global system. It also – in their eyes – cast doubt upon the model's post-2000 predictions. Subsequently they proceeded to modify the model. The members of the MIT System Dynamics Group did not share their conclusions; in fact, some (but not all) rejected the anomaly, and they unanimously upheld the model's predictions.

Having briefly discussed the idea of backcasting, I will now continue with a description of the history of the debate which surrounded it. Then I will discuss Lakatos's work on counterexamples in mathematics before going on to use his ideas in order to analyse the debate in more detailed terms. The debate is reconstructed from the principal exchanges in the literature between the groups at MIT and SPRU. There were, of course, other less formal interactions (through personal letters and meetings) as part of the overall SPRU critique of the system dynamics world-modelling effort. However, the argument in this chapter will confine itself to the explanation of the development of the formal record.

History of the Backcasting Debate

The controversy over backcasting originally arose when Cole and Curnow noted that the WORLD 2 model projected a population decrease between 1900 and 1904, and they subsequently suggested running the model backwards before 1900 in order to see from where this trend had developed. This population dip had not drawn much attention earlier because the output from the model had been presented in graphical form with a rather crude scale (for example, see figure 1.3). Actually, Forrester had commented that the death rate at 1900 was 'equal to or greater than the birth rate', but he implied that this was due to incorrect initial conditions which caused a 'small transient readjustment'. 'Such questions raised by the behavior of a model system cause us to re-examine and improve the model' (Forrester, 1971: 80).[3]

Cole and Curnow argued that the model's mathematical relationships were time reversible and that since the credibility of the predictions produced by the model depended to a certain extent upon its ability to reproduce trends between 1900 and 1970, extending its time-scale backwards would provide the opportunity for a better test of the fit between history and model trajectories. Setting the solution interval in the simulation to a negative value, Cole and Curnow found that the model retrodicted an exponentially growing population which reached a value of some 3.9 billion by the year 1880 (see figure 6.1). In the words of Cole and Curnow (1973a: 113): 'The curves are curious – they seem to indicate that the 20th century lies in the aftermath of a catastrophic population collapse.'

Cole and Curnow argued that at low levels of industrialization the model yielded poor estimates of death rates; in particular they contended that one

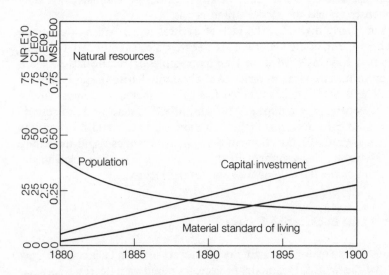

Figure 6.1 The backcast of WORLD 2 1900–1880

DEALING WITH MONSTERS   101

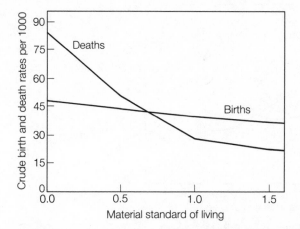

Figure 6.2   Crude birth and death rates as functions of MSL
Source: the specification of WORLD 2; Forrester, 1971: 132–4.

variable – known as DRMM (death rate from material multiplier) –
overestimated the death rate whenever material standard of living was
low.[4] When backcast, the level of population becomes augmented by
deaths and depleted by births: hence the errant values for the death rates
caused the population values to grow exponentially as the model was
retrodicted. This can be seen by a comparison of crude birth and death
rates as functions of material standard of living (MSL) which is itself a
function of capital investment. Figure 6.2 shows that (other things being
equal) as MSL decreases, the crude death rate rises much more sharply
than the birth rate – and, in fact, increasingly so. Thus, when the
WORLD 2 model is backcast, the level of capital investment falls –
followed by MSL – and so the population begins to explode.
    Figure 6.3 shows the function (line abcd) that had been chosen to
represent the relationship between DRMM and MSL. Cole and Curnow
decided to 'experiment' with this function and subsequently constrained
the range of DRMM from 1.5 to 0.5 instead of 3.0 to 0.5 as Forrester had
done. Figure 6.3 also shows the modified function (line abf). (Interestingly, Forrester himself had suggested that the original function might be
somewhat too steep on the left-hand side.)
    This single modification of DRMM enabled retrodiction of the model
beyond 1880 to the year 1850 (though other variables also become negative
by this time, not due to numerical errors but simply because the model
trajectories reach zero and then become negative). Back to 1850 the
population history of the model remains quite plausible and when the
model is run forward from 1850 it generates smooth population growth.

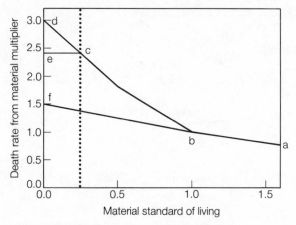

Figure 6.3   Alternative curves for DRMM
Source: the specification of WORLD 2; Forrester, 1971: 132–4.

This ceases in the twenty-first century, and the subsequent fall in the level of population is due more to falling birth rate than increasing death rate, as had been the case with the original model. Thus, the model's prediction (on population at least) was no longer as pessimistic. Modifying the DRMM multiplier was not the only possible way of enabling retrodiction with WORLD 2, and the SPRU team also suggested other possible changes.[5]

The main conclusions which Cole and Curnow drew were that Forrester's guesswork in setting the initial starting values for the WORLD 2 model was in error, and that the model gave poor estimates for death rates whenever material standard of living was low: in other words, that the model was not correctly formulated in this regard. They also advanced another – and perhaps more subtle – point, which was that had the model been initialized in 1880 on the basis of Forrester's arguments in *World Dynamics*, then the predicted collapse would occur some 20 years earlier. Similarly, if it had been initialized in 1850 the collapse would occur in 1970! The reason for this is that the model exhibits exponential growth within fixed limits: thus, starting the powerful growth forces at, say, 20 years earlier brings forward the clash with those limits. Therefore, seen as a practical and heuristic model testing tool, the questions raised in the context of backcasting illuminated WORLD 2's incorrect initialization and poor component formulation with regard to death rates, and also threw light on its basic mode of behaviour. These findings raised questions about the rest of the model, particularly in the light of the almost complete absence of empirical data in the model and the controversial conclusions Forrester had drawn from it.

According to Forrester, a good model is distinguishable from a bad one in the extent to which it 'captures more of the essence of the social system that it presumes to represent' (Forrester, 1971: 15). Further, he states that the 'computer gives the correct implications of the assumptions that went into the construction of the model' (Forrester, 1971: 15). However, the dip in population between 1900 and 1904 and the retrodicted population of almost 4 billion for 1880 are surprising features of the behaviour of WORLD 2 and represent anomalies which must ultimately be accounted for. They are anomalous because they conflict with history; put another way, pre-1900 history and the period between 1900 and 1904 are outside the scope of WORLD 2. Therefore, it cannot be accepted that the model captures the 'essence' of the global system; or, at least, there could be an improved model which captured more of its essence.

The response from MIT was not uniform; initially it was unequivocal, with the backcast being totally rejected. Later, however, the response from some other members of the group was more measured and the backcast was seen to be a genuine retrodiction of the model, though the model's post-2000 predictions were still upheld. The first response came from Meadows and other members of the WORLD 3 project team, who denounced the SPRU work on backcasting for a number of technical and other reasons. For instance, they argued that reversing the solution time increment 'must radically alter the entire dynamic character of the model'; that normally insignificant errors would tend to accumulate, with model elements exhibiting 'completely spurious excursions' (Meadows et al., 1973: 138). They charged that the SPRU backcast was such an excursion:

The discovery of one such excursion in the WORLD 2 population is cited as an imperfection of the model. In fact, the WORLD 2 population will also explode under reverse simulation from many different starting points. For example, if the model is initialised in 1940 with characteristic values for that date, and run backwards, population explodes by the year 1920. Since WORLD 2 does not always backcast its own behaviour, should we conclude that WORLD 2 is not even a good model of WORLD 2? (Meadows et al., 1973: 138–9)

For these and other reasons the MIT group saw backcasting as 'completely meaningless' (Meadows et al., 1973: 139).[6] However, aside from the above points – which undoubtedly have some relevance to the problem of backcasting – irrelevant factors were also cited. For example, Meadows's team argued that delayed relationships would be asymmetric in time and that any stochastic influences on the model's behaviour in the forward direction would not be recaptured when it was backcast.[7] Finally, Meadows's team concluded:

> Running a system dynamics model backwards tells us nothing about the model's utility in understanding the world. The meaning Sussex automatically assigns to backcasting illustrates the influence of analytical habits gained in the context of substantially different kinds of models. The Sussex authors suggest it is important 'to examine the great catastrophe of 1880' in WORLD 2. We believe it is more important to first understand the relation between the mathematical properties of multiloop feedback models and the dynamic attributes of real world systems. (Meadows et al., 1973: 139)

Now, arguably the main plank in the MIT retort was the charge that the SPRU backcast merely represented a spurious history. While (as noted earlier) SPRU did accept the possibility of spurious excursions, they argued that if errors were kept under tight control this need not be a problem, and that while the MIT backcast from 1940 to 1920 was unstable because of numerical errors in the computation, their own backcast exploded because of wrong assumptions in the model.

In a later article by another member of the MIT System Dynamics Group – Wright (1973: 1091) – it was accepted that the SPRU backcast was indeed unique: it 'had shown the legitimate predecessor state of the model'. (This has also been corroborated by a third, independent party – Erickson and Pikul, 1976.[8]) Although Wright accepted the legitimacy of the SPRU backcast, he did not accept their conclusions with regard to Forrester's model. While acknowledging that backcasting with system dynamics was indeed theoretically possible, and providing an example of a simple model which would retrodict unproblematically, Wright argued that practical difficulties limited its usefulness, and he viewed the SPRU backcast as 'lucky' in this respect.

> A retrodictive test of Forrester's *World Dynamics* . . . is shown to have found, fortuitously, an inconsistency in the model, but to have drawn incorrect conclusions about the importance of that defect for future behaviour and policy alternatives, to have suggested inappropriate and incomplete model improvements, and to have added nothing to understanding of the model. (Wright, 1973: 1085)

To try and solve the difficulties with the WORLD 2 model, Wright began by changing the 1900 initial conditions for capital investment; however, despite the fact that the model then exhibited smooth growth from 1900 in a forwards direction and yielded trajectories close to the original ones, the model still would not retrodict satisfactorily. He then turned his attention to the model's formulation. Though admitting that something was wrong with the model, Wright rejected the actual SPRU modification of the DRMM function. Instead, he altered the range of DRMM from 2.4 to 0.5 (see figure 6.3, line abce). He based his argument for this on the fact that the model misbehaved when MSL<0.25; the SPRU modification altered DRMM throughout the interval 0<MSL<0.5 while his modification was restricted to 0<MSL<0.25. In addition, he also chose to modify another variable, the capital investment multiplier (CIM), which influences capital investment rates. His purpose in doing so was to slow down the model's growth in capital investment when MSL<0.25; the effect of this was to overcome the problem pointed out by SPRU with regard to the timing of the model's collapse. The question as he saw it was: 'can these assumptions be modified to support reasonable 1880 values without damaging predicted future trends?' (Wright, 1973: 1092) In extending the modification of DRMM over a larger interval the SPRU team had also altered its values for post-1900 computations and, indeed, this accounts for the less pessimistic post-2000 trajectories. In challenging their modification Wright asserted: 'It may be that their formulation is correct; but it certainly does not follow that a discrepancy observed in the 1880–1900 range of operation (MSL<0.25) demands revising the formulation in other ranges' (Wright, 1973: 1092).

Beginning with 'reasonable' 1880 values, Wright argued that his modified model passed 'close' to Forrester's 1900 values and mapped out a path 'very similar' to the original WORLD 2. A second reason why Wright rejected the SPRU modification and the conclusions they drew concerning WORLD 2 was grounded in his different view of the purpose of a model:

A model need be accurate only for ranges of operation over which it will be exercised. . . . A nonlinear model will retrodict its referent system if its formulation is reasonable for the range of operation that occurs in the earlier period. It is possible for a model builder to choose, rationally and deliberately, component formulations accurate over the operating mode occurring after a starting point but inaccurate in ranges expected before that initial time. The model cannot be faulted if it remains in the acceptable operating range (Wright, 1973: 1092).

In 1974 Forrester again made reference to the misbehaviour of his model at the start of its simulation. He suggested that the model was incorrectly initialized and recommended changing its initial values; leaving the value for population, capital investment, pollution and natural resources at the previous levels, he argued that the value of CIAF – which represents the fraction of capital devoted to agriculture – should be increased from 0.2 to 0.4. Despite this modification, although the trajectories of the other variables mimic those of the original model (except that population no longer dips between 1900 and 1904), that for CIAF decreases for the first 37 years before following a path similar to the one of the original. In other words, curing the population dip was undertaken at the expense of introducing a declining level of capital investment in agriculture between 1900 and 1937 – a trend which has no historic foundation. Though Forrester's conclusions remained the same, he did not offer any hypothesis to account for (nor did he even note) the peculiar behaviour of this variable.

In addition, there is a more crucial point to be noted here, for Wright, too, had accepted Forrester's assertion that the original model was not correctly initialized. But Wright chose to alter the initial value of capital investment. The obvious question, then, is: what is the set of correct initial values for the model? Further, if both changes are tenable, why then could the fault not equally lie with the formulation of the model itself? In fact, there may be numerous combinations of initial values or, equally, numerous parameter formulations which could result in smooth population growth from 1900 onwards.

In 1976 Forrester argued that backcasting was 'apt to be meaningless' unless very special conditions were fulfilled (Forrester, 1976a: 32). Though citing the work of SPRU, he did not acknowledge any achievement or valid criticisms on their behalf.

At this point it would seem appropriate to summarize the main features of this debate. First, the groups at MIT and SPRU differed distinctly with regard to the basis and utility of backcasting. There were also some differences among the system dynamicists themselves, though they were united in their agreement that the SPRU backcast did not invalidate Forrester's conclusions. Second, originally the MIT group saw the backcast as meaningless and irrelevant, but Wright later saw it as legitimate. Thus, the debate shifted from one of whether or not the SPRU backcast was legitimate to a consideration of its implications, together with possible improvements to WORLD 2. Third, given that the model was supposed to capture the essence of the global system, the backcast represented an anomaly which needed an explanation. Similarly, the behaviour of the model between 1900 and 1904 was also anomalous. Fourth, in line with their contrasting approaches to modelling, each group held a different view of the purpose of a model, and of what should be expected from it. Fifth, SPRU offered a simple modification of the DRMM parameter which was rejected by Wright in favour of a less 'extreme' modification, together with a modification of a parameter-influencing capital investment. Sixth, Forrester thought that the 1900–4 population dip was due to incorrect initialization, but his modified set of initial values was different from that of Wright. Thus, even within the MIT group, there were different positions on precisely how the model should be modified.

Anomalies and Strategies for Coping with Them

In order to understand the different moves within the backcasting debate we need some concepts about how anomalies are dealt with. Suggestions are provided by Lakatos in his analysis of strategies for dealing with counterexamples in mathematics. In his book *Proofs and Refutations*, Lakatos (1976) set out to describe the logic of mathematical discovery and as illustration he took the example of the controversy surrounding the Euler–Descartes conjecture on polyhedra. This conjecture states that the relationship between the number of edges, vertices and faces of a polyhedron is given by the formula: $V - E + F = 2$; where V, E, and F represent the number of vertices, edges, and faces respectively. For example, take a simple cube; it has eight vertices, twelve edges, and six faces; thus yielding: $8 - 12 + 6 = 2$.

Lakatos discussed how various mathematicians adopted different attitudes towards polyhedra and counterexamples to the Euler–Descartes conjecture. At one extreme some thought that the conjecture captured the essence of all real polyhedra; at the other were those who saw the conjecture rather as a statement about those objects which were conventionally ascribed the status of a polyhedron (that is, that met some conventional definition). In the face of putative counterexamples (such as two tetrahedra joined at a vertex for which $V = 7, E = 12$, and $F = 8$, thus yielding $7 - 12 + 8 = 3$), different mathematicians consequently embarked upon disparate strategies in order to deal with them. Some treated the counterexamples as if they were monsters, grotesque challenges to the beauty of the conjecture. Others found them to be objects of curiosity. Ultimately, these strategies reflected different styles of thought – they were rooted in different conceptions of natural or proper order – and they led to different forms of mathematical knowledge.

I will now give a very brief and much simplified account of some of the strategies discussed in Lakatos's analysis, before employing them to understand the moves within the backcasting debate. First of all, imagine that we have some conjecture and a suggested proof for it. In fact, in informal mathematics, a proof procedure can be viewed as a series of subconjectures (or lemmas) derived from the main conjecture; Lakatos regarded a proof as a thought experiment for proving a conjecture. What are we to do if someone proposes an anomaly or counterexample? Such a case may be either a *local*, a *global*, or both a local *and* global counterexample. By global counterexample Lakatos meant one which refutes the conjecture; while local counterexamples conflict with specific lemmas in the proof. Local counterexamples usually give rise to the refinement of lemmas in the proof, but with global cases the responses are more complex. Looking at the history of the dispute surrounding the Euler–Descartes conjecture, Lakatos distinguished several distinct approaches for dealing with such counterexamples; but here I will consider only the four major possibilities.

First, there is the strategy of *monster barring*, in which the counterexample is declared to be a monster or 'pathological' case: it is said to be of no significance because it does not fit the definitions embedded in the proof. For example, in the case of the Euler–Descartes conjecture, some mathematicians proposed counterexamples which adherents of the conjecture refused to accept as genuine polyhedra. This strategy often evokes shifting definitions.

A second and more sophisticated strategy is to accept the counterexample as genuine, but to make a distinction between the 'correct' domain of application of the conjecture and the counterexample – which is thought to fall outside it. Other defining lemmas are added to the proof, and though the conjecture's domain becomes restricted, its underlying validity emerges intact. This strategy is called *exception barring*. The redrawing of the domain is, however, *ad hoc*, for it depends only on the particular counterexample and is no guarantee against there being others within the new domain.

A third strategy – one which is related to the last – is that of *monster adjustment*. Here, the counterexample is 'adjusted' by arguments which divest it of its threatening potential for (it is asserted) when seen in 'correct' terms, or from the vantage point of the 'right' perspective, it is no longer a monster at all. In fact, certain mathematicians – again when presented with a counterexample to the Euler–Descartes conjecture – suggested that there were hidden edges which only those with a trained eye could see. When these were taken account of, the conjecture was upheld.

Finally, there is the strategy of *proofs and refutations* in which counterexamples are welcomed and used to improve the conjecture. By inspecting the proof, a lemma which conflicts with a counterexample is incorporated into the conjecture; thus, counterexamples are assimilated and the conjecture becomes restricted to the domain of the errant lemma which any given counterexample challenges.

Before proceeding any further I must acknowledge the difference between Lakatos's mathematical example, the case of modelling, and the backcasting debate. I contend that the applicability of his scheme in this analysis can be defended on at least two counts. First, Lakatos raised the issue of these strategies in his discussion of physics: he saw structural similarities between mathematics and experimental science and indeed, his 'Falsification and the Methodology of Scientific Research Programmes' (1970) may be seen as *Proofs and Refutations* applied to the history of physics. (The latter point is also mentioned by Feyerabend, 1975.) Now, we may place modelling between the two poles of mathematics and experimental science – which placement, if accepted, supports my use of Lakatos. A second, though weaker, reason is that there is no good reason against using Lakatos's scheme for the case of modelling.

I said earlier that the backcast undertaken by SPRU had generated an anomaly, and I have suggested that the debate which ensued contains similar strategies to those identified and described by Lakatos. In order to substantiate this, I must first investigate what was at stake in the debate – in other words, I must see what constitutes 'proper order' for SDG – for it is against this backcloth that the strategies will become visible. To do this it is necessary to look for equivalents to conjectures and their proofs, and for local and global counterexamples. This will enable a tight rein to be kept on the use of Lakatos's concepts while at the same time demonstrating their utility outside pure mathematics. Of course in this case, unlike Lakatos's example, these analogues will be largely due to interpretation; they do not represent explicitly formulated conjectures or statements but follow from a reconstruction of the debate.[9] The legitimacy of the latter is rooted not only in documentary references, but also, as will become apparent later, in the order and understanding it can bring to the backcasting debate.

In the case of the world simulation model, one can see that the trajectories mapped out for the state variables are a form of conjecture about the behaviour of the world system. However, the focus on the world was only one particular instance of the application of system dynamics, which Forrester and his colleagues claim is a general systems theory – that is, it is applicable to 'all systems that change through time' (Forrester, 1971: 126). It is important to reiterate the point that system dynamics is not just a modelling technique but a systems philosophy and a theory of the behaviour of complex systems. At the heart of system dynamics is the tenet (which the system dynamicists took to be true) that systems are *real world* entities. This tenet is not just a practical metaphor for it gave substance to the system dynamicists' conception of the world. In other words, system dynamics is not so much an epistemological framework but rather an implicit ontological statement about the world. It is also necessary to make a distinction between the WORLD 2 model considered as a formal system – a referent system – and particular simulations which use it. The referent system or model incorporates all the relationships and parameters used in describing the interactions between the state variables; it is meant to capture the 'essence' of the real system. Thus, not only is it claimed that a referent system dynamics system can generate the same behaviour as a given system, but it also has the same properties – that is, those of any complex feedback system such as a natural tendency to seek equilibrium. The latter is a property that SDG believed the world system would manifest – leading to the predicted overshoot and collapse.

The main planks, then, in SDG's conception of proper order were: first, that all systems can be described by system dynamics; second, that all feedback systems share similar properties; and third, that a system dynamics model of a system will also exhibit those properties. Thus we may differentiate between the conjecture that system dynamics can describe all systems, its corollary that the world system can be described by system dynamics, and the subconjecture that the world system will collapse. Or, in more explicit form:

(A) conjecture: for all systems that change through time, their behaviour is given by that of their referent system dynamics system;

(B) corollary: the behaviour of the world system is given by its referent system dynamics system;

(C) subconjecture: the behaviour mode of the world system is exponential growth which will be followed by overshoot and collapse.

The world-modelling exercise was not concerned so much with (A) or (B): given their long experience and laboratory practice the MIT team treated these as almost self-evident. Rather, the exercise centred on the question of how the world behaves. MIT believed that, like any complex dynamic system, the world is equilibrium-seeking; and further, that it is undergoing exponential growth within finite limits and will therefore experience 'overshoot and collapse' – subconjecture (C). This is taken to be a subconjecture rather than a separate conjecture because it follows from the system dynamicists' theory of the behaviour of complex systems. In other words, the predictions of WORLD 2 did not stand or fall on the basis of the model but were rooted in SDG's beliefs about systems. What was at stake, therefore, was not the mere reputation of the group – indeed SDG were not newcomers to controversy – but the proper order of the world as interpreted through system dynamics.

Turning to the proof, this I take to be the simulation exercise with the model. The exercise of simulation is an attempt to reproduce a referent system-dynamics system, and to simulate its behaviour on a computer.[10] In analogy with Lakatos's idea of an informal proof taking the form of a thought experiment, simulation is a structured exercise which attempts to show that (B) and (C) hold – for SDG, simulation represented a laboratory experiment. 'Given the assumptions about how different parts of a complex system affect each other, the computer can then trace the operation of the system through time. It can carry through the arithmetic tasks and follow the rules of behavior as set down in the model description' (Forrester, 1971: 16). The simulation exercise can be seen as a series of subconjectures derived from (B) or (C); it is used either to show that the model (the referent system) does capture the 'essence' of the real system because it describes its behaviour, or to show the exponential growth followed by overshoot and collapse. The portion of the 'standard run' 1900–70 which allegedly reproduces historical trends, stands as the 'proof' of (B). And, (B) must be taken as part of the 'proof' of (C). SDG attempted to prove (C) by a series of simulations which purported to show that even with a wide range of alternative assumptions and policies the world system still faces collapse. Thus, the proof of subconjecture (C) is (B) and the 1970–2100 simulations.

Given this scheme, what do counterexamples look like? First, a local counterexample would be found when the model's behaviour (and therefore the referent system) does describe the behaviour of the real system, but a particular assumption is found to be in error. For example, a given assumption (either in the model or the simulation technique) may be invalid under certain conditions but does not affect the behaviour of the model, and so (B) or (C) hold. Second, a global counterexample would be found where the simulation output and the real behaviour deviate. Third, a local and global counterexample would be a case where the simulation output again deviated from real behaviour and the source is located in a model or simulation error.

What of the anomalies in the backcasting debate? The population dip between 1900 and 1904 was a global counterexample to (B) because clearly the referent system did not describe actual past world population data satisfactorily. (It was also a local counterexample if an error existed in the referent system – the model – or the simulation.) The backcast anomaly was also a global counterexample to (B). Ultimately, (C) was neither provable nor disprovable. However, (C) depended on (B), and so, if the latter is seen to have failed, both anomalies must be considered local counterexamples to (C), which would remain a subconjecture without proof.

Coping with the WORLD 2 Anomalies

The SPRU team deliberately set out to test the WORLD 2 model. In doing so they thought that a better model would emerge. Thus, SPRU had a pragmatic view of backcasting:

> In a non-linear dynamic model containing many parameters and many feedback loops, it is not practical to make all possible tests on the reasonableness of the model. 'Backcasting' can be expected to drive some variable to unrealistic values and hence show up inadvertently incorrect assumptions underlying a model. (Cole and Curnow, 1973b: 64)

Observing the anomalous behaviour at the start of the simulation, they generated another anomaly by running the model backwards. They suggested that the anomalies indicated that the model was in need of some reformulation. Had they thought that only an initialization problem was involved, the error in the DRMM parameter would have gone unnoticed. They subsequently reformulated the parameter in order to uphold (B) by modifying the referent system, but at the same time this generated an alternative prediction to (C). In other words, the model was changed so that it did indeed describe history (B) beyond 1900 but the original post-2000 predictions did not remain the same – the model trajectories no longer overshot and collapsed (C).

In one important respect the strategy of 'proofs and refutations' appears to be the closest to ascribe to SPRU; this is because they were prepared to assimilate the anomalies. Of course, strictly speaking, 'proofs and refutations' is a mathematical strategy, but in less narrow terms it embodies a distinctive methodological practice and it is this which was manifested in SPRU's response to anomalies. However, it has to be admitted that their modification of the DRMM variable really amounted to tinkering, for they had no more evidence than had Forrester as to the precise nature of the function. Indeed, SPRU noted that other model modifications would also allow retrodiction of the WORLD 2 model.

Turning now to the response of Meadows's team, it is clear that the backcast anomaly was not accorded the status of a genuine counterexample; rather, it was represented as a 'spurious excursion'. Further, while some of the MIT group's comments were apposite (and actually accepted by SPRU), others were red herrings. For example, their remarks about delays and stochastic influences were irrelevant to the case because the WORLD 2 model did not contain any explicit delays, nor did it contain any probabilistic functions – in fact, the predictions of a system dynamics model are completely determined by the choice of initial values. More importantly, the SPRU backcast was claimed to be 'completely meaningless', and Meadows's team made verbal recommendations about the important issues in question – of which backcasting was clearly not seen to be one – as if such recommendations alone could solve the problem posed by the model's anomalous behaviour. Further, much of the technical argumentation of Meadows's team may be viewed as a definitional flurry, which by seeking to stress the distinctions between forward- and backward-running models thereby upheld (B) and, by implication, (C). The strategy here was monster barring; the anomaly was roundly rejected as a 'monster', and we observe that the definition of the domain of systems to which system dynamics applied had shifted. Implicitly, (A) and (B) became:

(A)   for all systems that change *forwards* through time, their behaviour is given by that of their referent system dynamics system;

(B)   the *forward running* behaviour of the world is given by its referent system dynamics system.

And notably, subconjecture (C) remained intact.

In contrast, Wright's response was both more complex and more interesting. Remember that he accepted the backcast as genuine: he therefore accorded the anomaly the status of a true counterexample. Although he described the problem as a 'bug' and viewed the anomaly as 'grotesque', he was not a monster barrer. The different steps in his argument indicate why. First, he admitted that the model needed reformulating for the case of a low material standard of living but he did not think that the anomaly was sufficient to refute the main conclusions which Forrester drew from the model. In other words, the backcast anomaly was accepted as genuine but it was barred as an exception to (B), and was not seen as a challenge to (C). Wright asserted that a model need only be accurate for the range over which it is intended for use; although he allowed that Forrester did not make this range clear in the case of WORLD 2, he himself firmly limited the original model to 1900–2100 (Wright, 1976: 137). Thus Wright upheld (B) by barring the exception which the model did not cover – he was trying to delimit a safe domain for the model. The domain of (B) was reduced by extra conditions, both with regard to time, and to the levels of MSL. Thus, (B) became: the behaviour of the world between 1900 and 2100, when MSL>0.25, is given by its referent system dynamics system.

The second part of Wright's argument reveals the strategy of modified *exception barring* (Lakatos, 1976) – that is, having first accepted the exception to (B), he then proposed modifications which aimed to include it. Wright realized that the model should be able to replicate 1880–1900 history and therefore proposed to change the model so that the exception could be accommodated. (B) then became: the behaviour of the world between 1880 and 2100, is given by its referent system dynamics system; where the referent system in question was to be a modified one. Rejecting SPRU's particular modification Wright stated:

> One of the symptoms of whatever is wrong appears in the *World Dynamics* base run as a small population decline 1900–1904. At least, one wants to revise the 1900 initial values to erase that transient without affecting 1905–2100 behavior. . . . At early stages of industrial development, Forrester's original model over-estimates death rate and capital formation. An appropriate query is: can these assumptions be modified to support reasonable 1880 values without damaging predicted, future trends? (Wright, 1973: 1092)

So, the adopted strategy was to modify the model without affecting its original trajectories: or, in other words, to add to the referent system without changing (C). Wright admitted that death rate and capital formation estimates were in error when MSL<0.25, and he set out to bring pre-1900 history into the domain of (B). A closer look at his modifications shows the arbitrary nature of his strategy. Again referring to figure 6.3, we can see that Wright's respecification of DRMM (line abce) arguably gives the function a rather curious appearance. If MSL<0.25, DRMM is set to the value of 2.4, otherwise it is calculated in accordance with Forrester's original function. Further, figure 6.4 (line debc) shows Wright's effective change to the capital investment function (CIM); line abc shows the original function and again, for MSL<0.25, the parameter is changed (to 0.16), with the original function holding for MSL>0.25. It is evident that this implies a discontinuous change at MSL=0.25. In fact, the discontinuity ranges between values of 0.16 and 0.32 for CIM, which effectively means that capital investment doubles when MSL reaches 0.25. Alternatively, capital investment would suddenly double between 1899 and 1900. All this obviously raises crucial questions about the possible mechanisms which could account for such a discontinuous change, and Wright's procedure seems highly questionable.

Now, Wright's extra conditions were arbitrary because they were stimulated by the particular counterexample involved and did not guarantee against others. (Wright, however, believed that he had found a safe domain – hence his remark that the 'model cannot be faulted if it remains in the acceptable operating range'.) His modifications altered the model in an *ad hoc* way in order to bring the exception within its domain.

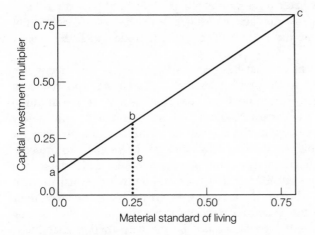

Figure 6.4   The capital investment multiplier
Source: the specification of WORLD 2; Forrester, 1971: 132–4.

This yields what has been described as characteristically 'segmented' or 'additive' knowledge: certain conditions hold for pre-1900 (MSL<0.25) while others hold for post–1900 (MSL>0.25) (See Bloor, 1978). Notably the switch in these conditions centred on a rather arbitrary boundary (either the 1900 boundary in time or the 0.25 value of MSL) and – as I argued above – implied a problematic discontinuity. Thus, to reiterate, his strategy was a modified form of exception barring: first the simulation of pre-1900 history was barred as an exception to the domain of WORLD 2; second, Wright claimed that the pre-1900 anomalous trajectories could be avoided by incorporating his model revisions; and third, he argued that the validity of Forrester's conclusions – based as they were on the 1900–2100 predictions – were unaffected by the anomaly.

As for Forrester himself, I have noted his shift in attitude towards the 1900–4 population dip, but he did not actually accord it the status of a real threat to his conclusions. He did not investigate the problem, but assumed, rather, that it was merely a question of initial values. In the event, he was prepared to give the CIAF variable an unrealistic history in order to 'correct' it and implicitly leave (B) and (C) undisturbed. His strategy then was to respecify his model simulation slightly. However, in the case of the 1900–4 population anomaly, I cannot easily ascribe one of Lakatos's strategies to him because in his formal statements at least he did not discuss it at length. Admitting this, one can none the less suggest that his routine approach to modelling prevented him from considering the possibility that there was some serious fault in the model's formulation, rather than that there was a small initialization error in the simulation.

Indeed, he himself had suggested that the DRMM multiplier might have been mis-specified (as was later concluded by SPRU and Wright), but (publicly at least) he did not consider it in connection with the 1900–4 anomaly.

This is reminiscent of what has been called 'monster adjustment'. In this case a potentially threatening anomaly is 'adjusted' and rendered harmless by the act of perceiving and designating it as an initialization error. In other words, Forrester altered the model's initial conditions only as a *consequence* of perceiving the anomaly as an initialization problem – a local counterexample – and he thereby adjusted the anomaly to preserve (B) and (C). In effect, just as some defenders of the Euler–Descartes conjecture had adjusted 'monsters' by contending that one had to learn how to 'see' such alleged counterexamples correctly, to uncover their hidden edges, so too Forrester was asserting that there was a true trajectory which was hidden or masked by the perturbation introduced through the specific initial conditions. Thus the model was to remain intact, but the conditions given to it during simulation would change. I contend that such a change is of a different order from the parameter changes invoked by SPRU and Wright. The former affects only the proof, while the latter also affected the referent system (the model) implied by (B). This can be illustrated by another analogy. One proof for the Euler–Descartes conjecture envisages a polyhedron to be made out of rubber which, after the removal of one face, can be stretched flat. By analogy, the choice of 'bad' initial conditions is comparable to finding that the rubber out of which one may fabricate a polyhedron is not isotropic and will not allow it to be stretched flat. With uniform rubber it would; similarly, with 'correct' initial conditions (assuming that they exist) the model would not give a population dip between 1900 and 1904. Because we know only Forrester's public reaction as opposed to his private one, it must be said that I may be in danger of over-extending Lakatos's idea of monster adjustment here. But, anyhow, I would argue that it is useful. For example, it enables us to understand how SPRU saw the anomaly as rooted in the DRMM parameter (that is, the referent system) while Forrester – wishing to uphold (B) and (C) – perceived it another way. Moreover, Lakatos described monster adjustment only in the face of global counterexamples, while the one in question here was global to SPRU but local to Forrester.

As regards the backcasting anomaly, Forrester allowed the possibility of backcasting, but argued that it was 'apt to be meaningless':

Running a simulation model backward to see if it retraces past history is often suggested as a way to validate a model. Such was done with the *World Dynamics* model by the Sussex group. . . . Yet, the procedure is apt to be meaningless unless a subtle combination of conditions falls within a narrow range in which the procedure is informative. . . . Practical, philosophical, and theoretical considerations overlap in a way that calls for clarification by new theoretical and interpretive work. (Forrester, 1976a: 32)

In other words, backcasting was a theoretical possibility, but was most unlikely to have any relevance to (B) and (C). The implication of Forrester's statement was that one has to learn how to interpret anomalous backcasts correctly; thus, he framed the issue of backcasting in such a way as to protect (B) and (C). Again I am tentative about labelling him here but could once more suggest monster adjustment. However, perhaps a better way of describing his response is not to say that he adjusted the backcast monster, so much that he monster barred the *technique* of backcasting. We should note that Forrester's reference to backcasting comes in a paper in which he set out to explain why people (particularly his critics) seemed to misunderstand system dynamics. Thus, rather than responding to a specific anomaly, Forrester was monster barring at the higher, methodological level of modelling techniques. Indeed, his implied distinction between the 'established' who know how to interpret backcasts correctly, and 'outsiders' who do not – in this case SPRU – is exactly the sort of differentiation drawn in terms of group boundaries that is found among monster barrers. Other instances of methodological monster barring can be found within the discipline of mathematics. Pimm (1980), for example, points to several instances, including Gordans's objection to a non-constructivist proof by Hilbert ('Das ist nicht Mathematik – das ist theologie'), and the controversy concerning the alleged computer proof of the four-colour problem.

Comments

A set of conjectural statements – encapsulating SDG's sense of proper order, their shared beliefs about the nature of the world – and proofs have been set out in accordance with Lakatos's scheme. Then I discussed the form of possible counterexamples in the case of modelling, and actually categorized the backcasting anomalies accordingly. Moving on to analyse the debate, I have shown that the strategies of Meadows's team and Wright correspond with certain responses described by Lakatos – that is, monster barring and exception barring. Further, the strategy of monster adjustment has been used to explain Forrester's responses to the 1900–4 population dip, and methodological monster barring was invoked to describe his reaction to backcasting; and, in methodological terms, SPRU's strategy accords with that of proofs and refutations.

The basic difference between SPRU and MIT was that SPRU were prepared to revise the model – in order to increase its credibility – at the expense of the original trajectories, and therefore of (C). SDG, on the other hand, revised the model only on condition that (C) was not challenged. They attempted to uphold (B) and (C) by *ad hoc* modifications to the referent system or the simulation exercise (that is, changed initial conditions).

Within SDG there was a variation in response to the anomalies; with Meadows's team monster barring, Forrester methodological monster barring and monster adjusting, and Wright exception barring. These variations highlight a difficult problem for grid/group theory – namely, how are such individual differences to be accounted for? In order to clarify the issue, it is useful to consider the following points. First, there is a problem which stems from the actual conceptualization of the grid/group scheme. More specifically, there is a difficulty concerning the nature or 'thickness' of the boundaries between the different sectors of the grid/group diagram – for example, at what point does, say, low grid/high group become high grid/high group? In other words, it is possible for a group to straddle the boundary between these two areas, thus giving rise to a mixture of responses. Secondly, and more importantly, it is necessary to reiterate the earlier point that the grid/group theory is not deterministic – thus a range of responses may emanate from the individuals within any given group. Indeed, as Bloor noted, one cannot use individual beliefs as a precise indicator of the nature of public knowledge; on the contrary, individual responses must be interpreted within the context of public knowledge.

> Individual evidence is always to be treated by putting it in a context where its typicality and its contribution to the overall pattern can be assessed. This overall pattern is precisely the system of boundaries and classifications – it is the style of knowledge – and this is what the theory is about. (Bloor, 1978: 26)

In the case of SDG it is significant that whatever the precise nature of their individual strategies, all members of the group resisted the anomalies so as to uphold their beliefs about system dynamics and the behaviour of the global system. Thirdly, there is the methodological point that I am not trying to establish that SDG fall into one sector of the grid/group diagram *per se*, and SPRU into another – one simply cannot ascribe absolute grid/group ratings. Rather, the point at issue is whether SDG were *comparatively* different to SPRU, both in terms of their response to anomalies and in their social experience. Given these points, it follows that grid/group theory allows for individual differences within the context of an overall comparison between the two groups – SDG and SPRU.

On the basis of the foregoing analysis, it is possible to suggest that the backcasting debate was marked by the social construction and rejection of error: that to a certain extent, whatever was judged to be wrong with the model – WORLD 2 – was mediated and reinforced by the social and cognitive environment of the group concerned. The source of the error, as seen, was not fully determined by the model itself: rather, there was an irreducible social factor, such that each group involved judged there to be different errors which were accorded different statuses.

It is important here to note that the development of the debate did not converge towards some ultimate single truth. Rather, the outcome (as far as each group saw it) was socially shaped or 'negotiated', by which I mean that it emerged through the processes of argumentation among the members of each research unit, and was interpreted in accordance with the prevailing pattern of grid and group. During the course of the debate, different positions emerged from the MIT group but the conclusions from the original model were upheld. What grid/group theory indicates in this regard is that, while the social environment of SDG did not prevent individual differences (there is always leeway, as opposed to determinism), it did constrain beliefs about system dynamics and the central point of the world-modelling exercise (namely, the articulation of the threat to the global system), and it was the protection of these beliefs that lay at the core of each response. In other words, the individual responses to anomalies among SDG must be placed in the context of their shared beliefs about system dynamics and environmental dangers. Further, though the SPRU backcast of WORLD 2 came to be seen as legitimate the MIT group continued to resist the general use of backcasting as a means of model testing. Without further information, grid/group theory must remain silent as far as the details of the individual variations among SDG are concerned.

On the one hand, SPRU, a project team characterized by comparatively weaker grid and group, treated the first anomaly as an object of curiosity, leading them to discover/construct a second one. SDG, on the other hand, at comparatively stronger grid and group, rejected, excluded, and adjusted the anomalies in relation to their conception of proper order and the predicted behaviour of the world system. In this case, then, I might suggest that weaker grid and group (SPRU) corresponded with a greater openness to anomalies; while stronger grid and group (SDG) restricted it; and in each case the growth of knowledge sustained by the two groups was different.

I have now completed the second stage of the comparative analysis; the discussion concerning each group's reaction to anomalies complements the evidence pieced together about their respective approaches to modelling; with some justification, therefore, it is possible to conclude that the thought style of SDG was characterized by stronger grid and group than that of SPRU.

7   Cosmological Beliefs

The final strand of my comparative analysis between SDG and SPRU will deal with their beliefs about knowledge, nature, man and society, and time. These will tell us about the content of their respective cosmologies and will enable us to consider whether their cosmological beliefs complement or contradict the evidence concerning their social experiences and thought styles.

The Cosmology of SDG

Knowledge

The system dynamicists' view of knowledge implicitly stood upon what may be described as 'rationalist' or 'Leibnitzian' ground; that is, system dynamics models were largely justified independently of empirical considerations (Mitroff and Turoff, 1973: 113-34). The justification of models lay in the alleged universality of feedback systems; these constituted structures which lay at the core of social systems. Whatever the variety of different geographical, historical, social, cultural, economic, or political contexts, the principles of feedback structures were considered to be applicable to all systems that change through time. Indeed, this is what underpinned the relative importances assigned to structure and data in system dynamics.

It must be noted that the system dynamicists actually displayed some diversity with regard to the use of data. With Forrester's later work – on urban and world dynamics – we find that he virtually eschewed the use of statistical and time-series data, strongly maintaining his thesis that complex systems were insensitive to the uncertainties in data. In contrast, there was a concerted effort on the part of the WORLD 3 project team –

headed by Meadows – to try and calibrate many of that model's parameters. Even so, Freeman (1973: 8) reports an admission by Meadows that perhaps only 0.1% of the data required for a world model were actually available.

The system dynamicists stressed the use of informal empirical sources; they set great store in 'learning by doing' and believed that a knowledge of feedback systems came from practical empirical experience with such systems. Moreover, the structure of a system dynamics model was constructed from descriptions based upon 'intuition and insight'. Speaking about the need to include the 'least precise but most comprehensive' information in system dynamics models, the WORLD 3 project team stated: 'Estimates of such unmeasured, intuitive variables are generally included . . . on the assumption that their inclusion, even with some inaccuracy, produces a more useful and accurate representation of the total system than does their omission' (Meadows et al., 1974: 22). Similarly, Forrester urged that it was better to include a parameter whose magnitude was uncertain but which was known to influence a system, rather than to omit it.

The system dynamics framework sought to explain real world behaviour and did so on the basis that all complex systems share similar properties. Such explanations were not primarily causal; in fact, the actual concept of causality was seen to be problematic. This was because mutual-causal processes – that is, processes where event 'A' causes event 'B' and vice-versa – were seen as an essential characteristic of feedback systems. They did discuss cause and effect to a certain extent, but it was only at a general level in terms of the properties (causes) of feedback structures and system behaviour (symptoms or effects).

Forrester asserted that an aid to understanding a given set of observations lies in the fact that they 'must fit into a limited number of categories' (Forrester, 1968: 4–1). This belief would imply that anomalous observations were unlikely to remain recalcitrant: they would be fitted into the existing categories rather than serve as the basis for new ones. This is another consequence of 'Leibnitzianism', for if all complex systems share the same properties there is no need to look beyond the existing categories – all observations are explained according to expected system behaviour modes. In fact, the alleged generality of system dynamics was but one instance of Forrester's belief in universal forms of knowledge. For example, although he allowed that physical laws such as Newton's laws of motion, the laws of thermodynamics, and Einsteinean relativistics are separate, he considered that they are but parts of some future 'broader unifying concept' (Forrester, 1961: 348).

The reliance on the formal theory embodied in system dynamics was combined with laboratory experimentation, and Forrester claimed that 'surprising discoveries' were the result. 'We observe that relatively simple structures produce much of the complex behavior of real-life systems' (Forrester, 1975b: 176).

The system dynamicists claimed that their method had the advantage that – when compared to other modelling techniques – social and psychological factors could be built into their models. Such factors were implicitly represented in parameters formulated to influence a model's rate or policy equations. For instance, WORLD 2 contains a parameter or multiplier which adjusts the death rate in accordance with the level of crowding. It was formulated so as to reflect the effects of psychological and social stresses: it was assumed that at high levels of crowding such stresses would raise the death rate and so the specification of this parameter causes the death rate to increase as crowding increases. Their confidence in this approach to 'soft' variables led to the statement that anything that could be described about a social system could 'be represented in a laboratory model'. This was complemented by the idea that an ultimate simplicity lay beneath the complexities of observed behaviour. Further, we can find repeated stress on the need to be explicit, and the assertion that formal computer models make all assumptions open to criticism.

> Since ours is a formal, or mathematical model it also has two important advantages over mental models. First, every assumption we make is written in a precise form so that it is open to inspection and criticism by all. Second, after the assumptions have been scrutinized, discussed, and revised to agree with our best current knowledge, their implications for the future behavior of the world system can be traced without error by a computer, no matter how complicated they become. We feel that the advantages listed above make this model unique among all mathematical and mental world models available today. (Meadows et al., 1972: 22)

Similarly, Forrester has asserted:

> The good modeller can discuss the issues surrounding his subject without contradicting himself. Such lack of internal contradiction is a goal that no public official can achieve based on a liberal arts education, and intuition. The modeller can know exactly the assumptions he has made. Without a shadow of a doubt, he can determine the dynamic consequences that follow from those assumptions. (Forrester, 1982: 104)

What is of interest here is their conviction about the certainty of the knowledge which they possessed; they assumed that all premises could be made explicit, and implied that they perceived clear, well–defined categories in all things – whether in the realm of physical systems or social systems.

Nature

As regards nature, we can discern a complex array of explicit and implicit assumptions which convey a distinctive view of the natural environment (some of these assumptions will only gain full import in the light of their views on man and society). The most explicit assumptions about nature are commonplace features of system dynamics literature: for instance, the titles of the books *The Limits to Growth* and *The Dynamics of Growth in a Finite World* are typical examples which encapsulate the simple, but powerful idea that nature is limited. It was assumed that nature contains a given, finite, and exhaustible stock of resources; there were also limits to the amount of pollution that nature can absorb; and constraints on the ultimate level of food production. Similarly, there was a posited limit to the possible levels of crowding; as population density rose, 'psychological factors, fear, and the threat from world conditions' would reduce the birth rate. Likewise, the death rate would rise as a consequence of 'psychological effects, social stresses that cause crime and international conflict, the pressures that can lead to atomic war, epidemics' (Forrester, 1971: 43). Hence, the limit to crowding was also another form of natural constraint – natural in the sense that it was somehow programmed into man as a biological species. Taken together, these limits underpinned the notion that the planet had a fixed 'carrying capacity' – i.e. it could support only a fixed level of population at a given standard of living.

Nature was seen to be under threat from man, his burgeoning numbers, industrial production, and agricultural activities. While it was suggested that there was a danger in the exponential growth of pollution, it was the alleged exponential growth of population and resource-consuming industries which were seen as the fundamental disturbing forces in the global ecosystem (Forrester, 1971: 11). However, despite the threat which man supposedly poses to the natural world he was seen to be fighting a losing battle – nature could not be subjugated for ever. Each technological advance was seen as merely a slight postponement of the time when the forces of nature would restore equilibrium. 'Fundamental forces of nature and the social system have been lying in wait until their time has come' (Forrester, 1971: 5). World equilibrium, therefore, was considered to be the inevitable natural state – man must live in harmony with nature.

The members of SDG declared that they were followers of Malthus (1830). While Malthus had only concerned himself with the limit imposed by food supplies, SDG pointed out the additional limits due to resource depletion, pollution, and the effects of crowding. Malthus too had spoken of natural checks on population growth but the system dynamicists gave a much more formal explanation for them – based upon systems-theoretic considerations. This explanation was rooted in the idea that a system was equilibrium seeking and required a set of 'pressures and stresses' in order to anchor it, and prevent its drift out of equilibrium.

Many people have charged that Malthus's work – intentionally or not – provided legitimation for the inaction of the British Government during the infamous Irish Famine in the 1840s; at that time it was suggested that the natural checks should be allowed to take their course, otherwise the future consequences would be even worse. Nature was therefore used for the purposes of moral justification. The character of the system dynamics message was very similar; indeed, Forrester – in contrast to Meadows's team – went so far as to suggest that world food production could be reduced, otherwise population would reach even higher levels and therefore more people would die in the coming collapse. But while differing with regard to this particular policy option, SDG appeared to unequivocally support the call to stop population growth.

The necessity of balance between society and nature led to the implication that perturbations of the 'natural order' are followed by a 'natural' response which restores equilibrium. Consider the following argument put forward by Forrester; it again resonates with Malthus's idea of natural checks on population growth. Discussing a hypothetical, overpopulated country, where 'misery abounds', he suggested that it would typically be especially vulnerable to natural adversities such as droughts or floods. 'The country is operating in the overextended mode where all adversities are resolved by a rise in the death rate. The process is part of a natural mechanism for limiting further growth in population' (Forrester, 1975b: 268).

Within system dynamics we find that a number of analogies were drawn between natural processes and social processes. For example, the growth and depreciation of capital was seen to be 'exactly analogous' to births and deaths in population – physical capital therefore mirrors social 'capital' (Meadows et al., 1972: 41). Put another way, natural processes were used as metaphors for describing social processes. This is not all; conflagration was also seen in terms of natural metaphors – war was viewed as a 'natural' outcome of a social system pressing upon natural limits; it was the social manifestation of a system moving towards equilibrium.

Man and society

Members of SDG appeared to hold a rather pessimistic view of man and his social institutions – they regarded their perspective as 'humble'. They assumed that in general people tend to be oriented only towards their own short-term self-interests and do not bear due responsibility for the future. Further, political institutions were also seen as being fallible in this regard – politicians were regarded as being tied to the short span of political office rather than to a long-term perspective. Institutions were viewed as relatively inert, with a tendency to tackle complex problems with simplistic solutions (Meadows et al., 1973: 151).

If we consider the view of man which they imputed to SPRU – and which they took exception to – we can again see the moral view of nature which they expounded. 'One possible concept of man, the one that is held by the Sussex group, is that Homo sapiens is a very special creature whose unique brain gives him the right to exploit for his own short-term purposes all other creatures and all the resources the world has to offer' (Meadows et al., 1973: 151). This view of man was seen to be 'firmly rooted in the Judeo-Christian tradition'. In contrast, SDG regarded the idea of man as ruler of creation to be a shortsighted fallacy, and put forward an opposite conception in which man was regarded – in allusion to Eastern religions – as but one species along with all others; he is embedded in the 'intricate web of natural processes that sustains and constrains all forms of life' (Meadows et al., 1973: 151). In line with this view, man and his social systems were regarded as being largely unchanging in nature (this being another manifestation of process–reduction which was discussed in chapter 3). 'In fact, social systems are dominated by natural and psychological factors that change very little' (Forrester, 1969: 110).

Their view of technology matched their pessimistic view of man: 'progress' was seen to have been obtained only at at the cost of 'natural beauty, human dignity, and social integrity' (Meadows et al., 1973: 151). 'Technical advances have not banished hunger or war. Instead, technical advances have only supported larger populations to be subjected to hunger and war' (Forrester, 1982: 99).

Of course not all men were considered to be shortsighted: the system dynamicists – among others – claimed to take a long-term perspective which they regarded as a moral responsibility. 'World modelling is so important that it should move in the most effective directions. The time has come to discuss the role of world modelling and the most promising approaches for fulfilling our obligation to civilization' (Forrester, 1982: 109). As they saw it, part of their duty was to help educate governments and the general public in order to prepare them for the transition to world equilibrium, and the consequent forfeit of freedoms that would be necessary to preserve it – we saw earlier that Forrester exhorted 'restraint, self-discipline, and intentionally increased pressures'. The system dynamicists argued that long-term values were needed – thus implicitly emphasizing man's roles and duties to society rather than his material well-being. People were exhorted to give up current aspirations for the sake of generations in the distant future.

The reflection on the nature of society was complemented by the realization that the individual might reject society's demands. Forrester recognized this and condemned it: for he believed that the failure to meet the system's requirements – such as a commitment to long-term goals – might cause the whole system to falter. The system dynamicists allowed that men have a degree of autonomy; they had created the socio-economic system and were not the victims of forces from without. In fact, to some extent they were the victims of their own policies. It was suggested that the goals of subsystems, and therefore individuals, should be subordinated to the goals of the system as a whole. This alleged harmony between system and subsystem was a generalization of the harmony between the self and society – each individual therefore had a role to play, a function to fulfil.

I have already discussed Forrester's beliefs concerning humanitarianism in a previous chapter, but can add to this by considering his ideas concerning equality, moral responsibilities, and people's links to the past.

> If all men are not to be equal at every point in time, then some boundary must be established around the concept that one is to be his brother's keeper. . . . If one has a responsibility for the future, an inescapable symmetry commits him to a legacy from the past. There is no basis for world equilibrium unless the sins of the fathers are to be visited on the sons. One can have no right to equality in the present, but only to an accumulated equality that reflects the actions of his heritage and the long-term goals of his ancestors. (Forrester, 1975b: 268)

Moreover, the 'stresses' he observed in the present – 'such social disorientations as drug addiction, rising crime rate, aircraft hijackings, genocide, and the increasing threat of a third world war' – were but the 'price for advantages that mankind reaped in the past' and which allowed population growth (Forrester, 1973: 73). These ideas sustained Forrester's belief that the transition to equilibrium might be most difficult for the developed nations – they were seen to be adopting technological means to put off the equilibrium state; moreover, this only rendered them more vulnerable and might cause the inevitable transition to be that much more painful.

The views of the WORLD 3 project team were somewhat more moderate than Forrester's, they believed that only a non-growth society could effectively address the problem of maldistribution of resources.

However, the possibility of egalitarianism in an equilibrium society was only a secondary matter, a spin-off, and not the prime motivation for ceasing growth.

Time

A common feature of system dynamics publications is the reference to the systems engineering field at MIT out of which Forrester's theory of systems developed – it had developed through more than 30 years of continuous effort directed toward the analysis and control of complex system behavior (Meadows, 1972: 5; see also Meadows et al., 1972, 1973, 1974). Thus, the system dynamicists cited their membership within a longstanding established tradition. The achievements of the past – largely in the domains of military and technological systems – lent legitimacy to their claim to have the knowledge to tackle the problems of the future. They perceived the past as being marked by distinct frontiers in knowledge; the frontiers of science and technology were seen to have been and gone, while that of understanding the behaviour of social systems was only just dawning (Forrester, 1975b: 234). The awareness of their roots in the past was matched by their long-term perspective and the symmetrical relationship which Forrester posited between past and future. These conceptions of time were also supported by their contention that the inherent delays of social and natural processes – up to 50 or 100 years – had the consequence that policies in the present determine the distant future, or at least constrain it. Conversely, the present was the outcome of previous, delayed, policies.

The argument concerning delays also carried a coercive edge, for it underscored their injunction to act now – otherwise, they argued, it might be too late to achieve an orderly transition to equilibrium and nature would impose one without men's wishes in mind. These delays – such as those inherent in population age structures, or the dissipation of a pollutant – were seen to be 'natural' and beyond technological control. Thus, time appeared to be seen rather as a superposition of natural cycles – future time was the unfolding of a myriad of delayed processes.

It was noted earlier that the time-scales often employed in system dynamics models tended to be very long – i.e. of the order of 200–250 years. We should further note that the urban dynamics model did not correspond to any given period in history; and despite the fact that the WORLD 2 model was purported to replicate the period from 1900 to 1970, Meadows's team argued that the role of time in a system dynamics model was only that of 'an indicator of lapsed chronological interval' (Meadows et al., 1973: 140). In other words, model time did not correspond to time in the abstract or physical sense, and it was not a causal factor in a model. This reinforced the notion that precise predictions of system states at specific points in time were eschewed – rather, as stated earlier, it was the sequence of behaviour modes which was the focus of predictive effort. Indeed, it was argued that because of the noise inherent in system processes, two otherwise identical systems might manifest quite different system states at any given time – their structural behaviour would, however, be the same. In this respect there was the implication that a certain temporal order inhered in the sequence of a system's behaviour modes and it seems reasonable to suggest that this was at the root of the SDG's arguments about the need for practical experience with feedback systems – such exposure yielded insights into the dynamic properties (behaviour in time) of complex systems.

Although physical time did not play a causal role in system dynamics models, the role allocated to 'natural delays' in the real world implied that time indeed had a causal role in the determination of system behaviour. 'Everywhere in the web of interlocking feedback loops that constitutes the world system we have found it necessary to represent the real-world situation by introducing time delays between causes and their ultimate effects' (Meadows et al., 1972: 143). It was these time delays between cause and effect that produced the overshoot and collapse of the world model rather than a more controlled asymptotic approach to the system's limits. We can therefore conclude that time had a *natural* dimension in system dynamics and as such imposed further limits on growth and human actions.

The Cosmology of SPRU

Knowledge

SPRU took neither a Leibnitzian approach to knowledge nor its opposite, Lockean empiricism, in which data are treated as prior to, and the justification of theory (Mitroff and Turoff, 1973). SPRU argued that the selection of data was subjective, and in fact theory-laden. Like SDG, they too accepted that the interpretation of time-series data was problematical but further noted that this also applied to 'recent poorly quantified trends' which SDG extrapolated into long-term behaviour modes. Although the alternative data they put forward in criticizing the models were 'optimistic' – in contradistinction to the 'selective pessimism' of MIT – the date were allegedly based on equally plausible assumptions. What this means is that, although the data advanced by SPRU did not necessarily refute the MIT models, they did establish an alternative viewpoint whose validity was on an equal footing. On this basis, then, SPRU rejected the exhortation to stop growth. For example, consider their criticism of the agriculture subsystem of WORLD 3: 'The assumptions about the physical limits of the critical variables in the agricultural sub-system of World 3 are pessimistic. By making more optimistic but, on the basis of available information, equally plausible assumptions about them, any physical limits to agricultural production recede beyond the time horizon of the model' (Marstrand and Pavitt, 1973: 56). Instead of empiricism, or rationalism, they avowedly choose a compromise Kantian approach – 'at least two theoretical representations are used, and data is collected, from which it is hoped that the "best" representation of the problem can be selected' (Clark et al., 1975: 34). This stance reflects both their diversity in method – their eclecticism and comparative orientation – and their concern to ground models in quantitative data. This of course did not guarantee objectivity which, they believed, lay 'in the eyes of the beholder'. Their view of knowledge is also evident in the formal and empirical tests they brought to bear on the world models.

The members of SPRU argued that the basis of knowledge lies in causal explanation. Their advocacy of the systems approach was limited to a broad view of problems, and they did not adopt the type of cybernetic approach taken by SDG – SPRU's use of the systems approach did not displace the analytical emphasis on causal explanation. 'A precursor to rational forecasting and planning must be an "explanation" of how the real world behaves. This entails the building up of descriptions about causal processes. "Explanation" to us means the inference of causal links between phenomena' (Clark et al., 1975: 38).

In addition to causal explanation, SPRU urged the separation and rigorous study of issues before any attempt to integrate them within a systems model.

> Even for world problem areas, however, the separation of issues is often beneficial. It is useful to identify particular pollutants, particular technologies and particular social institutions. Both separation of issues and the resulting specialization within disciplines are essential parts of the creation of knowledge necessary for their study. (Clark et al., 1975: 31)

This was a further qualification of their systemic approach: it required the in-depth study of the important factors in a problem area, together with a broad consideration of the set of factors which were taken to be relevant.

Nature

SPRU accepted that in purely logical terms the world's resources are finite, but they were at pains to add that this did not imply that they are necessarily exhaustible. Further, they regarded the attempt to quantify resources in terms of some fixed stock to be entirely problematic (Page, 1973: 33–42). In place of natural limits to growth, they perceived economic and technological constraints upon man's ability to exploit resources. While pointing out that there have been many (incorrect) pessimistic forecasts of resource exhaustion in the past, they noted the continued improvements in resource technology. Both in terms of exploration and recovery, technical improvements were seen to have made a mockery of such forecasts; they cited instances where advances had enabled the exploitation of progressively poorer ore grades – to the extent that previous waste or scrap could become a future ore resource. In addition, they maintained that much of the globe remains unexplored and argued that exploration – and therefore reserve estimates – have in the past been tied to effective demand. Strategic and economic interests were also considered to be important in this respect; for example, they referred to the growth in uranium exploration as a response to the tensions induced by the Cold War (Surrey and Bromley, 1973: 101).

Their position on the question of energy reserves was similar; for example, in reference to the oil crisis of 1973 they pointed out that oil prices were to some extent a reflection of OPEC bargaining power rather than of increased production or transportation costs. They did not see growth as being constrained by energy shortages.

> Contrary to the popular view, the real problem is not the prospect of physical shortage but the economic and social adjustments needed if . . . rapid growth continues. The solution lies in the pursuit of policies to foster the developments needed to ensure that adequate energy supplies will be available before reserves of conventional fuels become excessively depleted and to discourage the profligate uses of energy. (Surrey and Bromley, 1973: 105)

Much the same can be said of their view of food production – 'the major problems of feeding the less developed world are seen to lie in political rather than physical limits' (Marstrand and Pavitt, 1973: 56).

If nature was not seen as posing a barrier to continued growth, what of its capacity to withstand pollution? Their ideas on this matter have partly been touched on in relation to the question of aggregation but it is worthwhile returning to them. Speaking about the global aggregation of pollution in the world models they stated: 'By aggregating all pollutants, and assuming that they behave in some composite way, attention is drawn away from what are urgent, and still soluble problems, and diverted into speculation upon an imaginary race against time between "Life" and

"Global asphyxiation"' (Marstrand and Sinclair, 1973: 88). In other words, they did not support the idea of nature as some 'global entity' which was under threat from another 'global entity' in the form of pollution (as represented in the world models). This is not to suggest that they were disinterested in pollution but, rather, that they were sceptical about the terms with which it was discussed by SDG. Indeed, as the extract shows, they were concerned about those specific pollution problems whose solution was already feasible. However, they also stated their agreement with SDG on the need to develop new technologies which did not damage the environment (Freeman, 1973: 10). Having noted this point of convergence, it should be added that it was not the costs to nature which appeared to concern SPRU about pollution – rather, it was the cost to people; moreover, they implied that other costs of economic growth, such as work injuries, might be equally important.

Man and society

The Sussex team argued that social systems were qualitatively different from physical systems: first, because they contain the 'conscious actions of human beings'; and second, because the underlying laws which can appear to govern social processes, might in fact change continuously (Clark et al., 1975: 47). This helped to sustain an optimistic view of man and the possibilities of modifying social, economic, and political arrangements. In the face of possible physical constraints to growth – and in opposition to the rigidity and determinism which they imputed to the MIT models – they stressed again, and again, the importance of adaptive social and economic feedback mechanisms. 'If the world were confronted with critical shortages of particular industrial and construction materials, then all kinds of substitution mechanisms would come into play' (Freeman, 1974: 457).

This perspective stemmed from a view of man as an actor who responds to his environment rather than merely conforming to it; people were also seen to act on the basis of hope as well as despair.

Man is not pushed by a unified system mechanically into intolerable conditions but assesses the circumstances around him and responds actively by adapting his goals and values. . . . Man's fate is shaped not only by what happens to him but also by what he does, and he acts not just when faced with catastrophe but daily and continuously. (Jahoda, 1973: 211)

In his article 'The Luxury of Despair', written as a challenge to the views of Heilbroner (1974) – a neo-Malthusian along with Forrester and

Meadows – Freeman (1974) argued for what he believed to be the responsibilities of intellectuals. Not surprisingly, they vividly contrasted with those we saw implied by Forrester. 'Whereas he [Heilbroner] speaks of the responsibility of intellectuals to prepare the population for the reduction of freedoms, I would maintain that the responsibility of intellectuals now more than ever is to uphold those freedoms, which we know from very hard-won experience are vital to prevent the arbitrary abuse of power' (Freeman, 1974: 461).

Although SPRU were optimistic about the potential for future technological developments they did not regard them as inevitable. SDG believed that if present trends continued, then catastrophe was inevitable; but SPRU pointed out that, on the contrary, if present trends were to continue – with continuous technological improvement – then the opposite was likely to be the case. For them the form and use of technology was a question of social, political, and economic choices; they did not view technology as being either good or bad *per se*; nor did they consider it to be merely an artificial means of temporarily staving off natural checks.

> To pose the problem of new technology simply in terms of individual choice of good and evil is a big oversimplification. As so often in human affairs it seems that frequently there are two 'rights' rather than a 'right' and a 'wrong'. If this is so, then a great deal depends on the way in which social choices are made – on the institutional mechanisms and filters by which values are reconciled and interpreted. The problem is one of social debate and experiment, as well as one of individual ethical choice. (Freeman, 1971: 1042)

Indeed, SPRU noted that the internal logic of the world models implied that the creation of anti-pollution technologies would actually cause pollution to increase in absolute terms – either by stimulating more growth, or by the pollutive load associated with each unit of capital (whether that capital was devoted to industrial production or the removal of pollution caused by such production). Rather than seeking policies to avert some future catastrophe, members of SPRU drew attention to the contemporary predicament of the bulk of the earth's population; in place of equilibrium with nature, they sought balanced growth.

> Since we believe that brute poverty is still a major problem for most people in the world, and since in general we do not believe that the physical constraints are quite so pressing as the MIT team suggest, we do not accept their enthusiastic endorsement of zero growth as

the ideal for the world. . . . Some types of growth are quite
consistent not merely with conservation of the environment, but
with its enhancement. The problem, in our view, is a socio–political
one of stimulating this type of growth and of more equitable
distribution, both between countries and within them. (Freeman,
1973: 10)

Time

It is more difficult to develop an adequate picture of SPRU's perception of
time than in the case of SDG; there are none the less certain implicit
themes which can be discussed. To SPRU, the future appeared as
undetermined; they made references to previous forecasters – including
economists such as Malthus, Ricardo, Marx, and Keynes, as well as
population forecasters – and argued that all could be found wanting.
History was seen to have manifested continuous change; technological
developments were seen to have wrought qualitative shifts in the nature –
at least for some – of human existence. In so far as they perceived a
common element linking the past with the future it was that of flux. This
is not to imply that they denied that other factors remained static or
changed only very slowly; rather, it merely points out the importance they
attributed to change – it underscored their faith in the possibilities of
purposive human action. 'If we have learned anything from history it is
that men make it as much as they are made by it' (Jahoda, 1973: 212).

We may note that like the MIT group, SPRU also recognized that there
were certain important delays which had a bearing on global problems –
for example, they cited the delays inherent in research and development.
However, their position on this issue was far removed from the belief that
delays were such that growth must be stopped (there and then) lest it
might be too late.

In a series of tests on the world models, SPRU contrasted their
behaviour with that of accepted historical trends, arguing that the validity
of a model was partly determined by its ability to reproduce such trends.
They also advocated the use of time-series data for model calibration and
testing. Such procedures implicitly assume that events (data points) can be
fixed in relation to an abstract or physical conception of time. A choice
between models can therefore be made on the basis of which is better able
to reproduce the requisite values in accordance with their mappings within
physical time. I do not mean to indicate that SPRU would have dismissed
the system dynamicists' arguments about the temporal relationships that
might exist between behaviour modes (including such things as phase
shifts), but wish to suggest that SPRU required a model to pass a more
stringent test than SDG. This can best be seen if we consider SPRU'S

advocacy of a test known as two-sample testing. In this test, a time–series data base is split into two halves; one half is used to calibrate a model, and the other is then used as a control for assessing the model's ability to replicate it. Now the requirement that a model can generate data in accordance with their reference points within physical time is more difficult to fulfil than one which merely requires the reproduction of temporal sequences of behaviour (such as growth and collapse or oscillation). Indeed, the latter requirement can be seen as a subset of the first. I suggest that this difference should not only be considered as a technical or methodological matter – rather, I contend that there was a difference of perception involved here. Physical time was a reference line in SPRU's perspective, while the temporal order inherent in feedback systems, which was – by implication – only apprehensible from experience of such systems or through the perspective afforded by system dynamics, was the benchmark of SDG.

Conclusions

I have now completed the exposition of the different comparative elements taken for each group. Although some comparative remarks have already been made, this was to facilitate the exposition and I must now expand upon them and try to interpret the differences in terms of the grid/group theory of cosmologies. Earlier, in chapter 5, I argued that the social experience of SPRU was weaker in terms of grid and group than that of SDG; in chapter 6 it was found that SPRU's thought style – as given by their methodological orientation (including their approach to modelling and response to anomalies) – was also marked by weaker grid and group than that of SDG. Now, the task is to see if this difference is systematically present in the cosmological beliefs just considered.

SDG adopted a Leibnitzian approach to knowledge – in contrast to the Kantian position taken by SPRU. The former, based upon an all-embracing scheme, assumed that systems were real, as indeed it had to if its justification rested on formal rather than empirical ground. For SDG, the important features of the world lay in the systemic feedback relationships between its general or universal components (e.g. capital, population, resources). For SPRU, however, we have seen that the important features lay not in generalities, but rather in particularities – such as the variations between nations, institutions, or pollutants etc. Each group sought to make their respective view of the world explicit, but SDG related (and subordinated) the particular to the general, while for SPRU no general pattern existed and so they remained focused on particulars. Although SDG set great store by formal models, we should not conclude that their modelling was 'abstract' in the sense to which that term is applied to, say, theoretical physics. Rather, we have seen that system dynamics models were based upon intuitive observations of the behaviour of real systems. Informal empirical observations were regarded as plain concrete facts; although not theory-laden, they did require setting in an appropriate framework – which in this case was given by system dynamics.

The Kantian position of SPRU saw all facts as theory-laden and they preferred a pluralistic, comparative approach to knowledge. Instead of unifying frameworks and global entities, SPRU were more interested in particular technologies, institutions, or pollutants. The problems of formal data-gathering notwithstanding, SPRU advocated the necessity of using quantitative data because they were seen to provide a more objective basis upon which to build and test models. While SPRU placed a strong emphasis on causal explanation, SDG gave it less prominence and sought to classify societal problems according to the properties of feedback systems. Thus, on the grounds of their differences concerning formal empirical data, causal explanation versus categorization, and particular versus unifying frameworks, we can ascribe a lower grid rating to SPRU.

Turning to the conception of nature, we have found that SDG articulated an ecological view of a limited natural environment with which man must live in harmony. This position was complemented by the notion of natural checks on population growth, pollution, agricultural production, and industrialization. SPRU, on the other hand, viewed constraints as being largely rooted in social, economic, and political factors. They implied that society could improve upon nature through the appropriate use of technology – which once more denotes lower grid. SDG's conception of nature was elaborated to a much greater extent and accords with a high-grid/high-group cosmology, the interdependence and necessary harmony between society and nature being a hallmark of that cosmology. 'So here one should expect an intellectual effort to elaborate a transcendental metaphysics which seeks to make an explicit match between civilization and the purposes of God and nature. Synedoche in metaphors of society and nature shows their isomorphic structure and expounds their reciprocal support' (Douglas, 1978: 23). Douglas argues that the uses of nature for purposes of moral justification are all-pervasive with this cosmology. We have seen that a similar thread permeated the system dynamics worldview: whether it was in the use of naturalistic metaphors for describing social processes, the translation of the Malthusian idea of natural checks into systems-theoretic notions of equilibrium, or the necessity for pressures and stresses, we find a conception of a natural order underpinning a conception of society. Further, high-grid/high-group people 'use the incidence of misfortune to uphold the moral law. Disease and accident are either attributed to moral failures or invested with nobility in a general metaphysical scheme which embraces suffering as part of the order of being' (Douglas, 1973: 136). Again, this parallels and illuminates the notion of natural checks and the system dynamicists' idea of the necessity for pressures and stresses.

The two groups' respective views on man and society can be readily categorized into one of pessimism in the case of SDG, and optimism in the case of SPRU. The first stressed man's shortsightedness and the fallibility of social institutions – man is but part of the web of life, as dependent on the global ecosystem as all other species. The second looked to the potential for improvement – man is a species which makes history. With Forrester, all men could not be equal; but with the WORLD 3 project team we found a discussion concerning the possibility of global redistribution once the equilibrium state had been achieved. However, this was only a bonus of equilibrium, not the reason for seeking to control the approach to it. In contrast, with SPRU we found a stated commitment to the goal of egalitarianism.

The system dynamicists stressed the need for long-term values; man has to be held in check lest his self-interested orientation should lead to catastrophe. SPRU, in contrast, were concerned with the condition already faced by much of the world. While Forrester asked questions about the means of coercion necessary to sustain zero growth, SPRU argued for growth in order to remove the state of poverty endured by the underdeveloped countries.

The pessimists saw technology as a transient evasion of the natural order, the optimists saw it – when employed prudently – as a means of modifying the natural order. On all these points we can place SPRU in a lower grid position than SDG. However, SPRU's acceptance of the need for balanced growth, and for technologies which do not damage the natural environment, places them in a higher grid position than those who would countenance the most vigorous attempts to control nature. Thus, again we see that SPRU's views were not low-grid *per se*, but rather, were lower than SDG's.

Douglas argues that conceptions of time are employed in the role of justifying actions or coercing people to commit themselves to action. SDG justified their policy recommendations by appealing to the tradition within which they perceived themselves to stand (which in fact they did), and the long-term perspective they took of the future; the coercive edge of their views can be seen in the admonition to act *now* – for tomorrow might be too late. Historical tradition at MIT is well differentiated, and it was this which helped to support a long–term view of the future.

With SPRU we have seen that their view of time did not allow the possibility of making policies on the basis of forecasts into the distant future. For them the possibilities (but not the inevitabilities) of the future were matched by the changes wrought in the past – this served to legitimate their scepticism and caution about the SDG's arguments. Further, their favoured model testing procedures implicitly sought recourse to a physical conception of time to assess model behaviour. SDG, on the other hand, considered the qualitative temporal order which is inherent in both natural and social system structures to be sufficient. All cosmologies employ time in order to justify or coerce, but the distinction between physical time, and that embodied in system dynamics, indicates a cosmologically-based difference: SDG's conception of time was higher grid.

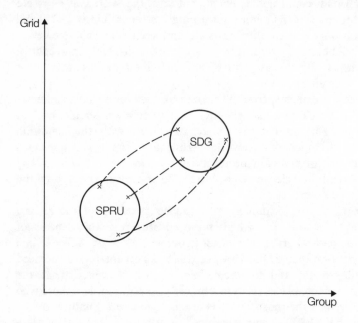

Figure 7.1   The relative grid/group positions of SDG and SPRU

With each of the comparative cultural elements we have considered, it has been found that SDG appear to have sustained a higher grid cosmology than SPRU. With the group dimension too, it has been found that SDG manifested the greater sense of group boundedness. Therefore, when considered together, this systematic cultural bias, in addition to the evidence we have concerning their social location and style of thought, supports the hypothesis that the social experience of SDG was indeed that of a higher grid/group setting than SPRU. Douglas's theory has not been tested here; rather, it has been used to show that on three different levels –

social structure, the style, and the content of knowledge – we can reach the same conclusions about the relative grid/group positions of SPRU and SDG (see figure 7.1). On a note of caution, it must be admitted that the concreteness of the evidence for each level is not the same. That for thought style is the most densely documented, followed by that for cosmological content. The evidence on social experience is the weakest. However, the findings for each level are mutually supportive and thereby render the overall conclusions that much stronger. Having established these connections, however, we cannot answer the question as to why either group came to be where they were – that is, we cannot draw causal inferences and say that the social experience of SDG caused their cosmology or vice-versa. Indeed, we can only say that with each group, knowledge and social experience were mutually supportive in their co–development.

I suggest that SDG's grid/group position changed, both during the processes of group consolidation and the closing of ranks which ensued when they came under criticism. All of this does not imply that SDG were in any way perverse or unique; rather, it may be that all theories exhibit similar characteristics during the course of their development. Douglas argues that no part of the grid/group diagram is without its own specific ills, all cosmologies have pros and cons and this is just as true for SPRU as for SDG. Further, all groups draw upon a conception of the natural order to support their position *vis–à–vis* social institutions and here we have examined two different conceptions supported by two different social experiences.

PART THREE
The Cultural Effect of
System Dynamics

8   Urban Dynamics: Knowledge for Social Policy

The discussion in Part Two was concerned with the ways in which social influences – at the macro-level of cultural tradition, and the micro–level of social experience at MIT – have shaped the development of system dynamics. Here I will begin to examine the other side of the relationship between knowledge and social structure – namely, the task now is to look at the exoteric role of this cultural artefact, as it emerged from the System Dynamics Laboratory and was used by its proponents to promote particular social policies.

It must be stressed that I will not try and answer the question of whether or not system dynamics has actually caused particular decisions to be taken by social or political administrators: even if it has been the basis for deliberate policy decisions, the associated officials may be unlikely to admit to it. Indeed, the mechanistic assumptions upon which such a question is based are simply inappropriate to the task of understanding the cultural role of knowledge. Rather, I am more interested in the potential societal role of system dynamics – that is, in its nature as a resource for negotiating social consensus, a corpus of knowledge designed for policy formation and large-scale social engineering. This requires that I consider the cultural role *implicit* in system dynamics. It is contended that this is a useful line of inquiry to pursue and is distinct from those critiques which have restricted themselves solely to questions concerning the likely efficacy of the recommended policies. Rather than attempting to explore this role in relation to system dynamics as a whole, I will concentrate on the system dynamicists' efforts at modelling cities, particularly Forrester's work as described in *Urban Dynamics* (1969). This will provide a sufficiently tight framework within which to illustrate my argument.

Earlier, I discussed the role of knowledge as a social binding agent that can cement people together in their various social groupings or figurations – that is, knowledge is an essential part of the social bonds that people form with each other; whether in terms of shared cognitions or as a means of coercion or legitimation. The nature of this bonding, the form and structure of the figurations, and some of the wider social and political consequences, are the social effects which are of interest here. More specifically, I will focus on the following five aspects of urban dynamics – management and control; a conservative or radical force; an explanatory resource; legitimation; the role of system dynamics experts.

The first area of interest centres on the instrumental role of knowledge in social management and control. The characteristics of the proposed urban structure, and the policies to achieve it, will be the focus of concern. This will enable us to consider a second area – namely, whether its potential role represents specific or general interests and goals of urban communities; and the extent to which the proposed policies were a radical departure from the conventional wisdom on urban problems.

The third area of interest concerns the use of knowledge as a resource for discussing the world and enabling people to set the chaos of experience into an intelligible framework. Here I will discuss the role of system dynamics as a device for explaining urban problems – an explanatory resource that organizes cognition – together with some attendant theoretical and social ramifications to which this leads. For example, in representing a theory of a particular social system, and given success in setting the agenda for debate, a model can theoretically 'close off' other alternative theories. This can have social consequences: in seeking to define the essence of an urban system, and being put forward as the theoretical framework within which urban problems are to be articulated, a model can close off other conceptions of social reality, and therefore alternative social structures.

The fourth area addresses those aspects of the urban model that served to legitimate it, and in particular the style of arguments that were mustered in order to justify it. Specifically, I will consider the different elements of the system dynamics worldview and cosmology which, on the one hand, cohered in such a way as to secure apprehension of this particular body of knowledge – such that it might appear self-evident; and on the other hand, thereby served to legitimate, and ensure commitment to, the specific policies and urban structures that were promoted.

Lastly, the fifth area of interest concerns the wider consequences of the spread of system dynamics and its use for the control and management of social systems. Earlier I argued that knowledge represents a power-resource – that those who define, control, and implement knowledge have a certain measure of power. In terms of social policy, knowledge defines what is possible and what is not: it distinguishes the practical from the utopian. Therefore those who devise policy have a degree of control over social relations and hence power. I will refer to the particular laboratory basis of system dynamics, and view its diffusion into policymaking as an extension of that laboratory. I will examine the role of system dynamicists in relation to politicians and the electorate; the effect of their proposed urban policies in ensuring social consensus through the integration of different classes into the proposed new urban structure – with the consequent acceptance of the cosmology which it would support; and the social and educational implications of the teaching of system dynamics as part of a wider process that might secure social consensus.

The Background to Urban Dynamics

In the 1960s the United States experienced a tremendous burgeoning of science and technology; scientific and technological rationality held out great hopes for many people as the generator of greater affluence and national pride. Science and technology took man to the moon, and technological applications of new knowledge increasingly penetrated many aspects of life for large numbers of the American population. Science and technology continued to restructure social relations in the workplace, developments which led many people – including politicians and administrators – to look to science and technology for solutions to social problems. This was the era when the so-called 'end of ideology' was debated and some writers opined that the only problems left facing society were technical and administrative ones.[1]

Amid the affluence of certain social classes, and the brash technocratic optimism of the time, the problems of urban decay continued to worsen – rioting and arson stalked the streets of many American cities. Within this contemporary climate it was natural that people should have looked to science and technology to solve the problems of urban decay – social engineering held out the promise of solving the urban crisis. 'Such hopes are manifest in the commonly stated expectation . . . that the technical skills which put men on the moon ought to be able to solve the problems of our cities or nation' (Greenberger et al., 1976: 324). In fact, it has been suggested that many engineers who were displaced as a result of cutbacks in the space programme during the late 1960s actually moved into areas of social policymaking (Greenberger et al., 1976; Brewer, 1973). The background of faith in technology and science provided the context within which certain groups began to use computer models in order to try and solve social problems. At the start of the urban project, Forrester consulted top city officials before retiring to his computer terminal to build the urban dynamics model. In other words, he constructed an esoteric variant of the background (exoteric) knowledge gained from his sources. Later, the urban policy recommendations emerged from the laboratory, shaped to play an exoteric policy role among the public and the various administrative officials who were originally consulted. This gave the urban model a certain air of legitimacy, but we will see later that, rather than offering a technocratic hope of solving the urban crisis, Forrester advocated a set of policies which appeared legitimate for quite different reasons too. *Urban Dynamics* was actually styled for exoteric consumption, and different groups involved in urban management and planning were invited to MIT for seminars at which the urban model was presented. Further, Forrester also gave testimony before government committees.

The urban model was greeted with a wide range of responses: some full of praise, others openly hostile. As an indicator of the range, two such reactions are worth noting. On the one hand, Krueckeberg (1969: 353) stated: 'Here is genuine systems analysis, and it is quite different from so much of the talky and marginal stuff. This is substantive, understandable, complete, cohesive, and directly instructive to what we are trying to do as planners.' On the other hand, Rochberg (1971) reported that some people judged some of Forrester's recommended policies to be comparable with Hitler's treatment of the Jews during the 1930s. Such criticisms notwithstanding, the US Department of Housing and Urban Development provided funding for further work with the urban model. In particular, they financed the application of urban dynamics to the city of Lowell in Massachusetts. This further research brought other members of SDG into the realm of urban modelling (Mass, 1974; Schroeder et al., 1975; Alfeld and Graham, 1976).

Management and Control

Having briefly set the context within which the urban model emerged, I will now piece together a picture of the policies and proposed urban structures contained in *Urban Dynamics*. Perhaps the most important characteristic of Forrester's approach to urban modelling was that cities were viewed as systems. Not just any kind of system, but most specifically, systems whose behavioural characteristics were determined by the properties of feedback structures – as described by system dynamics. Consequently, urban problems were explained in terms of the properties of complex non-linear feedback structures. These properties were thought to lead to a self-defeating style of urban management which was compounded by political expediency. Forrester sought to explain urban crises by asserting that city administrations pursued policies which were oblivious to the feedback characteristics of urban systems. Further, politicians were also charged with being too oriented towards the short horizon of their span of office, or towards the short-term political pressures of the 'underemployed'. 'Humanitarian impulses coupled with short-term political pressures lead to programs whose benefits, if any, evaporate quickly, leaving behind a system that is unimproved or in worse condition' (Forrester, 1969: 10). Thus, it was suggested that the conventional policies designed to relieve urban problems were ineffectual, or even a means of exacerbating the very conditions they were supposed to cure. However, it must be stressed that Forrester was not arguing that politicians were in any way inept; rather, he believed that because our intuitions about dynamics are formed by experiences with simple systems, we are incapable of inferring the behaviour of complex systems. This meant that city administrators simply did not have the training necessary to understand the workings of a complex urban system; in turn, this implied that cities required the skills of those competent in feedback systems.

In drawing attention to administrative failures Forrester located them mostly at a local level, and he asserted that the way towards urban revival lay in changed internal practices. The city was to be self-reviving, it had to become a 'master of its own destiny'. The overall goal of Forrester's alternative policies was to restore economic vitality to stagnating and declining areas. The focus of this effort lay in the integration of underemployed Blacks into mainstream economic activity. As noted in chapter 3, Forrester advocated a unified urban system which would be socially, economically, and racially integrated; he saw the 'extreme concentration' of social and economic groups as detrimental and believed that urban revival would be more easily achieved within one integrated system than in two separate and parallel systems.

The belief in the desirability of urban autonomy was tempered by two qualifications: first, urban goals should be subordinated to national goals; and second, Forrester envisaged some special situations in which the city would need assistance from outside. This might take the form of legislative action to force cities to adopt practices judged to be practicable for long-term revival: 'Such outside pressure may be necessary if internal short-term considerations make the reversal of present trends politically impossible' (Forrester, 1969: 129). What he meant by this, was that in cities where the electoral power of the lower classes precluded 'long-term' policies, the government might be forced to overrule the local political machinery and authoritatively impose the alternative policies which it deemed more correct.

Forrester did not just lay blame at the door of politicians who gave sway to the welfare demands of the underemployed, he also charged the latter with irresponsibility because they allegedly voted for benefits which cities were incapable of providing. The political power of the urban poor was seen as too great, a consequence of their overwhelming numbers (Forrester, 1969: 122). Forrester envisaged an urban structure with a more 'balanced' mixture of social classes. Since the political power of the lower classes was contended to be oriented towards short-term interests, which strengthened the downward forces of urban decline, his proposed solutions would work to restrict this power by constraining the population of the lower social groups within the city. The most controversial example was his suggestion that city administrations should enact slum-clearance programmes but desist from building low-rent public housing to replace them. In fact, it was suggested that slums should be demolished at the rate of some 5% per annum (Forrester, 1969: 71–106). Apart from the direct costs of construction, these low-rent housing projects also had an indirect cost-loading, caused by people who were thought to move to the city precisely because its housing was perceived to be attractive. Forrester believed that current laws and administrations encouraged an 'excessive' influx of the poor, while at the same time accelerating the exodus of the affluent. 'As the poor begin to dominate, their political power is felt. Their short-term interests increasingly dominate their own long–term welfare and that of the city' (Forrester, 1969: 119). This shifting balance of classes was thought to be one factor in soaring municipal costs. In addition, massive financial assistance to meet these costs was held to be ineffectual because the goals to which such aid was aimed were judged to be impossible. Not only did he state that much urban planning failed to distinguish the possible from the impossible, but he also suggested that the pursuit of unachievable goals could lead to a system state from which other achievable goals (that might have been possible) became foreclosed (Forrester, 1969: 119).

Forrester suggested that urban revival must be towards an equilibrium condition with a properly balanced mixture of social classes and a correct ratio of housing land to industrial land (Forrester, 1969: 125–6). He advised that such a balanced city would serve all sections of the population more effectively. Also, it must be noted that although there would be a hierarchy of social classes, these would not be rigidly separated, but would be integrated together.

The proposed policies did not envisage more coercive legal structures, and it was also expected that there would be less government encroachment. The suggested way forward lay in changing tax and zoning regulations so as to ensure that self-interested actions would lead to renewal (Forrester, 1969: 122–9). However, only certain parts of the population – the more affluent members of the community – were seen as the bearers of this revival. Among them we find owners of land and buildings (Forrester, 1969: 122). Current policies were said to lead to self-interested actions which produced degeneration, due to the migration of the affluent coupled with industrial and building practices that encouraged stagnation and inhibited renewal. For example, the tax structure was thought to penalize the people able to contribute most to the city, while at the same time favouring those who generated only costs. In contrast to this situation, it was argued that tax revenues should be closely correlated with the groups who voted for municipal expenditures. 'Only if the revenue is highly correlated with the people who require the expenditure will the city have a self-regulating system which generates a population able to sustain a healthy city and to pay for the urban services they require' (Forrester, 1969: 124).

Urban Dynamics also advocated a changed mix of industrial activities, to favour industries which were labour-intensive, profitable, and paid high wages (Forrester, 1969: 123). It is significant that the recommended urban policies would be more coercive towards the lower social groups while being largely favourable to the more affluent; the proposed measures would deter the influx of the underemployed but did not incorporate any regulations which would prevent the movement of the higher social classes (or of capital). Rather, the aim was to persuade these groups to stay in the city through incentives. Of course Forrester claimed that his proposals, despite their immediate effects, were for the long-term benefit of all. 'Policies that lead to urban revival will give the superficial appearance of favouring upper-income groups and industry at the expense of the under-employed' (Forrester, 1969: 121).

This rather elitist view can also be discerned in other proposals about tax-exempt institutions. Forrester argued that they should be judged on the basis of how they affected the city's cost and revenue balance; his point being that certain institutions put a cost-load on the city by attracting a disadvantaged population from the outside. In such cases he suggested that the institution in question could be considered 'detrimental' (Forrester, 1969: 124). In order to maintain its equilibrium it was claimed that the urban system must have a set of pressures against which to press. People were therefore exhorted to choose the behaviour mode they wanted for their cities and to accept the inevitable (even vital) pressures which would preserve that mode. Pressures, in other words, were to be actively maintained. '[A]n urban plan that aspires to a different equilibrium than we now have must be firmly based on a public understanding and willingness to live with the corresponding pressures' (Forrester, 1969: 128).

A Conservative or Radical Force

Having examined some of the major characteristics of the urban structure put forward in *Urban Dynamics*, we are in a position to discuss how that structure compares with existing urban structures, and its implications for the interests of the various urban sections. Although Forrester's programme was aimed at improving the city for all urban groups, his policies would have the effect of benefiting the affluent whilst penalizing the less fortunate. The interests of private enterprise and landowners were promoted – with zoning, tax, and legal regulations being changed in their favour. At the same time, these changes would shift an increased financial burden on to the poorer sections of society. Urban dynamics aimed to change cities in order to evolve new structures which would be organized in accordance with the dominant values and interests of the affluent classes.

To take but one example in more detail, let us consider the differential impact of the proposed revival policies on the upper- and lower-income housing subsystems. From the results tabulated in *Urban Dynamics* (Forrester, 1969: 101), it is evident that during the first 55 years of the revival, the ratio of the managerial/professional class to their corresponding housing type (premium housing) increases by some 11%. In contrast, the ratio of the underemployed to their housing stock increases by some 58%. Or, in more precise terms, the number of the managerial/professional class increases from 71, 100 to 108, 700, while premium housing increases from 110, 900 to 152, 800 units. The number of unemployed actually falls – from 377, 300 to 335, 900 – but their housing stock falls too – and much more sharply – from 310, 100 to 175, 300 units. Clearly, this implies a significant increase in overcrowding among the underemployed.

Society's master institutions were to remain intact and the measures to be adopted favoured those institutions at the expense of the poorer sections of the city. In three mutually supportive proposals, urban dynamics sought to curb the political power of the underemployed. First, through education, Forrester aimed to assure their consent for the type of economic revival which would 'initially' disadvantage them; second, he wished to restrict their numbers by directly limiting the provision of low-rent housing while simultaneously demolishing the slums; and third, in the last resort he reserved the right of the national government to ignore popular support for welfare policies and impose opposite policies of its own.

Yet Forrester did not unequivocally support all affluent sections of society; we cannot simply reduce his model to a mere emblem of 'bourgeois' ideology which singularly projected the interests of the rich. Indeed, he questioned certain property rights of landowners which, in conjunction with tax and zoning regulations, were thought to lead to urban deterioration. Also, it must be borne in mind that Forrester envisaged an equilibrium condition for cities because he believed that growth was not indefinitely sustainable; this implied a change of imperative for private enterprise whose traditional ethos has always been growth-oriented. In this regard, urban dynamics can be considered to have had some measure of autonomy, in the sense that although committed to the long-term interests of capitalism, Forrester was not precluded from making policy recommendations which might be disadvantageous to some sections of private enterprise. For example, he cites certain arguments against large-scale transportation networks that would undoubtedly run counter to the interests of some building contractors (Forrester, 1969: 127–8). Moreover, his injunction against low-rent housing schemes was a threat to those companies that had traditionally been dependent on public housing contracts. Further, urban dynamics was more detached than those views which saw urban problems solely as a natural outcome of city life (Goldsmith, 1971: 1); Forrester insisted that the persistence of problems was due to bad internal practices (we will return to this point in the section on legitimation). This degree of autonomy is something which has been ignored by those critics who have sought to reduce system dynamics to a mere reflection of capitalist interests.

On balance, however, urban dynamics remained tied to the interests of the more affluent classes, for it did not challenge society's dominant institutions. Forrester argued for an urban structure which would be organized in their interests and which would effectively penalize lower-income groups in order to secure those interests. While urban dynamics was conservative in the sense of preserving the wider social order, it was in fact a radical departure from conventional urban policy, promising, as it did, large-scale social engineering. Moreover, it stood as criticism of urban administrators, and marked a break with the received wisdom which had long been rooted in the idea of dealing with urban problems through large financial programmes. Forrester did warn that his policy recommendations required further study, that they were an opening of the topic rather than a set of final conclusions; however, this did not prevent him appearing before the National Sub-Committee on Urban Growth, where he suggested that its name be changed to the Sub-Committee on National Equilibrium, and offered the results of the urban model as a guide to national policy on urban problems.

It is possible to suggest several ways in which the urban model could be put to practical use by administrators. For example, the model could be employed as a means of justifying specific policies that had already been decided: merely serving to provide a veneer of technological legitimacy for the vested interests that lie behind a particular set of policies. In such a case, knowledge serves a purely instrumental function, in that it is employed by the politician for his or her own ends. There has in fact been some speculative discussion suggesting that the urban model can be considered to have played this role. For example, Greenberger et al. (1976: 68) note that the model might 'masquerade as an oracle' and be used by local officials to legitimate previously planned slum-clearance programmes. Further, in a 'Rand Corporation Report' by Averch and Levine (1971), the urban model was viewed as 'likely to be influential in Washington and elsewhere'.[2] In a similar vein, Whithed (1972) argues that the policy suggestions contained in *Urban Dynamics* might be utilized by people who wished to avoid public investment in urban programmes, their positions being buttressed by the scientific aura surrounding the computer model. Also, he identifies a certain convergence between the aims of the model and various moves to limit the immigration of the poor into American cities.[3]

Another possible perspective for considering the policy role of *Urban Dynamics* stems from considering the dominant cultural view of technology at the time it was built. We cannot just assume that an actor such as a politician is someone entirely independent of the knowledge they use to authenticate policy. A more complex situation arises when such an actor actually sees a model as an authoritative source of social policy; this may be a case in which politicians call upon technological expertise in good faith in order to try and solve urban problems. Indeed, at any given time politicians reside within a climate of opinion where some means of gaining knowledge are considered to be more efficacious than others. Thus they are to some extent constrained by the systems of knowledge upon which they can legitimately draw. In this case it is possible to cite evidence – though admittedly circumstantial – that the urban model has indeed been used in a genuine way. In fact the practical implementation of urban dynamics to real cities was attempted in a number of projects, but apart from the city of Lowell in Massachusetts, most of these efforts ended in failure.

> Most of these attempts did not get outside the classroom. Of those that did, some . . . could not make the model fit the city. In Lowell, where this was not a problem (partly because Forrester and his colleagues were directly involved), the Urban Dynamics model and the ideology that accompanied it got a good reception and fair hearing (Greenberger et al., 1976: 157).

In the city of Lowell the model was employed as an educational tool to explore different policy alternatives (Mass, 1974; Schroeder et al., 1975). Although noting that the policymakers there claim that the model was never used directly to formulate policy, Greenberger et al. report that,

among other measures, Sullivan (the manager of the city who was a friend
of Collins – one of Forrester's colleagues) decided to stop sales of city land
for low-income public housing projects. Their argument is that Sullivan
feared such housing would attract underemployed persons to the city –
which of course was exactly in line with the theory of urban dynamics.
Further, we should note that Forrester's imputation of a strong link
between housing availability and migration was rather unorthodox; most
studies would appear to have found that job availability is a much more
important factor in migration (Averch and Levine, 1971). Thus, Sullivan's
policy would appear to have been rather unorthodox too – lending further
support to the connection between his decision and recommendations
contained in *Urban Dynamics*.

I have now discussed two possible ways in which the urban model might
be used in real policy situations: that is, as a legitimating cloak, and as a
source of authoritative knowledge. The urban model was a response to the
urban crisis, a response which sought to solve that crisis in the interests of
the dominant institutions of society. The means employed reflected one of
the dominant types of thinking – technological rationality aimed at social
engineering – allied to the highly fashionable use of computers.

An Explanatory Resource

Urban dynamics was directed towards the control and management of
cities, this dimension of instrumental control was complemented by its
role as an explanatory resource – a means of 'talking' about cities and
urban problems, and thereby offering a medium for the negotiation of
social consensus. Urban dynamics provided a framework within which
urban problems could be discussed; in doing so, it offered a language
which could appear to be objective and value-free. Even among those
critics who were quite negative about Forrester's model, there were some
who perceived the potential role for urban dynamics as an instrument for
structuring urban issues: 'Forrester . . . has provided a language in which
different disciplines can argue together precisely. These are accomplish-
ments without precedent' (Fleisher, 1971: 54). However, in explaining the
condition of cities, urban dynamics reflected a particular theoretical
position which closed off other non-system-theoretic explanations.
Theories of contradictions and class conflicts, for example, were excluded
from discussion. In addition, only certain goals were defined as possible;
other goals were said to be impossible or utopian. This theoretical closure
had indirect social and political consequences in terms of the range of
urban structures that were deemed to be attainable. In particular, this
closure parallels Crenson's concept of the 'framing and raising' of political

issues. 'Political issues can create political consciousness. They also tend to shape or restrict that consciousness. Political agenda items like the economic development issue do not produce a general expansion in the scope of political discussion, but expansion only in certain directions' (Crenson, 1971: 171). Thus, urban dynamics framed the urban question in a particular way, defining problems in a manner that was connected to the proposed solutions – that is, the definition of urban difficulties was influenced by the set of solutions which were deemed feasible. It provided a 'new' way of looking at the urban question, but while claiming to be objective it restricted the consideration of other perspectives and therefore other possible solutions. Embodying a theory of urban interactions, and the causes of failure of previous urban programmes, it also constituted one of the set of exemplars concerning the feedback properties of all systems. In other words, the properties of urban systems were located within the overall system dynamics schema: the domain was new but the feedback dynamics remained the same. Together the general systems theory of system dynamics, and its set of applications, constituted the boundaries within which any discussion of urban problems was to be articulated.

In addition to the claim that the urban model could explain the existence and persistence of urban problems, it was also claimed that it provided an explanation for the failure of previous urban programmes (Forrester, 1969: 1–11). Again the explanation was rooted in the properties of complex feedback systems, particularly the principle of counterintuitivity (that is, the idea that complex systems behave in a way that is counter to the intuition of the untrained observer), and no attention was given to the alternative explanations which abound in the rather large literature on urban problems. A consideration of some of these different explanations can reveal other features of cities which urban dynamics closed off; it can also help to give further resolution to the picture of the urban theory which urban dynamics aimed to consolidate. Considering the concepts which Forrester eschewed, rather than the ones he implicitly or explicitly adopted, might seem unfair. However, I am merely following Mannheim's idea that the absence of concepts may indicate a wish to avoid coming to terms with certain phenomena (Mannheim, 1936).

In the case of *Urban Dynamics*, we are told that documentary information was explicitly ignored when formulating the urban model; instead Forrester relied partly on the information of 'practical men' who knew the urban scene 'first hand' (Forrester, 1969: x). The point here is not to criticize Forrester because he deliberately avoided the literature but rather to emphasize that he avoided certain concepts, of which the idea of conflicts of interest is one of the most notable. To develop this line of argument a little further, it is useful to refer to some alternative views of the failure of urban programmes. For example, Gans has been a major critic of urban programmes, particularly the urban renewal programme which was devised to clear slums, relocate their inhabitants in decent housing, stimulate rebuilding, and revitalize downtown areas of cities (Gans, 1967). In contrast to the aims of the programme, Gans maintains that clearance of slums made way for many luxury housing developments and some middle-income projects. As a result, the people who were dispossessed were unable to afford the cost or rents of the new properties and many simply moved into other slum areas. This led to further decline in those areas and increased overcrowding, together with the concentration of racial minorities into ghettoes. He cites startling figures to support his case: 'a 1961 study of renewal projects in 41 cities showed that 60 % of the dispossessed tenants were merely relocated in other slums' (Gans, 1967: 466–7).

He also contends that certain areas were cleared not because they contained the worst slums, but because they offered prime sites for luxury developments. Because public funds were used to undertake the clearance work, and to make the land available to private developers at a reduced cost, he concludes that the low-income population was in effect subsidizing its own removal purely for the benefit of those in a better financial situation. Finally, he argues that another failure of the renewal programme was that some cities scheduled clearance projects just to clear away non-white poor people who were seen as standing in the path of the progress of private enterprise (Gans, 1967: 471).

Other programmes ran into quite different problems; in particular, the housing subsidy programmes were subject to criminal abuse by the illegal tactics of several groups, including bankers and speculators. Mercer and Hultquist (1976) contend that the subsidy programmes failed the very people that they were designed to serve while benefiting others who were not in need. Moreover, investigations have revealed 'scandalous and often criminal actions' within these investment schemes, and as the extent of the abuses became clearer, the Nixon administration suspended much of the federal housing apparatus (Mercer and Hultquist, 1976: 105).

None of these difficulties were mentioned by Forrester, nor were any of the other factors – such as discrimination against Blacks – which could be cited. Yet such problems are a pointer towards the failure of urban programmes and also direct attention towards causes of urban problems that lie outside the narrow framework adopted by Forrester. He was concerned with the management and control of urban systems and therefore needed a systems-theoretic explanation for the causes of urban problems and the failure of previous programmes. His denial of contrarieties was partly grounded in his cosmology, preventing him from seeing or admitting the possibility that society may be rent with contrarieties or conflicts of interest. Also, his belief in the oneness and unity of the world led him to ignore the basis of class conflicts; although he admitted that goal conflicts existed, he saw them as due to shortsighted interests which should be subordinated to the 'true' common interests of urban systems.

Because Forrester's explanation was pitched at the level of the city, it also failed to consider the nature of the links between the city and the rest of society. Consistent with its theoretical closure, we might also usefully note that the theory precluded even a consideration of the possibility that urban problems might be generated in the wider societal system; for example, by contradictions within the capitalist system itself. This form of argument has been developed by Castells, who has sought to examine urban crises within the context of the wider crises of capitalist societies (Castells, 1977). Central to this line of argument is the contradiction between the privatization of profits and the socialization of costs. Forrester saw economic activity as an almost independent sphere of social reality and did not consider the argument that the state, or local government, pay part of the cost of reproducing labour power. 'Enterprise of the right kind costs the city very little by its presence. It polices its own internal land area. It buys water and other utilities . . . it demands little of fire departments. Industry of itself does not require schools. . .' (Forrester, 1969: 124). The socialization of costs is reflected in schooling, housing, medical provision, and transport systems. In effect it subsidizes the costs of production, and yet the profits of that production are privatized. These issues defy a crude reduction to the structure of system dynamics models – they cannot produce or encapsulate serious patterned conflicts or contrarieties of this sort. As well as denying the possible importance of conflicts and contradictions in the explanation of urban crises, they were also denied any relevance in social life in general. As an explanatory device, the urban model therefore upheld the legitimacy of the social order and its dominant institutions: urban dynamics reflected the unity of the city, an imaginary unity which it constituted within the sphere of esoteric knowledge and embedded in a computer program.

Legitimation

A policy model may serve to project and legitimate specific social structures, and can do so in a characteristic way determined by the worldview and cosmology which accompany it. If someone builds a computer model it is because in his or her worldview such a task is deemed to be a valid way of exploring social policy. Within urban dynamics we find the use of esoteric computer simulation techniques, a theory concerning the complexities of counterintuitive feedback systems, and the technocratic promise of social engineering – not of the piecemeal variety, but large-scale control of social systems. The mere utilization of scientific and technological resources can serve to provide justification for a model in the eyes of other observers. Thus, the fact that some people associated the urban model with science and technology served as a form of legitimation for the policies that were advocated. However, the legitimizing resources of the scientific/technical aura which surrounded the urban project were not the only sources of justification that we may discern; they were perhaps only the most explicit aspects of legitimation that shrouded Forrester's work. To expose others I will again have to return to the cosmology of the system dynamicists.

In chapter 4 I argued that cosmologies carried a baggage of implicit assumptions concerning the nature of man and the cosmos; these assumptions provide the ultimate justification, the fundamental legitimation, for a society. In any discussion about social reality such assumptions will govern the form in which the arguments are couched. This will also be the case when formal mathematical modelling is applied to social policy. It is Douglas's contention that people use concepts of nature in order to legitimate their social institutions; nature is seen as a resource for talking about society. In grounding their justifications for the dominant social relationships within the context of the grand meaning of nature and the cosmos, people legitimate the prevailing social order. Nature is the final arbiter of what is right and what is wrong, what is deviant and what is natural.

But we can expand this idea a little further by observing that the perceived logical or causal order of the world is a reflection of that implicit in the self-evident assumptions in which cosmologies are grounded. In other words, the assumed or intuitive order of the world is really a product of social relations, of the experiences that confront each person in his or her interactions within a particular social environment. 'Apprehending a general pattern of what is right and necessary in social relations is the basis of society; this apprehension generates whatever a priori or set of necessary causes is going to be found in nature' (Douglas, 1975: 281). Thus, in maintaining their social environment people generate a set of beliefs, seemingly validated because they are seen to encapsulate 'natural laws', which serve to legitimate it, to endow it with meaning and make it reasonable in their eyes. Alternative beliefs are denounced as utopian, impossible, or – most efficaciously – 'unnatural'. Therefore the roots of legitimation go deeper than the question of merely labelling what is natural, and what is not, for the beliefs which describe the cosmos share a pattern of assumptions – an intuitive causal order – that actually reflect the very self-evidence of the social environment. People not only see beliefs as legitimate because they state that which is natural, but, more subtly, because they match their own intuition. Given this theoretical basis, let us now apply it to Forrester's urban theory and consider the elements which gave it a self-evident quality.

Two key assumptions seemed to govern the operation of Forrester's model; these were the concepts of 'attractiveness' and the 'unlimited environment' (Forrester, 1969: 12–37). Forrester assumed that cities have a multiplicity of components of attractiveness such as housing and jobs etc. These were thought to determine the rates of immigration and migration to and from the surrounding environment. (It was assumed that people move to the most attractive area, whether it is the city or the environment. Further, that environment was taken to be limitless – i.e. it could absorb as many people as possible who wanted to leave the city; and it could also supply an inexhaustible influx of people who might wish to enter.)

The total attractiveness of the city was fixed so that there would always be a trade-off in its different attractiveness components. Forrester asserted that urban revival would come from manipulating these components while keeping the total attractiveness the same. The only conceivable way for the total to increase would be if the whole surrounding environment increased in quality. Any change within the city effected an interchange with the environment such that some new balance was obtained. For example, if the city appeared attractive because it temporarily had a surplus of housing, it would attract an influx from outside; this population change would lower the city's housing attractiveness component and a new balance with the surroundings would be achieved.

Perhaps the most salient factor in all this is the notion of the desirability, if not the inevitability, of urban equilibrium. The idea that there must be a balance – in expenditure, in population, or whatever – appears as a powerful fact of life; and it was seen to be proved by the causal order of feedback systems. So long as one goes along with the concept of the urban system as a 'master of its own destiny', while neglecting the importance of the links with the environment, the arguments about balance have a strong intuitive appeal. (Similar ideas to these have, of course, been a thread in the policies toward local authority spending implemented during the 1980s by the Thatcher government in Britain.) We can also find statements directed towards the nation. We are told, for example, that a healthy city is not a 'drag' on the country and could even benefit the nation as a whole.

Forrester eschewed the extreme optimism of those technological rationalists who have contended that the only problems in advanced capitalist societies are technical; at the same time he did not reduce the causes of urban problems to purely natural ones. In the latter form of argument, urban problems are viewed as the inevitable outcome of natural laws wherein the only solution is to abandon the cities and create new small-scale alternative communities. The balance between these two extremes is revealed by his assertions about what is possible, and what is utopian in society – these being grounded in terms of what he considered to be natural. For example, we are told that urban areas have a characteristic life-cycle and evolution, with ageing and deterioration as natural features; stagnation and decay are to be seen as episodes in the cycle of the occupation of land. But, further, we are told that the 'natural condition of the aging city tends toward too much housing and too few jobs for the underemployed population' (Forrester, 1969: 121). In other words, the causes of a large underemployed urban population were *natural*. However, Forrester also argued that these natural conditions were encouraged by tax and zoning practices; the implication being that a reversal of these practices could halt decline and lead to a new and better equilibrium condition – though pressures would still have to be maintained. Forrester regarded the city as an 'organic living complex', its evolution was not seen as the intentional plan of designers, but as the outcome of a 'self-directing system' which people had set in motion. Although he did not believe that urban problems were eternal, or naturally fixed properties of urban systems, he did seem to view cities as though they were natural products in the occupation of geographical space. 'Urban difficulties are not a matter of location so much as a phase in the normal life cycle of occupied land.' (Forrester, 1969: 11) Such a view resonates with what Castells has described as the urban ideology. 'The urban ideology is that specific ideology that sees the modes and forms of social organization as characteristic of a phase of the evolution of society, closely linked to the technico-natural conditions of human existence and, ultimately to its environment' (Castells, 1977: 73–4). In seeing urban systems as something natural, people may tend not to see the conflicts of interest which are incipient to their development; hence problems come to be seen either as natural inevitabilities, or as aberrations, rather than as potentially indigenous properties of certain types of social organization.

The path from decline to revival was thought to lie in social management and control (Forrester, 1969: 122). But there were limits as to what could be done – as revealed in the notion of natural and unnatural goals. Discussing outside help for the city, Forrester argued that it could not be sustained indefinitely if the effort was aimed at an 'unnatural' goal that cities could not maintain themselves. Further, the idea that all sustainable system modes required pressures or 'negative forces' – such as a housing or job shortage – recurred throughout his discussion of urban systems (Forrester, 1975b: 180); it reflected the commonly found notion that things must get worse before they get better, that treatment can be painful. How else could the lower classes be persuaded to accept policies which would 'initially' put them at a disadvantage? These ideas are an example of how negative aspects of the world became integrated into the system dynamicists' cosmological scheme (and thereby justified) – the maldistribution of social advantages took the form of a pressure which had to be accepted and even actively maintained.

Forrester also talked about 'misfits' – by which he presumably meant those who did not match up to the acceptable norms, or – as we might suggest it can be seen – the grid of rules inherent in his cosmology (Forrester, 1969: 122). Such people were to be prevented from entering the city – which required a balanced mixture of social classes (hierarchy) and an equilibrium with the surrounding environment. Further, it was to be protected against the 'excessive' influx of the unemployed, with a shortage of housing and high rents as possible deterrents. So here we find a discrimination in terms of 'group': those who do not keep to the norms of the dominant majority are to be excluded from the city. Moreover, we have seen that Forrester charged the underemployed with irresponsibility – this being a moral accusation which formed part of the rhetoric of attributing blame for urban stagnation. Such an element of scapegoating can be a powerful source of appeal in any social policy: if something is wrong in society – so the rhetoric goes – surely there must be some group who are at the root of it; if these culpable people are excluded then things will improve.

Forrester's thoughts on the provision of social benefits complemented these policies because he considered the welfare system to be 'an active part of the social trap that keeps people from becoming self-supporting' (Forrester, 1975b: 199). Put another way, he was asserting that welfare cases were products of the welfare substructure and he wished to redraw the boundary of the urban system so as to exclude the welfare subsystem. In seeking to alter the urban structure he was upholding the legitimacy of a social order whose problems were alleged to be partly rooted in the welfare substructure. (As noted earlier, opposition to welfare and to New Deal ideas generally had a strong tradition amongst certain sections of American society.) Further, if welfare cases were created in the manner in which he suggested, it meant that other causes might not exist; it implied that there was a poverty trap but not the glimmer of a suggestion that the creation of poverty might be connected to the creation of affluence.

Role of System Dynamics Experts

In this section the task is to examine the wider role that system dynamics might play in society. For example, we might look for a congruence between system dynamics – considered as a belief system – and the structure of relationships through which it would be practised or taught. To use a metaphor, the focus of interest will be on how the laboratory – in this case the System Dynamics Laboratory – can become extended, out into the world where particular problems are to be solved, and can modify social relationships. We can consider the potential social and political implications of the role of the experts who understand, teach, and implement this body of knowledge.

It is contended that as a system of knowledge, system dynamics entails features which somewhat distance it from techniques such as statistical or other types of computer modelling. Generally speaking, practitioners of such techniques cannot make choices about social values within the theoretical terms of the methods themselves. In contrast, system dynamicists explicitly seek to make objective statements about values in terms of the theory of feedback systems. For example, it has been claimed that system dynamics reveals constraints upon the possible choice of value structures if social systems are not to collapse; in this sense it is more akin to a social theory than a technique. Further, these constraints were not thought to be due to any inherent weaknesses in system dynamics, but rather were seen as the real limitations of social systems. (Of course I do not mean to suggest that techniques are value-free, or that they are not used to influence value-choices.)

In addition to this difference, system dynamics has at times been promoted by assertions that posit a privileged epistemological position for it. These claims were rooted in the ontological primacy which feedback systems were accorded, together with the contention that only the expert use of computers could reveal the complex behaviour of our social systems. The system dynamicists were not just claiming that system dynamics was useful, they saw it as vitally essential for the future of society. These somewhat unique features call for a consideration of system dynamics in different terms than might be appropriate to techniques proper, such as, say, cost–benefit analysis or event simulation. In this regard, one issue that needs to be considered concerns how this corpus of knowledge began to diffuse into society. In fact, system dynamics has been disseminated in two essential ways: first, at an educational level – in schools, colleges, and universities; and second, it has been adopted by a wide range of groups to be used in different problem domains (an indication of this variation was given in chapter 1).

Those who 'own' knowledge have the ability to exercise power; in this sense the claims of the system dynamicists were indirect claims for power. In discussing the control and management of urban systems, they sought to carve out a special role for themselves and for urban dynamics. This role would insert them into a distinct network of relationships with politicians and the electorate; it was only they who could carry out the simulation modelling and reveal the possibilities of urban systems, the sustainable behaviour modes, and the attendant pressures and stresses. Thus, urban dynamics was a knowledge resource by which the system dynamicists could seek to create a new pattern of social relations – among themselves, politicians, and the electorate. It was also a symbolic system which could then serve to mediate and reinforce that pattern. In such a situation the traditional role of the politician would change; choices were to be made concerning the possible ensemble of pressures under which people might live, but the task of ascertaining what was possible was for the system dynamics expert and his or her computer. For instance, Alfeld and Meadows suggested a central role for such experts; in discussing a potential move towards urban prosperity they maintained that at the 'centre of such a process is the use of dynamic modelling techniques to evaluate new programs and suggest ways for improving old ones' (Alfeld and Meadows, 1972: 65–6).

Implicitly, the role of the politician was to become one of delivering policy options (drawn from system dynamics models) to urban residents. He or she would adopt the persona of a public relations officer, informing the electorate of what social systems would and would not allow. The political machinery would be structured towards the choice of behaviour modes, but the criteria by which possible modes could be decided, would remain in the hands of the expert and effectively beyond open political discussion. Thus, the problems of any particular city were to be taken over from urban administrations and brought into the System Dynamics Laboratory where solutions could be found. The solution set was then to be handed back to the politicians for implementation.

> People would never attempt to send a space ship to the moon without first testing the equipment by constructing prototype models and by computer simulation of the anticipated space trajectories. . . . Why, then, do we not use the same approach of making models of social systems and conducting laboratory experiments on those models before we try new laws and government programs in real life? (Forrester, 1975b: 212–13)

In terms of legitimacy, scientific laboratories are rather special institutions; they are shrouded by a form of mystique; for example, laboratory practices can appear mysterious and the knowledge produced is esoteric. This view of laboratories can be observed not only in the public imagination, for scientists too give credibility to the myth. As recorded in Part One, Meadows had been uneasy about the publicity campaign that had accompanied the launching of The Limits to Growth, and he was adamant that the media would not be allowed into the System Dynamics

Laboratory. Within a laboratory, complex real-world problems are translated into puzzles which can be more easily solved. Outside in the environment, the forces of nature and the perversity of numerous contingencies serve to thwart the endeavours of scientists; but once inside the laboratory the roles are reversed. To take an example, Latour (1983) argues that when French farmers were faced with a problem of anthrax, Pasteur succeeded in reformulating their perceptions of their interests such that they were won over to the necessity of bringing their problem into his laboratory – only there could the anthrax organism be tamed. In other words, the laboratory was a powerful rhetorical resource for establishing the sequence of steps which would lead to a solution of the anthrax problem.

Similarly with system dynamics: urban problems were translated into a computer model in a laboratory where they could allegedly be solved. Moreover, just as Pasteur's laboratory facilitated the control of the anthrax organism, and its elimination – these being impossible in the outside general environment due to innumerable contingencies – so too the System Dynamics Laboratory allowed controlled experiments on models of social systems. However, an important distinction here is that while the anthrax organism actually did come to reside in Pasteur's laboratory, system dynamics translations were purely symbolic.

But once laboratory puzzles have been solved, how are the solutions to be implemented in the outside world? Latour describes how Pasteur found it necessary to organize farmers' vaccination procedures – they had to follow strict rules in accordance with laboratory practice, otherwise their efforts would be swamped by the unpredictability of the environment. That is, the laboratory became extended out on to the farm. The proposed reorganization of urban systems can also be usefully construed by thinking of the changes as a laboratory extension. First, for instance, system dynamics has been offered as a 'packaged technique'. For example, Dynamo – the computer language in which system dynamics models are encrypted – is written for those people who have little or no mathematical/ programming expertise.[4] Also, computer programs are available for checking the dimensional consistency of model equations etc., and a number of system dynamics textbooks and workbooks are now available. These, coupled with the non-data dependent character of system dynamics, aim to secure a correspondence between the use of system dynamics inside the laboratory and that outside – whether in schools and universities, in cities, or in corporations and other policy contexts.

Second, one condition for the success of urban revival was the requirement that the city should be as controllable as its laboratory model. In order to effect revival programmes in cities, they had to be managed and controlled. In other words, urban dynamics defined a role for system dynamicists in urban systems, it created the need for, and indeed legitimated, their position as system managers.

Third, on another level, system dynamics actually organized the perceptions of those who adhered to it. In Kuhnian terms, the system dynamics paradigm brought with it a general theory of feedback systems, together with a set of exemplars, which served to order the cognitions of its adherents. Again, it was not a mere technique but a theory of the world. Trained professionals in system dynamics would see themselves – that is, their role as system managers – and the world around them in a distinct systems-theoretic way; and the administrators with whom they had to interact were to be encouraged to adopt the theory too. Indeed, the system dynamicists organized a series of presentations of the urban model to which they invited city administrators and politicians: the aim being to convince them of the importance of system dynamics.

Fourth, the policy recommendations of urban dynamics also constituted an extension of the laboratory: the city was to be reshaped such that its structure matched that of the model in the laboratory. For the practical implementation of urban dynamics would change urban structures in such a way as to exclude those substructures which do not conform with the ones advocated by the theory; these exclusions would centre upon the welfare subsystem and highly concentrated social and economic areas. This indicates a further intricate strand in the relationship between knowledge and social structure; for when Forrester advocated the integration of underemployed Blacks into mainstream economic activity, we can understand this as a policy which would submit them to the dominant public grid. Moreover, the elimination of the ghettoes would also help to eliminate the cosmologies which they support. These people would be incorporated into a new urban structure in which the cosmology represented by system dynamics would aim to be the dominant cosmology of the whole city. Hence, urban dynamics not only promoted a theoretically closed view of cities; for the recommended policies would concretize an urban structure which would support the cosmology implicit in the theory – thereby reinforcing the proposed policies. Thus, another effect of urban dynamics was the promotion of a social restructuring which could close off alternative perceptions and dissent. Within the new urban structure the expert's perceptions would be consistent with the theory of urban systems, and the perception of the urban residents would be such as to make the policies appear self-evident.

Finally, it is worthwhile elaborating on the role of system dynamics in education. In chapter 5 I discussed the self-image of the system dynamicists: distinctly bounded groups – I argued – reinforce their own social identity by promoting their philosophy, they may see themselves as special, as having a unique mission. 'The approach is easy to understand but difficult to practice. Few people have the required level of skill' (Forrester, 1975b: 212). Further, because system dynamics was thought to have a universal validity, there was an implication that someone trained in the nature of feedback systems could enter any subject area or field without prior experience of the subject concerned.

> The same dynamic structures recur within different fields and in the connections between fields. When a structure is understood in one setting, it is understood wherever else it may be found. . . . By creating an educational system on a common dynamic foundation, we can hope to develop a modern 'Renaissance Man' with a command of universal concepts that allows him to move between fields in a unified framework. (Forrester, 1975a: 4)

Courses on system dynamics have in fact been taught within different educational institutions in several countries. Other groups have adopted the urban dynamics model as a teaching tool or urban simulation game (Belkin, 1972). Because of SDG's desire to extend system dynamics into all levels of education, we must infer that the system dynamicists were indirectly making a bid for power over the content of curricula. On this view, the teaching of system dynamics can therefore be thought of as a medium for the dissemination of the social cosmology and style of thinking which are implicit within it. In this context it is useful to note a point raised by Douglas; speaking about how pieces of knowledge are classified within the classroom she states: 'as they are connected in the curriculum so they enter the minds of the pupils, and, though the details of the content will fade, the connections are likely to guide their judgements and perpetuate the system of power which the curriculum represents' (Douglas, 1973: 10).

While it is not necessary for us to be drawn into the debate concerning the wider pedagogical implications of this idea, we can use it to throw some further light on the teaching of system dynamics. Of course these remarks can only be general for I have no detailed information on how system dynamics is actually taught. The relationship between teacher and the pupil is part of a control system in which the curriculum is an example of a symbolic system which mediates and reinforces hidden power relations. In the context of the school, these relations are represented by the groups who decide upon the content of the curriculum. In seeking to extend the teaching of system dynamics throughout the educational system, Forrester and his associates were indirectly seeking to exert some measure of control within the system of power that determines the curriculum. Thus, within different social environments – whether the school or the political machinery of cities – system dynamics had the potential for reorganizing those structures in accordance with its implicit cosmology.

At different levels within the education system we might expect to find different roles implied by the knowledge being disseminated. At the lower levels we could expect the knowledge to be geared towards its passive acceptance – along with the rest of the curriculum. The system dynamicists believed that only a few people have the special skills which are required for practising system dynamics; thus at the higher levels we would find the elite – the prospective system managers or controllers.

If we refer once more to Bernstein's work, we can allude to another interesting facet of the teaching of system dynamics. Bernstein has argued that most subjects are ordered hierarchically so that as one ascends the educational ladder the 'ultimate mystery' of the subject is only revealed at a late stage (Bernstein, 1971: 213). This mystery is not, however, revealed as order or coherence, but rather as disorder – i.e. sophistication involves an appreciation of the very provisional and contingent nature of our knowledge. For example, a young budding physicist may believe that he or she will ultimately discover the truth of the universe when the top of the educational ladder is reached; however, he or she eventually finds that truth is not quite what they had been led to believe on the basis of the way in which the subject is organized. For the majority, however, the picture is different because they never reach this insight. 'For the many, socialization into knowledge is socialization into order, the existing order, into the experience that the world's educational knowledge is impermeable' (Bernstein, 1971: 214).

Returning to system dynamics, I might suggest that its social and educational implications are somewhat at variance with those outlined by Bernstein. Rather than revealing disorder and the provisional nature of knowledge, system dynamics seeks to consolidate order – the general or universal order which underpins all systems. Even for those at the higher stages – such as Forrester and others in the System Dynamics Laboratory – this is the quintessential feature of system dynamics, and so one might conclude that its educational dissemination carries no potential for ultimate critical reflection. Hence, as with those at the lower stages, those who are trained to be practising system dynamicists would share the same socialization into the notion of the coherence and permanence of their knowledge.

Summary

Seeking to take a holistic view, composed of multiple perspectives, this chapter has advanced several arguments about the potential role of system dynamics as a knowledge resource which mediates and reinforces social relations. The picture that has emerged reveals several interconnecting dimensions by which this could be effected. In no part of the discussion have I meant to imply that these social effects were within the conscious control of Forrester or other system dynamicists; rather, they express the possibilities of a system of knowledge which has evolved within the social context in which these systems analysts reside.

I have shown that the idea of laboratory extensions can illuminate the role of the system dynamics in policymaking. The urban policies would necessitate the creation of a special niche for the system dynamicists – a self-reinforcing social position which would insert them into a special relationship with politicians and the electorate. With regard to the latter, I have pieced together a picture of an urban structure which, given the argument concerning cosmologies and social structures, would perhaps constrain them towards an acceptance of the role of the system dynamicists and the policies which they recommend.

Several interwoven threads of legitimation pervade the theory, each displaying a distinct facet whose function was to make the theory appear rational or self-evident in people's eyes. Taking a position between technocratic optimism, and one which might construe all urban problems as a natural outcome of city life, Forrester put forward a mixture of ideas whose justification arose from different sources. From the moral indictment of the irresponsibilities of the poorer classes, to the promotion of capitalist enterprise and technocratic ideas of the need for changed urban administration, the theory spanned a whole gamut of notions which served to lend it legitimacy. Again this supports the conviction that system dynamics cannot be reduced simply to a reflection of capitalist or technocratic interests.

Urban dynamics was a claim for power: it sought to stake out a position for system dynamicists and carried an assertion of authority to speak about the nature of social systems. This claim bore the hallmark of the time – namely, the ceding of authority to those who commanded the use of esoteric techniques in technology and the physical sciences. Beneath the technical glare we can discern a strong moral position: system dynamics offered to fulfil the promise of social engineering while remaining rooted in a traditional conservative view of lower-class people and societal duties.

I have explored several interconnected strands within the exoteric role of system dynamics and have tried to show that its potential role was complex and multifaceted; this has given rise to far more questions than it has been possible to answer here. Nevertheless, the insights generated stand as an original contribution to the understanding of the cultural role of system dynamics.

9 Simulations of Doom: Personal Needs and the Credibility of Disasters

In this chapter I turn the spotlight on the reception which greeted the system dynamics world models. These models are the most widely known and extensively publicized of the various system dynamics projects, and have generated both widespread support and criticism, particularly in North America and Western Europe. As noted earlier, *The Limits to Growth* book sold over three million copies.

In addition to seeking an explanation for the enormous popularity of the thesis underpinning the models, I am specifically interested in the spectrum of beliefs (and disbeliefs) which they stimulated, and will employ some psychological and sociological ideas in order to examine the differential reactions of different audiences. Other researchers have often tackled the question of the popularity of *The Limits to Growth* as part of an overall investigation of the rise of environmentalism (Cotgrove, 1975; Enzensberger, 1974; Sandbach, 1978, 1980). However, none has sought to deal in detail with the variation in reaction to the world models.

I contend that the message of the world models was a focus for personal concerns – that it played on certain personal needs. These included the need for cognitive security – that is, the need to be able to explain one's life and endow it with meaning and a sense of purpose. The principal psychological reactions on which I will concentrate are the mechanisms of projection and displacement. Because the world models became a lever of protest for various groups, they provided a resource by which those groups could project their dissatisfactions and lay blame at the door of the establishment, scientists, technology, industrialists, or whoever. In doing so, these groups were protecting themselves against their own complicity in global problems (complicity which would be painful to admit). This type of reaction is an example of what psychologists call displacement –

that is, the substitution of an acceptable explanation for one which would be painful to admit or sustain. To take another example of these reactions, we may note the way in which some people make a fetish of nuclear weapons (Elias, 1978a: 24). The nuclear bomb is a symbol on to which some people project their fears; they blame scientists for its presence – thus displacing a more objective explanation for the existence of hostilities between nations and substituting a more welcome one. Moreover, the projection and displacement divert attention from people's own sense of helplessness in the face of hostilities. Such reactions are closely bound up with preserving cognitive security and I will argue that personal needs are discernible amongst a number of different responses to the models even where those responses were superficially disparate.

In addition to personal needs, it is important to note that the world models did not enter a social vacuum. Rather, they emerged at a time of considerable social change – including economic upheavals and the decline of traditional values and institutions – which some people saw as a portent of a threatening future. My contention is that it is in relation to the prevailing social context that the public appeal of the models is best understood. The world models must also be seen in relation to the environmental movement of the 1960s and early 1970s which was itself part of the wider social context. I cannot hope here to provide an explanation of this movement: the reasons for the rise of environmentalism are obviously beyond the scope of this investigation. However it must be acknowledged that the world models contributed to the development of the movement and I will consider the millenarian overtones of environmentalism.

Basically the approach I take is to propose that the models represented a complex message which was interpreted in divergent ways by various groups with different cosmologies. These groups ranged from those who saw the message as confirming their belief in the imminent collapse of Western civilization, and who subsequently sought survival in small alternative communities, to those who viewed the message as a justification for increased international regulation and the formation of a 'world government' or some other supranational institution.

The message encapsulated many intuitive feelings about the state of the modern world. In fact, it embodied age-old ideas about the relationship of man to man, man to society, and man to nature – though casting these ideas in a somewhat modern form. These 'natural symbols' – to use Douglas's term – vary from cosmology to cosmology; this variation offers some prospects for understanding the different reactions to the models.

The plan of the chapter is as follows. First, I discuss the actual details of the message contained in the models. Second, I will deal with the psychological impact the message could have had on its audience and refer to the millenarian overtones of environmentalism. This will then lead on to a comparison between the belief system represented by system dynamics and that pertaining to astrology. The theme explored here will be the personal needs which the world models fulfilled. It will be argued that they afforded a form of belief system which sought to explain the contrarieties of the world and endow it with meaning and coherence. Third, using Douglas's ideas as a background for analysing the social roots of beliefs concerning pollution, the argument will proceed to differentiate the responses to the message. More specifically, consideration will be given to the types of response to the message which could be expected in the light of the grid/group theory of cosmologies. Finally, some actual responses will be examined in relation to those expectations.

The Message of the World Models

The messages of the world models – WORLD 2 and WORLD 3 – can be considered as being basically the same. There were of course some differences, *The Limits to Growth* being somewhat less pessimistic than *World Dynamics*, but for the purposes here it is reasonable to refer to the message of the two models collectively as 'the limits to growth' (LTG). The use of the term 'message' is based on the idea that the world models encapsulated a number of different themes whose interpretation depended on the particular audience in question; or, in other words, the meaning of the message was not an autonomous entity. Any simple treatment which assumed that the message of the models had only one meaning would therefore be inappropriate. Instead, I will try to point out the range of elements within the message and thereby pave the way for understanding the divergent inferences drawn by different groups.

The LTG message contained the ominous prediction that the world was facing a total catastrophe. This prophecy appeared to be different in kind from earlier predicted disasters because it was apparently based upon the behaviour of computer simulation models – a feature which set the message apart from religious and other apocalyptical prophecies. It had overtones of scientific objectivity because it came from a group who were among one of the world's leading scientific/technological elites.

The potential collapse could be caused by one of several factors, acting singly or in concert. Among other possible scenarios we find pollution crises, starvation, and industrial collapse through the exhaustion of natural resources. The global collapse would give way to an equilibrium condition with a much lower level of population, and the 'shift from growth to equilibrium may be initiated by catastrophes such as wars, or epidemics' (Meadows, 1973: 33).

The concept of system viability was used to focus doubts about the future, and the modellers questioned whether man was about to fall into an abyss of his own creation – a social and technical system which he could no longer control and which was driving the whole race towards disaster (Forrester, 1971: 8). In addition to arguing that the viability of the world system was threatened, the system dynamicists advocated measures which would supposedly bring the global system into an equilibrium state and thus guarantee its viability. Indeed, the conception of viability was directly linked to the means of sustaining it – i.e. equilibrium. These measures were directed towards curbing the growth in population, industrialization, and pollution; this would require a shift in values from those oriented towards short-term interests and material growth, to those compatible with long-term equilibrium (Forrester, 1971: 125).

Forrester advocated an enhanced role for religion in the proposed equilibrium society and suggested that churches were guardians of the future. His assumption was presumably that a stronger religious orientation could provide the stricter moral codes required to secure the forfeit of expectations in a world of no material growth. The system dynamicists argued that because of the alleged slow response time of complex systems, people were to take action soon, for it would take some time before their efforts came to fruition. They suggested that if people postponed action then it might well be too late to avert the catastrophe.

Equilibrium would occur when growth in the global systems' positive loops had been arrested by the negative loops, thus yielding a balance of forces and harmony; that is, 'a condition of constant population, constant use of resources, and constant generation of pollution, all limited so that the equilibrium condition can be sustained indefinitely into the future' (Forrester, 1975b: 256). So, the equilibrium society would have no conceivable end – its social order would be perpetual.

The concepts of system viability and equilibrium were further linked to the ideas of order, conservation, the purposive nature of systems, harmony, and balance with nature. A world in equilibrium would be a world of order and harmony between man and nature, and between the different subsystems. We were told that man must not seek to conquer nature but try to live in harmony with it, thus reflecting the rising concern with ecology (e.g. Commoner, 1971). In the early part of the 1970s, ecology became a widely used term in Western societies and served as a focus for a series of related concerns. The LTG message was seen by many people as a vital part of the argument for environmental protection, for it purported to show that environmental abuse threatened not only the extinction of obscure species of animals, but the existence of man himself.

Although appearing to many as scientists, Forrester and his associates distanced themselves from the scientific and technological rationality which they saw as being tied to short-term interests – designed to treat the symptoms of the world's problems rather than the 'true' causes. They were therefore much opposed to technological 'fixes'. In fact, they claimed that the method with which their models had been formulated embodied a new and distinctive way of thinking about the world – that is, a dynamic systems approach which they believed was the only way of comprehending the behaviour of a complex system. The method used in constructing the models was holistic, the WORLD 3 project team was multidisciplinary, and a long-term view was taken of the future of the global system.

Forrester and Meadows both acknowledged that the models did not consider the political changes that would be necessary to achieve global equilibrium, restricting themselves only to a consideration of the viability of the physical infrastructure which underlies the world. Yet this admission was not just a statement regarding the limitations of the models; it also served to set their work above the sphere of politics, to make them appear more objective. Further, we should note that in painting their systems analysts' view of the world, conflict was seen largely as a symptom of exponential growth or competition for limited resources. It was seen as being rooted in short-term considerations. The message of the world models was therefore projected above short-term political squabblings, class conflicts, and other similar conflicts of interest – it purported to address the long-term future of the whole globe. The main elements of the message are summarized in figure 9.1.

Millenarianism and Personal Needs

In Sandbach's (1978) search for an explanation of the rise and fall of the 'limits to growth' debate, he refers to Barkun's thesis that the environmental movement was a millenarian one (Barkun, 1974). Though a detailed examination of this idea would go beyond the scope of this book, nevertheless Barkun's conjecture does have some relevance for anyone seeking an understanding of the social effects of the world models. Barkun links millenarianism to disasters and has suggested that real or imaginary catastrophes reduce people's threshold to susceptibility by exploiting their fears and anxieties. Further, he argues that people are then more readily moved to 'abandon the values of the past and place their faith in prophecies of immanent and total transformation' (Barkun, 1974: 6).

Disasters may take many forms; among others, Barkun refers to natural catastrophes, demographic shifts, economic depressions, and industrialization. But also, he suggests that in some societies people experience a prolonged sense of unease and uncertainty (a non-specific 'sense of dread') which similarly increases the plausibility of impending disaster;

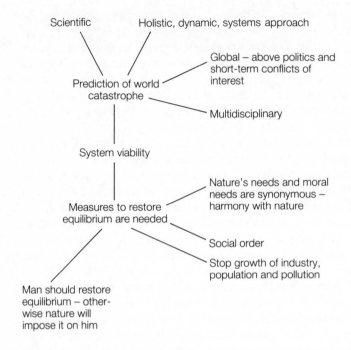

Figure 9.1   Elements of the message of the world models

and in reference to America's recent history he describes the cultivation of a 'disaster imagination', elements of which include nuclear holocaust, over-population, race war, and ecological imbalance. Thus we can see that the global collapse associated with the message of the world models fitted in with this picture of unease very well; the credibility and appeal of the message being dependent upon its efficacy in touching existing fears and anxieties. Are we then to conclude that the world models helped to cause a millenarian outburst? In fact, this is too simple a picture – to understand why, we must refer to Barkun's theoretical assumptions.

One major problem with Barkun's thesis is that it stems from functionalist premises and implies that the normal condition of society is some kind of steady state. Disasters, of whatever form, are seen to disturb this equilibrium and precipitate millenarian outbursts. Secondly, while there may indeed be a historical correlation between disasters and millenarian movements there is not necessarily a causal relationship.

Another view of millenarian movements has been developed by Cohn (1970) who offers a socio-psychological account in which he seems to suggest that such movements are a collective delusional action, a form of paranoid fantasy which seeks to alleviate the anxiety attendant upon the various contrary experiences, deprivations, and disasters in the societies in which they occur. In other words, they are a means of meeting certain personal needs. 'This phantasy performed a real function for them, both as an escape from their isolated and atomized condition and as an emotional compensation for their abject status' (Cohn, 1970: 285). In contrast, Douglas has argued for a more sociological interpretation of Cohn's material – which in fact is drawn largely from millenarian movements in the Middle Ages. She pinpoints weakness of social structure as a common element in the movements he has documented. Douglas's account of millenarianism therefore stands in sharp contrast to Barkun's functionalism. For her, the sources of millenarianism are located in the social structure itself. Indeed, certain societies are conjectured to be actually prone to millenarianism. This still allows a role for elements such as disasters, real or imagined, and deprivations; but in her analysis the role is that of a triggering agent rather than an external perturbing force in an otherwise well-balanced system.

Douglas's position offers a better way of considering the relationship between the world models and the millenarian features of environmentalism: the millenarian aspects of environmentalism are to be located in the lack of structure in modern societies. She contends that the lack of strong social articulation leads people at the fringes of society to express their marginality in millenarian movements. In becoming converted to such movements, people express the need for a more meaningful belief system, one which offers redemption and an alternative to the lack of coherence in their lives. In this respect, therefore, the world models carried a message which mapped on to the contemporary millenarian tendencies of the period. '[F]or lack of a discriminating principle, we easily become overwhelmed by our pollution fears. . . . An unstructured society leaves us prey to every dread' (Douglas, 1975: 246–7). The message should not be considered as a solitary, independent triggering agent – an imaginary disaster as it were – but as a social product of the times, and a knowledge resource for symbolizing those times, which both explained them and provided a vision for the future in the form of a perpetual equilibrium society.

Ironically, despite the fact that the message was taken up by various millenarian groups, it was not the intention of the system dynamicists to promote collective radical action. Rather, they sought to solicit those individual actions which would secure a future equilibrium state. To be sure, some did draw radical conclusions from their message, but with Forrester in particular, we find a primary emphasis upon individual values, self-restraint, and the forfeit of aspirations. This implies that the millenarian response, with its attendant radicalism, is not sufficient to explain the popularity of the message. In fact, the focus upon individual adjustment, and subordination to the requirements of the proposed equilibrium society, has direct parallels with the idea that systems analysis and popular ecology have authoritarian implications. This notion has been echoed by a number of writers; for example, Lowe and Worboys assert that popular ecology represents a deeply conservative response to a perceived crisis of authority in Western societies (Lowe and Worboys, 1978: 19). Sullivan (1976: 245) states: 'The real danger in the new perspective is that its grave tones may, in the sombre mood of the present, support a drift toward fatalism and acquiescence in a new totalitarianism.' Also, it is worth adding that the development of systems analysis and its extension into many different areas of social management has been seen by some as a reflection of increasing authoritarianism (Habermas, 1971; Lilienfeld, 1978).

While the authoritarian implications of systems analysis and popular ecology are relevant to the social effects of the world models, we cannot hope to cover so much ground here. However, one important effect which we can consider is the unquestioning individual adjustment (though perhaps on a mass scale) to the message of the world models. This is particularly relevant when we bear in mind the authoritarian overtones of some of the policy recommendations explored by Forrester (for example, one of his policy options for securing world equilibrium included a proposed reduction in food production). Though this type of response is different from that of millenarianism in terms of the social actions which might ensue, it is possible that it reflects similar personal needs. Further, like millenarianism, passivity may be deemed to be non-rational (Douglas, 1973: 186–8; Cohn, 1970: 281–6). For example, it can be argued that the LTG message had both a rational and non-rational aspect: it was rational to be concerned about the environment but arguably non-rational to think that the question of ecology or the environment was above or beyond politics. 'If the ecologists are right about the crisis facing spaceship Earth, this is not the time to move beyond politics or to end politics. If they are right, we are challenged to excruciatingly political decisions about the distribution of power on this planet' (Neuhaus, 1971: 161). This notion of rationality and non-rationality should not be taken in any absolute sense, for it would be incorrect to dismiss certain strands of environmentalism, including the world models, as non-rational and just leave the matter there. Rather, we should try to understand all beliefs as a 'rational' way of coping with certain situations. I have already suggested that the mechanisms of projection and displacement have a bearing upon the apolitical overtones of the LTG message, and it is to these and similar phenomena that we must look to gain an understanding of the passive response.

System Dynamics and Astrology

How are we to understand the mixture of rationality and non–rationality in the responses to the LTG message? And why should people respond positively to its authoritarian implications? In fact, this type of reaction has been discussed before by Adorno in his studies of various authoritarian mass movements in the 1950s. One aspect of his work focused on the content of newspaper astrology columns and various astrological magazines. Adorno was interested in the personal needs which this material exploited; astrological beliefs were seen as a symptom of something that was of greater importance within the wider culture of contemporary North American society. '[W]e want to analyze astrology in order to find out what it indicates as a "symptom" of some tendencies of our society as well as of typical psychological trends amongst those this society embraces' (Adorno, 1974a: 81).

Adorno contended that the aid and comfort offered by astrology requires adjustment to the absurd and contradictory nature of society as seen by many people. Astrological adepts behave rationally to the extent that they are concerned with themselves and controlling their lives, but this is done by conforming to existing social conditions rather than by seeking to change or question them. This is perhaps the more interesting aspect of astrology and one which is present in the message of the world models as well. It is this feature which differentiates its implied social effect from millenarianism where collective radical actions – rather than individual passivity – may ensue.

My conjecture is that Adorno's study can yield some illuminating insights into the nature of system dynamics and the public response to the message of the world models. He was concerned with the susceptibilities and needs that are exploited by cultural phenomena such as astrology, and it would be interesting to examine the similarities between astrology and system dynamics to see if the latter might fulfil or exploit similar personal needs.

One way of structuring the task is to consider the comparison along the following lines. First, I will examine the style of their respective messages – specifically, the way in which each seems to be derived from an abstract source of authority, and the sense of impending doom which pervades their respective predictions. Second, I will refer to their structures as belief systems – in particular the way in which they offer a coherent picture of the world which is based upon a holistic fusion of physical and social reality. I will also refer to the mechanisms of projection and displacement. Third, attention will be turned to their social effects: this will include the solicitation of individual adjustment to social conditions (rather than radical change), together with the expression and reinforcement of people's sense of dependence or helplessness.

Message style

Adorno's study was restricted to those people who take astrology for granted, just like other aspects of culture such as economic forecasts, the cinema, or music. Astrological advice mediated through newspaper columns is seen as emanating from a depersonalized source – the stars – and is interpreted by an expert. Adorno considered astrology columns to be an abstract source of authority which 'attempts to satisfy the longings of people who are thoroughly convinced that others (or some unknown agency) ought to know more about themselves and what they should do than they can decide for themselves' (Adorno, 1974a: 17).

My argument is that scientists and computers are similarly surrounded by myths which also serve to portray them as abstract authorities. Just as there is no way of arguing with the advice of astrology columns, there is (for most people) no way of challenging the authority of a computer: indeed, for some it stands as a symbol of legitimacy. On the one hand, computers have become increasingly employed in all sectors of society, and yet on the other hand a remarkable degree of mystique and ignorance surrounds them. Popular names and images such as 'robots' (an obvious human projection) and electronic 'brain', only serve to perpetuate the myths. (The trade name of one contemporary microcomputer is 'Newbrain', another is known as 'Superbrain'.) Also, the media abound in reports containing statements such as 'Computers show that . . .', or 'Computers predict that. . . .'. The devices themselves are often made the subject of the sentence while the people who program them remain hidden or appear as mere interpreters. Moreover, this confusion is not just to be found among the general public; for experts in computing, such as certain artificial intelligence researchers, have attributed human capacities to machines. Because the LTG message was based on computer simulations it is suggested that the aura surrounding the world-modelling project exploited the same susceptibility to 'authoritative sources' as that exploited by astrology columns.

Another obvious similarity between these two belief systems is the element of doom which gilds their respective predictions. Discussing the nature of the imagery employed by astrologers, Adorno suggested that 'the heavy employment of the "impending doom" device is hardly accidental. It encourages the addressee's destructive urges and feeds on their discomfort in civilization, while at the same time stirring up a bellicose mood' (Adorno, 1974a: 24).

Here Adorno was referring to Freud's theory of the death instinct.

Without being drawn into the controversy about the existence or otherwise of such an instinct, we can at least draw a parallel between 'destructive urges' and the contemporary interest in disasters. In fact a similar element has been observed by Enzensberger, who has conjectured that scenarios of ecological catastrophe played upon the 'delight in the collapse of things' which many people appear to harbour (Enzensberger, 1974: 9). Of course, in more recent years Western society has witnessed another popular form of interest in disaster – the threat of nuclear war. While not wishing to deny the danger in the arms race, it is no exaggeration to say that many people appear to dote on images of total incineration and 'mega-deaths'. Whatever the fundamental explanation of people's interest in disaster, it is plausible to suggest that the images of catastrophe carried by the LTG message exploited that interest in the same way as does astrology. Importantly, in addition to articulating threats, both astrology and system dynamics present a remedy as well: each claims to have knowledge that can be used to exert a measure of control over our lives.

Structures as belief systems

The appeal of astrology lies in the fact that it transforms 'free-floating' anxieties into a definite symbolism; it offers coherence in a world where none may seem to exist and it attracts those who are searching for a meaning to existence. '[I]t also gives some vague and diffused comfort by making the senseless appear as though it had some hidden and grandiose sense while at the same time corroborating that this sense can neither be sought in the realm of the human nor can properly be grasped by humans' (Adorno, 1974a: 84).

System dynamics also offered the promise of coherence by purporting to explain the cause of many disparate societal problems; in locating this explanation at the level of the global system, mankind, and nature, it furnished it with ultimate legitimacy. Moreover, we should not forget the system dynamicists' claim that the human brain is incapable of following the behaviour of a complex feedback system and that computers must be employed to aid this function. In other words, the understanding of feedback systems, the prediction of future world behaviour, was somewhat beyond human competence alone.

Like astrology, system dynamics forced together separate fields of inquiry. Astrology attempts to conflate psychology with astronomy, while system dynamics forced together the properties of physical and social reality – e.g. of electronic and social systems – under the mantle of a general systems theory. In fact, astrology occupies a gap in knowledge left by the division of labour in science, a gap which is located between astronomy and psychology. The conflation of these two sciences is 'non-rational' and another source of the mystery which surrounds astrology, in that it interrelates fields which, at the present state of knowledge, cannot meaningfully be integrated. System dynamics, too, occupies a gap – that between all the disciplines which it has attempted to interrelate. It also had overtones of mystery, derived from its offer of insight into the workings of the world, an offer which was based upon an allegedly new way of thinking.

Although appearing to be a source of mysterious knowledge, astrology sometimes attempts to portray itself as a science. From one point of view it represents the logical outcome of a mechanical deterministic approach to science: human fate is seen to be ruled by the stars which are themselves ruled by mechanical laws. Similarly with system dynamics: though rejecting a linear monocausal approach, system dynamicists reduced social phenomena to the determined behaviour modes of feedback systems. While appearing to be based upon a different way of thinking (a holistic systems approach), it reduced the intricacies of social reality to the simpler properties of physical reality.

Astrology claims to have an insight into the fate of mankind; yet we can see that it in fact projects the social world on to the heavens and therefore displaces a more objective explanation of the events in people's lives. 'Superstition is insight, because it sees together the ciphers of destruction scattered on the social surface . . . from the transfigured society, whose forms it has projected into the skies, it promises itself the answer that could only come from real society' (Adorno, 1974b: 9). If people wish to understand their own lives, or the world around them, they cannot find the answer in the stars, for the real explanations are more likely to lie in society itself. The projection of social phenomena on to the movements of the stars is paralleled in system dynamics by the projection of societal problems on to the properties of feedback structures and nature. 'The battle between the forces of growth and the restraints of nature may be resolved in a number of ways' (Forrester, 1971: 2). Moreover, in a sense system dynamics also purported to explain the 'ciphers of destruction'; bringing together all the disjointed and contrary events and experiences within modern societies, it sought to offer an insight into the workings of the global system which generated them. It neatly summarized all the feelings of malaise and the attendant premonitions that something cataclysmic was about to happen. For example, Forrester believed that system dynamics could explain a vast array of different phenomena – from revolutions and economic crises, to global interactions and social evolution. System dynamics offered a panacea which promised to render all societal problems intelligible.

Social effects

I have already suggested that astrology and system dynamics could encourage individual adjustment to existing social conditions rather than radical change. This is a crucial similarity in their social impact and is complemented by the way in which they may function as ideologies which make conditions bearable. With astrology, this particular aspect of Adorno's thesis rests upon the concept of dependence. He discussed the dependent state of modern man, 'caught by a world of administration' where people feel as if they are powerless pawns. Though modern man may in fact be no more dependent than his ancestors, Adorno argued that he experiences his dependence in a more personal and conscious way. In giving credence to astrology, people express their sense of dependence by seeking to attribute it to a higher and more justifiable source.

This brings us to the concept of displacement which was introduced earlier. In attributing dependence to the stars or to nature and feedback systems, people can justify it while avoiding the admission that they are themselves partly causes of it. Further, these beliefs function in such a way that they reinforce the dependence. 'What drives people into the arms of the various "prophets of deceit" is not only their sense of dependence and their wish to attribute this dependence to some "higher" and ultimately more justifiable sources, but it is also their wish to reinforce their own dependence' (Adorno, 1974a: 82). On this view, astrology should not just be interpreted as an expression of dependence, but also as an ideology *for* dependence: 'an attempt to strengthen and somehow justify painful conditions which seem more tolerable if an affirmative attitude is taken towards them' (Adorno, 1974a: 83).

System dynamics can also be seen to have functioned as an ideology for dependence; it encouraged acceptance of the status quo rather than the collective radicalism found in millenarian movements. For instance, Forrester claimed that in choosing the system mode we wish for our social systems we also choose the pressures under which we must live. If people accept this they are thereby forced to take an affirmative attitude to pressures and stresses.

System dynamics offered to bring structure and coherence into the uncertainty of a crisis-ridden world. By forcing the realization that pressures and stresses were inevitable they could become less debilitating. Instead of leaving people prey to the chaos of seemingly disjunct fears and anxieties, it introduced an element of certainty which was rooted in the grand concepts of nature, the global system, and mankind; this could bring comfort and strengthen the conviction to face up to an existence under pressures, self-restraint, and the forfeit of aspirations.

In projecting their dependence on to the global system and nature, the powerlessness which people felt could become more dignified. Curiously though, while the LTG message resonated with intuitive feelings of dependence, it also seemed to make people appear important. This was because the viability of the proposed equilibrium society required *individual* acts of adjustment. Thus, although the message reflected the social world as it appeared to many people, it also countenanced their credibility by appealing to their sense of (or wish for) personal importance. Making the powerless feel important is of course another aspect of astrology, for while human fate is thought to be governed by the heavens, each horoscope is ultimately individual.

The analogy drawn between astrology and system dynamics has highlighted some of the other personal needs which the message of the world models may have touched. But one problem with the analogy is that it addresses only the personal needs of individuals and cannot tell us anything about why some people resisted or were not susceptible to the message of catastrophe. As with millenarianism, it is necessary to consider the social milieu of the people to whom disasters are likely to appear credible. In fact, Adorno maintained that astrological beliefs could only be understood in relation to social reality as perceived by adherents. The ultimate explanation for such beliefs was thus held to lie in society itself rather than in the psychology of the individual believers. Extending this view to system dynamics, we need a sociological framework to complement what has been said thus far; moreover, it must be capable of explaining the response of those groups who *rejected* the message, thus providing a 'control' for the argument. Again, even among those who reacted positively to the LTG message it is possible to discern a range of responses – from suggestions for authoritarian utopias to proposals for libertarian communes – and so the ideas of projection and displacement, and of personal needs, are simply not fine-grained enough to deal with the specificities of the observable reactions. To achieve a more detailed understanding it will prove useful to return to the grid/group theory of cosmologies.

The Social Roots of Environmental Beliefs

Modern man is not alone in fearing for the safety of his environment, Douglas tells us that most tribal environments are also held to be in danger. Though the natures of the perceived dangers are not the same, she argues that we allocate responsibility for pollution in the same way as do people in primitive societies. Pollution, in her view, is a social construct which is loaded with moral persuasiveness and used as a means of coercion.

For instance, in certain tribal societies, accusations of witchcraft, unnatural sex, and pollution are amongst many similar charges which may be made against specific sections of the community. Douglas argues that these accusations are a means of enforcing power or exerting political control. An accusation of witchcraft or pollution is rooted in a system of knowledge which defines what is 'natural' and 'unnatural'; which distinguishes the honest man from the man-eating witch, the pure from the impure. Thus, those who exert control in this system and its classifications also influence the social system for which the system of knowledge is a necessary support. 'Pollution ideas, however they arise, are the necessary support for a social system. How else can people induce each other to co–operate and behave if they cannot threaten with time, money, God, and nature? These moral imperatives arise from social intercourse. They draw on a view of the environment to support a social order' (Douglas, 1975: 242–3). Within primitive cultures, charges concerning pollution often take one of two distinct forms. First, an accusation of witchcraft (of being a source of pollution, a danger to the rest of society) may be issued by the leaders in order to exert control over some individual or group. Second, the converse of this is that ordinary members of the society may suspect their leaders of corruption and accuse them of witchcraft. The typical targets of the charges depend upon the relative power of the leaders and their followers.

Transferring this line of thought to modern society, Douglas suggests that this age-old formula may well underlie the modern debate concerning the environment. If this is indeed the case, then we must consider the environmental debate in political terms. Douglas maintains that the 'centre' (the leaders) and the 'border' (peripheral groups) of modern societies translate their political objectives into views about pollution and the environment. For example, if a border group considers the 'system', or industrialization (which is often identified with it) to be a bad thing, then pollution may be seen to emanate from social institutions. According to this type of view, man is seen as naturally good whereas institutions are seen as a cause of corruption in men and pollution in nature.

Despite the view that ecology is above or beyond politics the debate over the environment is therefore essentially a political one. Each party to the debate has its own conception of man, nature, and pollution; there is no objective or scientific theory about pollution and the environment; in Douglas's terms they mean different things to different groups.

Figure 9.2 shows how the message of the world models may be interpreted in two distinct ways. One is a centre interpretation and the other represents a border view. For example, a group which is opposed to the establishment, and the industry and technologies identified with it, could latch on to the system dynamicists' concern about growth and

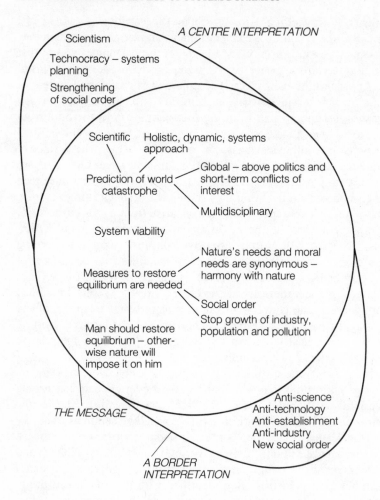

Figure 9.2   Different interpretations of the message

technological fixes in order to reinforce its own position. The important point about this, in relation to the argument developed here, is that each group in the system dynamicists' audience received the same message but drew different conclusions from it. In other words, there were different exoteric interpretations of the esoteric message: different aspects of the message became built into the commonsense, 'self-evident' outlooks of various groups.

In addition to this social dimension of pollution beliefs there is also the psychological dimension referred to earlier. To charge someone else or some other group with pollution is to externalize its causes and project guilt on to parties other than oneself. Thus, in addition to masking the social and political interests of border groups, pollution charges may also mask their complicity in the production of the pollution which they despise.

The concept of the environment as a potential weapon of social control is not the only one which has a bearing upon the message of the world models and their reception. Douglas also draws our attention to the social bases of credibility and to the problem of pollution fears in unstructured societies. Each concept of the environment masks a certain form of social structure and is rooted in a moral consensus that both protects that structure and is in turn reinforced by it. Further, each environment has dangers which are organized into a system of knowledge which allows people to cope with them.

> In essence, pollution ideas are adaptive and protective. They protect
> a social system from unpalatable knowledge. They protect a system
> of ideas from challenge. The ideas rest on classification. Ultimately
> any forms of knowledge depend on principles of classification. But
> these principles arise out of social experience, sustain a given pattern
> and themselves are sustained by it. If this guideline and base is
> grossly disturbed, knowledge itself is at risk. (Douglas, 1975: 245)

Thus the basis of belief in any particular danger (the credibility of the threat), is maintained by a moral consensus within the society. Conversely, the absence of a moral consensus leaves us open to the multiplicity of dangers that may usually confront us without our being aware of them. 'In a sense the obvious risk to the environment is a distraction. The ecologists are indeed looking into an abyss. But on the other side another abyss yawns as frighteningly. This is the terror of intellectual chaos and blind panic' (Douglas, 1975: 245). Douglas conjectures that the lack of structure within modern societies actually increases our pollution fears and leaves us 'prey to every dread' – hence one reason for the millenarian tendencies found in environmentalism. A society with a strong moral consensus embraces a view of the environment which provides discriminating criteria which control danger and allow people to live with many risks which actually surround them. In modern societies, however, the social structure is weakened, scientists are in conflict about what is dangerous and what is not, and we are confronted by an intractable array of reports about possible dangers – from our diet and the air we breathe, to the medicines we consume and the technologies which sustain our material comfort.

These arguments are of considerable relevance to the set of responses which greeted the world models. I have already hinted that these responses reflected the diversity of beliefs in Western society and the discussion of pollution fears is an example of why this is so. To develop this line of reasoning further, in the following section I will discuss the ways in which different cosmologies might be expected to have influenced the reactions of various groups to the message of the models.

Expected Responses to the Message

If we examine the various general conceptions of the universe which the grid/group diagram contains, we can begin to discern the possible variations in belief and interpretation which greeted the world models. With high classification there is a close matching between the purposes of society and nature, which are seen to be in reciprocal interdependence. This of course is similar to the position of the world modellers themselves, and so the response of people with high classification cosmologies is easy to see because the style of thought underlying the message of the models would be similar to their own. We might thus expect a strong concern with maintaining social order, equilibrium with nature, and also an emphasis on the idea of natural laws.

With small-group cosmologies the distinction between inside and outside is transferred to thoughts about nature. Just as society is split between 'them' and 'us', so too nature is divided into the pure and the dangerous. The LTG message could appear to symbolize that part of nature which was 'good' – especially as it was seen to be similarly exploited by the larger society from which the people in the group have withdrawn. Also, we should note that this cosmology is open to millenarianism – the withdrawal from mainstream society and its rewards means that these groups are lured by the threats and promises of millenarian movements.

At high-grid/low-group, people are insulated from each other. This social insulation produces a corresponding insulation between cognitive categories and therefore a low degree of reflexiveness. Hence, these people patch together a cosmology which is often eclectic and contradictory and in which no dominant theoretically-elaborated concept of nature or the environment is to be found. They see the world demarcated by impersonal rules which oppress them. 'Some more than others feel their lives controlled, not by persons, but by things. They wander through a forest of regulations, imponderable forces are represented by forms in triplicate, parking meters, inexorable laws. Their cosmos is dominated by objects of which they and fellow humans are victims' (Douglas, 1973: 90). These people also tend to identify with nature. For our purposes here this has two interesting features. First, some form of union with nature offers a tantalizing escape from the oppressive grid of society; second, the topical themes which centred upon the technological exploitation of nature can be seen as a symbol of the exploitation experienced by these people themselves. Further, Douglas argues that people with strong grid cosmologies are prone to recurrent outbursts of millenarian fervour, periods of belief that some total transformation of the world is at hand. However, another possible tendency – which is noticeably disparate – is passivity. In other words, some of these people might just accept the message as true without seeking to question it. So here we have a social environment that tends to support the form of millenarian and passive responses described earlier.

In contrast, at the other extreme – low grid – we find a characteristic high degree of reflexiveness; there is a tendency for boundaries to be made and broken almost at will and scepticism is a dominant trait. Here, the competition between individuals is strong and exacting in its toll. Nature, however, is identified with all that is innocent and pure, and stands in stark opposition to society. In contrast to earlier conceptions of nature, some groups in modern society (notably those at low group) embrace a unique vision of the natural world. What seems important about these modern conceptions is that nature is no longer viewed as a source of danger. As Douglas points out, nature has come to be seen as an innocent party rather than as an instrument of God's revenge. (People sometimes, for example, viewed adverse weather as a reaction of the gods.) The innocence of nature is a reflection of the alleged innocence of the individual: both are seen to be murderously assaulted by society. Hence, it is possible to suggest that the message could appeal to some of these people because its stress on harmony with nature would resonate with their own feelings *vis-à-vis* society.

However, because of its refined critical apparatus, this cosmology is not prone to millenarian tendencies and people who predict the end of the world are subject to much scrutiny and have to compete like the rest to make their voices heard. Within the individualist environment at low grid we can in fact distinguish another variation on this cosmology. This is represented by autocrats who exert much control over other people; an example of this type of cosmology is referred to by Douglas as 'Big Man'. The Big Man is a remote and powerful leader who is often geographically separated from the bulk of his followers. 'Their ephemeral social contacts and imperviousness to personal pressures enable them to see the cosmos as a rational order not dominated by people but by manipulable objects. These objects are the impersonal rules which govern their transactions. . . . For them it is a rational world whose laws are perfectly intelligible and unmysterious' (Douglas, 1973: 165). So, to these leaders, the world is rational and is to be exploited for their own purposes. Douglas suggests that this cosmology has much in common with certain powerful figures in modern societies who view the world as a morally neutral technical system which is accessible to their own resources. If the message of the world models appealed to these people, we can expect to find that they responded with suggestions for increased regulation and control. Further, those with a particularly technocratic point of view would be biased towards the emphasis of technological solutions to the problems raised by the system dynamicists. On the other hand, in so far as the proposed global equilibrium was construed as a threat to capitalist interests, we might also expect to find negative responses. The low-grid cosmology demands freedom for individual transactions and so talk of regulating production – and thus contracts or transactions – would tend to be resisted.

In line with the discussion of comparative method in chapter 4, it is worthwhile restating the point that the beliefs pertaining to any given cosmology are only intelligible within a comparative framework. Thus, rather than seeking to identify responses purely on the basis of cosmologies viewed in isolation, we must look for differences between responses in comparative terms. To this end it is useful to consider some general trends within the grid/group diagram and thereby use these to aid the identification of responses. For example, we could envisage a continuum of responses running from a plea for unfettered growth at low grid/low group to a no-growth position at high grid/high group. In between these two extremes we would expect to find advocates of balanced or directed growth. Further, running from top (high grid) to bottom (low grid), we might expect a shifting emphasis between order and liberation. This differentiates another no-growth cosmology (at low grid/high group), only this time the stress would be on an alternative society based on individual liberation or alternative communities rather than some form of world government as at high grid.

I have now indicated why and how, on the basis of different cosmologies, various groups might be expected to have responded to the world models. In the following section I will describe some actual responses in connection with the expectations set out here. These reactions will be considered in relation to the cosmology which appears to be held by the group or individual involved; however, I am not offering a definitive identification of these cosmologies because to do so would require a more detailed study of the people concerned. Nevertheless, we can discern important cosmological characteristics among these people and it is contended that these form a sufficient basis for understanding their particular interpretations of the message. Also, I am not attempting to offer a precise description of the social environment from which different responses emanated. This is in line with what was said about making individual predictions with the grid/group diagram in chapter 4, but it does not affect the differentiation of responses according to cosmological beliefs; it merely requires us to observe the possibility that an individual's beliefs are not necessarily always correlated with the social environment in which he or she resides.

Indeed, it is perfectly possible for a person in a given social location to articulate a cosmology which actually corresponds to a different social environment. In other words, we may well be dealing with that person's wished-for pattern of social relations. However, we should expect Douglas's theory to hold in as much as specific configurations of beliefs will still be found together. For example, one is unlikely to find advocates of zero-growth who think that nature should be dominated and controlled by technology. Thus, the goal is to seek to explain various responses to the message on the basis of different interpretations which were refracted through the cosmology held by the particular people involved – whether that cosmology reflected their actual social location, or merely their wish for a different social order.

Exoteric Interpretations of the Message

In this section we will consider some different responses to the message; most of the selected examples were generally favourable. However, I will endeavour to highlight the similarities and differences between them. We may begin by considering several reactions which were rooted in various ideas of authoritarian utopias – i.e. alternative societies based upon centralised authoritarian control – where grid and group would be strong (O'Riordan, 1970). First, we can consider the case of Ophuls who said of the LTG message:

> Admittedly only crude first efforts, these computer simulations of the global ecosystem nevertheless provide a graphic picture of the way in which exponential growth is rapidly thrusting up against natural limits; they seem to show that only quite radical changes in policy will allow us to avoid catastrophic situations in the inevitable transition from growth to equilibrium. (Ophuls, 1973: 227)

Ophuls's proposed solution, which he saw as unpalatable but nonetheless necessary, was to establish Leviathan – or in Douglas's terms, to build up grid and group. 'Only a Hobbesian sovereign can deal with this situation effectively, and we are left with the problem of determining the concrete shape of Leviathan' (Ophuls, 1973: 225). A different utopian vision was provided by the *Blueprint for Survival*, which was published in

1972 and resonated with many of the issues raised by the system dynamicists (Goldsmith et al., 1972). In fact, the *Blueprint* employed the results from the world-modelling project in order to bolster its own case. Goldsmith, a co-author of the report and editor of *The Ecologist*, thus responded favourably to the message. 'The only sensible reaction to the Blueprint for Survival and the Limits to Growth is that their conclusions are obvious – painfully obvious' (Goldsmith, 1972: 3). The picture of the proposed utopia which emerges from *Blueprint* is again a rather authoritarian one. Though Goldsmith was favourable towards small-scale communities he saw them as being integrated into an overall social system which would be marked by hierarchy and order – in which individuals were to be differentiated into different niches.

> Undifferentiated individuals competing for the same ecological niche cannot co-operate in any way. . . . It is only when as a result of competition, they have been found to specialise in such a way that each one learns to exploit a different sub-niche, that co–operation is possible. . . . Competition is the means whereby a hierarchy is set up. In the right conditions. . .the competing individuals eventually arrange themselves so as to constitute a hierarchy and learn to accept their respective positions within this hierarchy. (Goldsmith, 1974: 125)

In fact, Cotgrove (1975) argues that Goldsmith's outlook represents a traditional view of community – that is, one which is characterized by explicit forms of authority and hierarchy, and a belief in natural differences and inequalities; further, in this view, the purposes of society and nature are closely matched and so the optimal social organization is one that allows people's 'true' nature to exert itself. These beliefs of course echo the earlier description of high grid/high group cosmologies in chapter 4.

Another writer with similar 'authoritarian' views is Hardin – he also responded positively to the WORLD 3 model. 'The book is receiving wide notice and thoughtful discussion. Perhaps this time the message will be remembered. Perhaps, this time Cassandra will be believed. Let us hope so' (Hardin, 1972: 23). In his 'The Tragedy of the Commons' (1968) Hardin called for mutual coercion to enforce population control. In Cotgrove's words, this was as a forceful expression of the 'emphasis on order and traditional authority emerging from the will of the community' (Cotgrove, 1975: 24).

> The most important aspect of necessity that we must now recognize, is the necessity of abandoning the commons in breeding. No

technical solution can rescue us from the misery of overpopulation. Freedom to breed will bring ruin to all. At the moment, to avoid hard decisions many of us are tempted to propagandize for conscience and responsible parenthood. The temptation must be resisted, because an appeal to independently acting consciences selects for the disappearance of all conscience in the long run, and an increase in anxiety in the short. (Hardin, 1968: 1248)

And in similar vein to Ophuls, Hardin argued that it was necessary to cede power to a hierarchy of custodians (Hardin, 1968: 1246).

In chapter 4 the comparative analysis between SPRU and SDG illustrated a cosmology which was at lower grid and group than that of the system dynamicists. SPRU were committed to directed growth, but a similar view was also taken by Bray, a British Labour MP and a member of the Club of Rome. He also rejected the message of the world models; reviewing *The Limits to Growth* he stated: 'There may well be a role for simple global material flow models, even of the simplicity of that in this book, but to have any practical implications for policy they will have to be more firmly based in reality, and better linked with the more complex systems behaviour models which man has found necessary throughout history' (Bray, 1972b: 112). Rejecting the call for zero-growth, he advocated growth to meet human needs.

[T]he continued growth of GNP . . . is needed to meet the many human needs in all nations, including provision for a rapidly expanding population for the next 50 to 100 years. In practical human and political terms it is much easier to redress serious inequalities, and to provide for new needs within nations and between nations if men feel their own conditions of life are improving. (Bray, 1972a: 19)

Another expression of the need for controlled growth can be found in *Catastrophe or New Society*, a report on a world-modelling project conducted by a group in Latin America (Herrera et al., 1976). In this project – which was an explicit reaction to the pessimism of LTG – the aim was to explore the transition from the present world economy towards one in which resources would be allocated according to the goal of meeting basic needs for all people. In opposition to the views characterized by LTG we find the statement:

The stance of the present authors is radically different: it is argued that the major problems facing society are not physical but sociopolitical. These problems are based on the uneven distribution of power, both between and within nations. The result is oppression and alienation, largely founded on exploitation. The deterioration of the physical environment is not an inevitable consequence of human progress, but the result of social organizations based on destructive values. (Herrera et al., 1976: 7–8)

What of the cosmology of the Big Man: this is to be found among those objectors to the message who called for unfettered growth; these were technocrats and leaders of large corporations – advocates of unrestrained economic forces and the market economy. Such a position which called for growth *per se* was represented by Gaines, senior Vice-President and economist for Manufactures Hanover Trust. In 'The Doomsday Debate' he wrote:

> It is growth, after all that will provide the products and services needed to eliminate want worldwide and to reduce pollution without reducing the real scale of living of people. Also, growth provides the incentive for technological breakthroughs that will restrain our consumption of limited resources by developing economically usable substitutes. (Gaines, 1972: 1)

Another 'Big Man' cosmology may be attributed to Peccei, the head of the Club of Rome. He welcomed the world models but did not agree with the system dynamicists on the matter of halting industrial growth.

Cotgrove draws attention to the fact that some of the environmentalist groups displayed tinges of what Mannheim (1936) described as 'orgiastic chiliasm'. This refers to certain feelings of ecstatic immediacy which attend the idea that a sudden and total transformation of the world is at hand. It is a characteristic which is found among some millenarian groups and it can be discerned to a varying degree amongst certain supporters of the LTG message. For example, it can be seen in one form in the publication *Towards Survival* which gave qualified support to the message. Notably, the editors of this publication sought to draw membership from those who 'are already convinced, from their own thinking, reading and observing the world around them, that we are entering the most crucial period in the history of mankind' (Towards Survival, 1972). For another example we can turn to Allaby, who was one of the co-authors of the *Blueprint for Survival* and therefore also favourable to the LTG message. He viewed the environmental movement as a kind of revolution; interestingly, it was to be like a 'religious conversion' rather than a violent political upheaval.

Their revolution may involve a certain amount of violence, but this will be accidental and incidental: there will be no barricades, blood will not flow in the streets. The environmental revolution will be gentler and more violent than that, for its target is the very fabric of society itself. It can succeed only if it changes the hearts of the majority of men. . . . The revolution in this sense is much more akin to a religious conversion, a 'turning about at the seat of conscious-ness'. (Allaby, 1971: 76)

These examples provide evidence for the millenarian interpretations which might have emerged with insulated, or small-group cosmologies; the LTG message appearing to confirm the millenarian outlook to which these groups were prone. Further, I might add that the temporal uncertainty pertaining to the date of the predicted catastrophe would resonate with the millenarian's sense of immediacy – the exact timing of the total transformation was unknown, but its signs were already at hand, it was imminent.

The LTG found a ready audience amongst many other groups who were associated with the counter-culture of the time. These sections of the environmental movement have been the subject of a large investigative literature (for an introduction and source of further references see: Cotgrove, 1975; Cotgrove and Duff, 1980; Enzensberger, 1974; Lowe and Worboys, 1978; Sandbach, 1980; Sills, 1975; Sullivan, 1976); without referring to specific named groups it is useful to draw upon this material in order to paint a general picture of their reactions. For example, some groups expounded views which were almost the complete antithesis of the aims of the traditional environmentalists. Cotgrove labels these people 'liberal environmentalists' (this dichotomy between traditional and liberal corresponds to the order/liberation distinction made in reference to the grid/group diagram).

By contrast, the 'eco-activists', 'eco-freaks', and other environmen-tally oriented expressions of the counter-culture are opposed to almost everything that the traditional community stands for. Indeed many of its activities – the challenge to traditional sexual ethics, the use of drugs, the rejection of hierarchy and institutionalised rule-governed behaviour in the pursuit of liberation – are amongst the indicators of social pathology which traditional environmental-ists' reassertion of community seeks to cure. (Cotgrove, 1975: 29)

However, despite these important differences, like the traditional environmentalists the libertarian groups were also opposed to reductionist modes of thought. They believed that the apprehension of the world required an ecologically-oriented holistic way of thinking. It is therefore not surprising that the world modellers' concern for nature, coupled with their systems approach, should have proved appealing.

Finding society (the centre) oppressive, some liberal environmentalists opted for a survival strategy. Withdrawing into self-sufficient communes, they adopted alternative philosophies and lifestyles – sometimes with a strong religious orientation, typically culled from Eastern thought. As we saw in chapter 7, Meadows's project team also admired the view of nature expounded in Eastern philosophies. These people became, or wanted to become, a small group or sect. Enzensberger referred to them as 'eco-freaks'. 'They live in rural communes, grow their own food, and seek a "natural way of life". . . . Their class background corresponds to that of the hippies of the 1960s – of reduced middle-class origin, enriched by elements of peripheral groups' (Enzensberger, 1974: 8). Such people would typically have come from social environments which were individualist or insulated; the move to form groups being a reaction against the lack of personal bonds and experience of control by impersonal rules. If members from individualist environments, their action also corresponded to a rejection of the competition it involves – a renouncement of its rewards and a longing to escape its pressures.

Once formed into sects, the sectarians would have perceived a strong boundary between themselves and the outside (the centre) and the catastrophe predicted by the models would have been a powerful reinforcement of this boundary. Indeed, Douglas suggests that the stronger the boundary is, the greater is the degree of hate and vengeance with which prophetic threats are loaded. Hence the world models would have been appealing not only because they could be seen to justify the withdrawal from society, but also because they resonated with this potent element of small group cosmologies. In *Risk and Culture* Douglas and Wildavsky discuss the sectarian nature of some American environmentalist groups – such as 'Friends of the Earth' – who are considered to adopt typical border strategies: 'attacking centre programs on behalf of nature, God, or the world is a border strategy' (Douglas and Wildavsky, 1982: 137). Further, they assert that 'FOE maintains an almost utopian vision of future society in which all forms of life will exist harmoniously without political, economic, and technological restraints. We hear the sectarian overtones of love, cosmic unity, and resistance to centre machinations' (Douglas and Wildavsky, 1982: 136).

In most cases these responses bear out, and in no instance refute, the general style of the expectations set out in the previous section. Although I have only looked at a few cosmological characteristics it would of course be possible – as in the case of SPRU – to carry out a more detailed analysis. I have primarily focused on the differences between responses to the models, but a number of the selected examples shared the conviction that the world situation was problematic. Further, they all had their own particular prescriptions for a better future – for example, prescriptions which might take the form of a new utopia or a revival of the utopia perceived in past traditional societies. The different views – from technocratic optimism and the promotion of unrestrained growth, through the idea of directed growth and the meeting of basic needs, to the call for an end to growth – were complemented by different beliefs about nature and society. In concert, these beliefs led to various interpretations of the world modellers' message from which disparate inferences were drawn. For example, we have seen that the idea of ending growth was a feature of the authoritarian utopias advocated by Goldsmith, Hardin, and Ophuls, in which man would yield to natural laws. In contrast, those who advocated more libertarian forms of utopia – in which grid and group would presumably be weaker – placed an emphasis upon directing growth for human purposes. Thus, the more positive affirmations of the message emanated from those who posited utopias which, being implicitly marked by strong grid and group, had something in common with the equilibrium state adumbrated by the system dynamicists.

We can conclude that the social effects of the message of the world models were neither simple nor homogeneous within its target audience. (Further, to the extent that the debate still persists, these effects may be detected as long as discussion continues.) The message resonated within a social context in which certain groups were looking for a coherent view of global problems, and system dynamics offered a suitable mapping of the world which was appealing for a variety of social, political, and psychological reasons. The environmental debate – to which the world models were a stimulus – was a forum for different political interests where various groups employed different conceptions of the environment, including different interpretations of the message, in order to argue for their own particular goals. Further, we have seen that these conceptions can be distinguished by considering the cosmology employed by the groups involved, and that this also informs their specific interpretations. In other words, the message did not simply diffuse amongst different groups, but was subject to various exoteric interpretations.

The world models played upon certain personal needs which are particularly pertinent to the millenarian and passive responses. System dynamics offered a belief system which shared important similarities to that of astrology, in terms of style, structure, and social effect. Moreover, the analogy with astrology not only illuminates the personal function of system dynamics within the passive response, for it also increases our understanding of the other responses too. A belief in imminent catastrophe has a social dimension, but we have seen that it also has a psychological basis in a fascination with destruction. This is also the case with projection and the need to maintain cognitive security.

It should also be mentioned that the focus on society as a systemic whole appeared among many of the responses. As implied earlier, a systems view of society can tend to negate the idea of class conflicts and as such its apolitical – if not suprapolitical – stance appeals to certain people. On a personal level, it might be that some people seized upon the LTG message because it absolved them of complicity in the global problems with which they were concerned. By ignoring the role of conflict amongst the causes of contemporary problems, people could ignore their own complicity in them – or at least their own individual helplessness in the face of such problems and conflicts. Of course this does not mean that such people absolved themselves of blame entirely. Quite the contrary, the stress upon system interdependence – often allied to the rhetoric of 'we are all in the same boat' – admitted blame; but because it was equally apportioned it can therefore be considered to have become its own negation.

I have tried to open up an area of discussion on a topic where I felt that the conventional explanations for the appeal of the world models have not done justice to the variety of social and personal factors which are implicated in the various responses of different people. Though the discussion remains somewhat speculative, especially with regard to the millenarian and passive responses, speculation must precede more detailed empirical investigations if important insights and new areas of inquiry are not to become prematurely foreclosed.

10   Conclusions

Before proceeding to a general discussion, I will recap on the main parts of the argument developed in the preceding chapters. My investigation has shown that system dynamics cannot be narrowly defined as a mere technique and is best viewed as a body of knowledge with several dimensions – each of which makes sense only in relation to a specific nexus of questions. In other words, system dynamics is not a 'thing in itself'; rather, its perception depends upon one's perspective. For example, technical questions about the computer simulation stages of system dynamics modelling fall within the appropriate domains of mathematics and computer science. This, however, is not an area which has been of interest here; rather, the analysis here has sought to address quite different questions. For instance, I have shown that system dynamics may be considered as a type of social theory, or a social cosmology which mediates and reinforces specific patterns of social relations.

I began the analysis by drawing an analogy between the worldviews of Forrester and Parsons. This showed that they shared a number of important theoretical beliefs and value orientations, and this gave plausibility to the idea of seeing whether – like Parsons – Forrester too could be considered to be located within a middle-class conservative tradition which was primarily concerned with the problem of maintaining social order. Looking at the development of system dynamics, we saw that this idea could enable us to explain its inherent theoretical shifts and domain expansions.

The development of system dynamics has been marked by its extension to successive new domains – from the corporation, to the city, the world, and then national economies – with consequent expansions of its theoretical core. Each new application has been addressed to a specific social crisis, which it has sought to ameliorate without challenging the controlling institutions of society. In each case the basic concern was the restoration of social order. With the emergence of the world models the system dynamicists raised the idea of arresting economic growth. The environmental crisis was perceived as a portent of severe social breakdown and the preservation of social order was again of the imperative – even if it meant halting growth, which would challenge both the short-term interests of capitalism and its traditional growth-oriented ethos.

Of course halting growth could conceivably undermine the whole logic of capitalist production, as Habermas has pointed out:

> Capitalist societies cannot follow imperatives of growth limitation without abandoning their principles of organization; a shift from unplanned, nature-like capitalist growth to qualitative growth would require that production be planned in terms of *use values*. The development of productive forces, cannot, however, be uncoupled from the production of *exchange values* without violating the logic of the system. (Habermas, 1976: 42–3)

Whether Forrester himself perceived this implication is another matter; his views on halting economic growth were a reflection of his deep commitment to social order rather than a challenge to capitalism *per se*. It does show, however, that his thought had a certain detachment in relation to capitalist interests.

The next task – undertaken in chapters 4 through 7 – was to obtain a more detailed description of the system dynamicists' style of thought and their social experience. To do this I employed the grid/group theory of cosmologies and compared the System Dynamics Group with the Science Policy Research Unit. The ensuing analysis showed that on three different levels – thought styles (including questions of modelling methodology and response to theoretical anomalies), the content of cosmologies, and social experience – we could reach the same conclusions about the relative grid/group position of each group. On each level it was found that SDG were in a relatively higher grid/group position than SPRU.

The system dynamicists appear to have had no doubts about the efficacy of system dynamics; for them it described the properties of a world that is actually systemic. The exploration of their social cosmology indicates a social component in their unshakeable faith – it was correlated with their social environment: the greater fixity of their cognitive categories *vis-à-vis* the control group (SPRU) correlated with a higher grid/group setting. Their cognitive categories were taken as veritable truths and no other view of the universe was open to them.

In chapter 8 I investigated the social and political effects of system dynamics. Given the lack of empirical evidence – itself a consequence of the very nature of the politics of expertise – the discussion therefore encompassed speculative areas. For example, on the question of the use of system dynamics for policy formation, I have argued that a system dynamics model may not just be used to promote social cohesion – through economic, social, and political measures – but may also be used to negotiate consensus through education. This brings us back to the difference between system dynamics and techniques – which remain solely esoteric or narrowly technical; system dynamics aimed to map out the policies for the control and management of social systems, but also sought incorporation in curricula at all levels of education. The teaching of system dynamics – and therefore socialization into the cosmology that carries it – would aim to secure a broad social consensus.

In my discussion of the urban-modelling work I set out reasons why the policy recommendations could be perceived as legitimate by politicians and the electorate. I also argued that these reasons were pertinent to system dynamics in general. Douglas contends that men use their cosmologies in order to coerce each other, that they make appeals which usually contain some reference to time, money, God, or nature. The analysis of system dynamics shows that we can find all four elements. Taking time first; the system dynamicists argued that time was not on man's side, that the outcome of his actions can take many years to produce their full effect. Thus, although their prophecy of world catastrophe located it some time within the coming century, they argued the necessity for taking action now. Second, the monetary dimension can be discerned in the stance against massive financial programmes for alleviating the problems of cities and the belief that successful schemes must be intrinsically low-cost. Third, though the concept of 'God' was not employed in any direct way, I have noted Forrester's discussion of the prominent role of religious institutions in any future equilibrium society. Fourth, system dynamics is imbued with unambiguous views concerning the natural ordering of the universe; whether it is the necessity of urban pressures, urban goals, or a world equilibrium, all were perceived as being a reflection of a natural state of affairs.

The arguments presented and developed in chapter 9 have been the most speculative. The scope of the problem of understanding the effects of the world models was both challenging and somewhat daunting in its prospect. Despite this, I sought to explain some of the more manifest features of the episode, such as the differential interpretation of the message. I also raised the question of millenarianism and therefore issues about the general social context of the time. While avoiding the inference that the prophecy of catastrophe caused a millenarian outburst amongst the young and disaffected, I nevertheless contended that it did provide a convenient focal point, as well as a resource for those groups with millenarian tendencies. Just as millenarians are usually vague about the.

precise timing of the total transformation which they await, the world models also avoided exact predictions about the date of world collapse. On a personal level this temporal uncertainty reflected and strengthened an uncertainty due in part to the unstructuredness of the social environment within which millenarian groups resided.

Following on from this discussion I drew an analogy between system dynamics and astrology which showed that the former had a potential for touching or exploiting other personal needs and susceptibilities. The analogy therefore revealed some aspects of system dynamics – for example, the fascination with disasters – that have not emerged in previous studies. The most problematic implication to emerge from the comparison between system dynamics and astrology concerned its potential for eliciting the unquestioning acceptance of the proposed policies, and I briefly expanded on this issue in terms of its social ramifications. I drew attention, for example, to the fact that a number of writers had argued that systems analysis had authoritarian implications. While not pursuing those arguments, the comparison showed their relevance to system dynamics. Moving on from the question of individual personal needs, I acknowledged that an explanation pitched at such a level could not cope with the diversity of beliefs and disbeliefs which greeted the message of the world models and that a sociological explanation was required. Turning once again to Douglas's grid/group diagram I showed how it could be used to differentiate and make sense of the range of reactions.

This study has shown that system dynamics has authoritarian tendencies which can be discerned at several levels. First, there is the nature of some of the policy recommendations – from reducing food production to the control of urban populations by manipulation of the low-rent housing market. Second, there is the abstract form of system dynamics modelling and the air of objective authority which emanates from the use of computers and esoteric techniques. Third, there are the pedagogical and wider consequences inherent in the teaching of system dynamics. Fourth, there is the role of system dynamics experts in policy formation. While I have examined only the case of system dynamics, it is worth noting that the discussion has also implicitly raised questions about the wider uses of systems theories generally.

I contend that this investigation has fulfilled the three objectives set out in the preface: namely, it has examined the cultural tradition from which system dynamics emerged, and which shaped its development; secondly, it has analysed the relationship between the system dynamicists' social experience and the intellectual style and content of their work and beliefs; and thirdly, it has illuminated the social role of system dynamics in mediating and reinforcing different patterns of social relations.

The pursuit of these goals has been effected with the expectations of two academic communities in mind: sociologists of knowledge and systems theorists. In terms of the former, the most elaborate and empirically substantiated argument is that presented in chapters 4 through 7. As for the systems community, I have sought to marshall unconventional tools – drawn largely from sociology and anthropology – in order to explain the development of one specific strand of the systems movement. The construction of this explanation has been informed by the need to provide different perspectives and to adopt a broad holistic view of the problem. I have not attempted to advance systems theory in itself, but the investigation has provided an interpretation of the development of system dynamics which could inform decisions about future goals of the systems movement. Both at the knowledge level of how our social constructions arise, and at the policy level of how social change might be effected, this case study of system dynamics may help to stimulate some debate concerning key issues central to those goals. Of course this is not to suggest that the account articulated here is in any way total, merely that it has opened a unique window on the subject. Indeed, it is partly in relation to existing accounts that mine is to be judged; this is the theme of the next section.

Relationship to Other Lines of Inquiry

I have examined system dynamics in relation to various theoretical ideas concerning the relationship between knowledge and social structures. Implicit in what has been said is the awareness that 'knowledge' and 'social structure' are themselves theoretical constructs – abstractions, or fast-frozen glimpses of the much wider and deeper phenomenon which we refer to as culture. In chapter 2 I argued that approaches such as those based upon the dichotomies of internal/external history, science/ideology, base/superstructure, or cognitive/social, could not yield the type of understanding of system dynamics which I sought. The different features of system dynamics which have been uncovered would have been closed off if those approaches had been followed. For example, I noted Forrester's commitment to capitalism; but we have also seen that this does not exhaustively explain the social underpinnings of his work, which in fact had a certain autonomy in relation to the social context which nurtured it. Other critics have viewed system dynamics purely in relation to capitalist interests; the rigidity of the base/superstructure model which they have explicitly or implicitly adopted has prevented them from seeing that it cannot account for a number of the more important features of system dynamics. For instance, they could not explain the moralistic imperatives within system dynamics, nor could they account for the moral compulsion and legitimacy of some of the policy recommendations with which we have dealt, or the variation in beliefs which greeted the world models. Neither could these other approaches explain Forrester's ideas about halting economic growth.

The same applies to those critics whose analysis is grounded in some version of idealism. In such an intellectual framework the question of the social constraints upon the system dynamicists' thought can hardly be formulated. To take just one example, idealism cannot explain the observed correlations among social experience, thought styles, and cosmological beliefs found in the comparative analysis of SDG and SPRU. Moreover, neither economic reductionism nor idealism could account for the domain expansions and theoretical shifts which have marked the development of system dynamics; and the same can be said of analyses based on the internal/external dichotomy.

I have also sought to circumvent the problems which arise if analysis proceeds by trying to establish whether or not system dynamics is science or ideology. For science too is a cultural product, and we have seen that it is not possible to elude the social mediation of ideas concerning pollution, nature, or the relationship of the self to society. Thus, I could not have understood the social effects of the world models if they had been viewed as mere ideology, for the understanding would only have been tenable in relation to the assumption that there could be a scientific concept of the natural order which was devoid of social implications and meanings. Further, the anthropological approach has revealed the factors which have lent credibility to the message of the world models. Arguments based on a dichotomy between science/ideology assume that scientific knowledge is accepted as being true because of the force of reason. They would not, however, have any substantive hypotheses to explain why so many different groups – including scientists – gave credence to the idea that the world faced a catastrophe. Going beyond the fact that some people perceived the system dynamicists as scientists, and therefore regarded the message as objective, I have tried to show that the models symbolized important cosmological issues which were consequently interpreted in line with the cosmological beliefs of different groups. If system dynamics had been viewed as either science or ideology, then I could not have explained this variation, nor the differential inferences which different groups drew from the message.

Moreover, if I had adopted the received view of the transmission of scientific ideas – which is typically based on a production-diffusion model – again I would have failed to grasp these specificities. In Fleckian terms, I have tried to show that the public reception of scientific ideas is not one of mere diffusion, but can be a process of multiple interpretation within the cosmologies of different exoteric circles.

In terms of the sociological study of science, the analysis of the response to theoretical anomalies has shown that the work of Douglas and Bloor may also yield useful results outside the domain of the natural sciences and mathematics. Indeed, the study of system dynamics has shown the applicability of their conceptual tools to a subject breeching the gap between the natural and social sciences.

Reservations

Though this amounts to a justification for the approach which I have taken, it is not intended to suggest that it has explained everything, or indeed that other problems have not arisen as a very consequence of the approach. Certainly there are other questions about system dynamics which cannot be accommodated within the scope of this framework. Some of these are due to lack of information concerning the System Dynamics Group but others are methodological in origin. In the first case I have already mentioned (in chapter 8) that I do not have sufficient data to draw inferences about the consequences of the nature of system dynamics teaching – that is, in terms of the pedagogical relationship between teacher and taught. This is important because this relationship is one of power; it is a control system which is mediated by the curriculum. As such it is – as Bernstein has shown – another example of the interaction between social relations and symbolic systems. In principle, however, we could discuss this further if the requisite information were obtained.

I do not wish to imply that the social effects of system dynamics can be considered in a vacuum – that is, without detailed attention being paid to the social locations in which it is disseminated; this would fall into the traps of philosophical idealism. Rather, as the argument in chapter 9 has shown, groups in different social contexts may take what they want from system dynamics and incorporate it into their own socially constructed views of the world. Thus, system dynamics may become modified because of the different cognitive constraints imposed by alternative social structures.

On the methodological front, I could not adequately deal with the individual variations among the system dynamicists. While not disallowing the possibility of dissent within the group of people who embraced system dynamics – indeed, I noted the differences in opinion concerning backcasting – the theoretical net constituted by the grid/group theory could not capture the specificities of these differences. Rather, it has been public knowledge which has been the focus of concern here.

Another and more complex methodological question centres on the fact that I have relied on textual extracts for my source of empirical evidence. Critics might demand direct empirical observation or a consideration of more informal sources. Others might also require that the investigation should start not with beliefs as given by evidence in texts, but with discourse. Indeed, the development of the formal record of system dynamics which I have sought to explain here is but one type of discourse and so I am not in a position to address others.

It may be objected that throughout the argument I have been treading a thin line between a socio-anthropological explanation of the development of system dynamics and an evaluation of its content. While not denying that a certain evaluative element has tended to follow the exposition – rather like a shadow, now hidden, now exposed – I feel that it has been restricted to the purpose of bringing the system dynamicists' perspective into sharper focus. Thus, if I have said that system dynamics eschewed the idea of class-conflicts, I have – to use Mannheim's term – shown its particularity. In other words, I have not been trying to show that system dynamics was either true or false, but rather, that its perspective was particular to a specific style of thought – itself related to a particular social context.

> [T]he different perspectives are not merely particular in that they presuppose different ranges of vision and different sectors of the total reality, but also in that the interests and powers of perception of the different perspectives are conditioned by the social situations in which they arose and to which they are relevant. (Mannheim, 1936: 255)

There is also another sense in which this investigation has been evaluative; this has surfaced in connection with the discussion of the social effects of system dynamics where I pointed to its theoretical closure and potential authoritarian characteristics. I would argue that these were a legitimate subject of investigation, but in the very act of unmasking them I have inevitably made evaluations. To balance this I might assert that other global theories, or world hypotheses, have their own particular closures too. Further, I have focused on the disadvantages of a cosmology marked by higher grid and group than the selected control, but in fact Douglas's work shows that all cosmologies have their own characteristic problems and woes.

Other critical remarks may be made with regard to the overall theoretical basis of this piece of work. Where it has seemed pertinent I have endeavoured to draw attention to the problematical and less rigorous aspects of the arguments; but there is also the question of the eclecticism manifested in the number of disparate intellectual strands from which I have borrowed in order to expand the scope of the investigation. These strands are variously similar and dissimilar and on certain points I have perhaps given insufficient attention to their critical evaluation. Instead, I have chosen to use them as theoretical tools – if, at times, somewhat brutally – in order to develop my case.

Given the nature of the subject matter, I might perhaps crave leniency and ask to be judged finally on whether I have succeeded in shedding some light on areas where hitherto there has been darkness, confusion, or controversy.

Notes

Preface

1 For example, see: J. R. Burns, D. W. Malone (1974) Optimization Techniques Applied to the Forrester Model of the World, *IEEE Transactions on Systems, Man and Cybernetics*, SMC-4(2), 164–71; F. E. Burke (1973) Ignorance about Limitations to Growth, *Nature*, 246, (23 Nov.), 226–30; H. S. D. Cole, R. C. Curnow (1973) 'Backcasting' with the World Dynamics Models, *Nature*, 243, (11 May), 63–5; J. G. M. Cuypers (1973) World dynamics: Two Simplified Versions of Forrester's Model, *Automatica*, 9, 399–401; A. R. Gourlay, J. M. McLean, P. Shepherd (1977) Identification and Analysis of the Subsystem Structure of Models, *Applied Mathematical Modelling*, 1 (June), 245-52; D. C. J. de Jongh (1978) Structural Parameter Sensitivity of 'The Limits to Growth' World Model, *Applied Mathematical Modelling*, 2 (June), 77–80; K. E. Sahlin (1979) System dynamics models: some obscurities, *IEEE Transactions on Systems, Man and Cybernetics*, SMC-9(2), 91–3; M. Stonebraker (1972) A Simplification of Forrester's Model of an Urban Area, *IEEE Transactions on Systems, Man and Cybernetics*, SMC-2(4), 468–72.

2 For example, see: H. M. Enzensberger (1974) A Critique of Political Ecology, *New Left Review*, 84, 3–31; J. Galtung (1973) 'The Limits to Growth' and Class Politics, *Journal of Peace Research*, 12, 101–14; R. Golub, J. Townsend (1977) Malthus, Multinationals and the Club of Rome, *Social Studies of Science*, 7, 201–22; R. Lilienfeld (1975) Systems Theory as Ideology, *Social Research*, 42(4), 637–60; R. Lilienfeld (1978) *The Rise of Systems Theory: An Ideological Analysis* (New York: J. Wiley and Sons).

Chapter 1 The History of System Dynamics

1 A. Peccei is an Italian industrialist who is a former director of Fiat and Olivetti. The Club Of Rome describes itself as: '*Not* a political organization, either of the right or of the left, but a free assembly of individuals seeking to find a more objective and comprehensive basis for policymaking.' A. King

(1974) The Club of Rome Today, *Simulation in the Service of Society*, 4(8), 1–7. See also: A. King (1981) The Club of Rome and its Policy Impact, in W. M. Evan (ed), *Knowledge and Power in a Global Society* (Beverly Hills, California: Sage Publications), 205–24; A. Peccei (1982) Global Modelling for Humanity, *Futures*, April, 91–4; A. Peccei (1969) *The Chasm Ahead* (London: Macmillan Co.); A. Peccei (1973) The New Threshold, *Simulation*, 20(6), 119–206.

Chapter 2   System Dynamics – a Cultural Artefact

1 K. Popper (1959) *The Logic of Scientific Discovery* (London: Hutchinson). Popper's demarcation criterion centres on the idea of falsifiability, whereby a hypothesis is judged to be scientific if it is intrinsically open to falsification through empirical testing. Kuhn offers a very different picture of science in which he differentiates between 'normal' and 'revolutionary' science. Kuhn argues that normal science is distinguished by the activity of 'puzzle-solving' in which scientists solve puzzles that have been defined by the tools of the paradigm within which they work. Unlike Popper, however, Kuhn does not see any one criterion as being decisive. See also: T. S. Kuhn (1970) *The Structure of Scientific Revolutions* (Chicago: The University of Chicago Press); T. S. Kuhn (1977) Logic of Discovery or Psychology of Research, in *The Essential Tension* (Chicago: University of Chicago Press).

2 This idea is derived from Douglas and other work in the sociology of knowledge. For example, Bloor argues – according to his 'strong programme in the sociology of knowledge' – that the same types of causal explanation must be sought in explaining *both* true and false beliefs. See: D. Bloor (1976) *Knowledge and Social Imagery* (London: Routledge and Kegan Paul); B. Barnes (1973) The Comparison of belief-systems: Anomaly Versus Falsehood, in R. Horton, R. Finnegan (eds), *Modes of thought* (London: Faber and Faber), 182–198.

3 L. Laudan (1981) The Pseudo-Science of Science?, *Philosophy of the Social Sciences*, 11(2), 173–98. For a reply see: D. Bloor (1981) The Strengths of the Strong Programme, in the same issue, 199–213. See also: H. Meynell (1977) On the Limits of the Sociology of Knowledge, *Social Studies of Science*, 7, 489–500; E. Millstone (1977) A Framework for the Sociology of Knowledge, *Social Studies of Science*, 7, 111–25; M. Mulkay (1980) Sociology of Science in the West, *Current Sociology*, 28(3), (Winter), 1–184; S. Woolgar (1981) Interests and Explanation in the Social Study of Science, *Social Studies of Science*, 11, 365–94. For a reply to Woolgar see: B. Barnes (1981) On the 'Hows' and 'Whys' of Cultural Change (Response to Woolgar), *Social Studies of Science*, 11, 481–98.

Chapter 3   Social Engineering: From Corporate Power to Crises of Social Order

1 A criticism of Gouldner's position on this point is to be found in: S. M. Lipset, E. C. Ladd, Jr (1972) The Politics of American Sociologists, *American*

206 NOTES TO PAGES 60-101

Journal of Sociology, 78, July, 67-104. This issue of the *AJS* also contains other critiques of Gouldner; earlier reviews appeared in Volume 77, No. 1. For other criticisms see: J. Urry (1972) More Notes on Sociology's Coming Crisis, *British Journal of Sociology*, 23, 246-8; C. E. Swanson (1971) in a review symposium on Gouldner's book, *American Sociological Review*, 36, 317-21. In the same series of reviews, a more positive critique comes from S. E. Deutsch (1971), 321-6.

For other critiques of Parsons's work see: C. Wright Mills (1970) *The Sociological Imagination* (Harmondsworth: Pelican Books); D. Lockwood (1956) Some Remarks on 'The Social System', *British Journal of Sociology*, VII, 134-46; D. Walsh (1972) Functionalism and Systems Theory, in P. Filmer (ed.) *New Directions in Sociological Theory* (London: Collier and Macmillan), 57-74; R. W. Friedrichs (1970) *A Sociology of Sociology* (New York: The Free Press).

For Gouldner's reply to some of his critics: A. W. Gouldner (1975) *For Sociology* (Harmondsworth: Penguin).

Chapter 4 Cosmology, Knowledge, and Social Structure: Technical Issues

1 In describing the development of his thought Bernstein (1971: 122) includes a quotation from Sapir which encapsulates the importance to be attributed to the role of language in the construction of reality: 'It is quite an illusion to imagine that one adjusts to reality essentially without the use of language and that language is merely an incidental means of solving specific problems of communication or reflection. The fact of the matter is that the real world is to a large extent unconsciously built up on the language habits of the group.'

2 For a very basic discussion of some of the issues involved, see: Open University (1977) Language and Social Class, *E202 Schooling and Society*, Unit 23, Block IV (Milton Keynes: Open University Press).

Chapter 6 Dealing with Monsters: Methodology and Thought Styles

1 I do not advocate the general use of backcasting simulation models, nor do I explore its ultimate legitimacy. Moreover, it must be said that neither of these two groups regarded backcasting as being in any way fundamental to the wider debate on world simulation models. This does not however detract from its usefulness for the purposes here.

2 It should also be noted that not all difference equations can be backcast; for example, the SPRU team cite the case of Bessel's difference equation for certain parameter values.

3 In the light of what was to follow his remark was most significant for several distinct ways of improving it emerged.

4 DRMM is a weighting factor which adjusts the death rate in accordance with the level of material standard of living – MSL – which is itself related to the level of capital investment. Thus:

DEATH RATE = P DRN DRFM DRCM DRPM DRMM

where P is the level of population, DRN is a nominal value for crude death rate and DRFM, DRCM, DRPM are other weighting factors representing food consumption, crowding and pollution respectively.

5 For example they changed the level of capital that is devoted to agricultural production – by this means a high value of DRMM due to a low level of MSL may be compensated by increased food per capita.

6 Meadows and his project team did acknowledge though that if the 1940 values were entered with extreme accuracy (in error by less than 0.001%) then the model would backcast over limited ranges. However, they further noted that the approximation errors in the computer simulation language used with system dynamics models – *Dynamo* – were of the same order of magnitude.

7 World 2, however, contained neither delays nor stochastic processes.

8 They have shown that a confluence of histories does not occur. To do this they computed a series of different model trajectories between 1880 and 1900 based upon a well-distributed set of starting values near to the 1880 values derived from the SPRU backcast. They found that 'no other nearby histories came close to matching Forrester's model at 1900'.

9 Lakatos's account too was a rational reconstruction, but in his case the conjectures and proofs advocated by the disputants were more explicitly stated – though precisely what was meant by them was not.

10 All of the assumptions implied by the referent system are considered subconjectures within the 'proof'. The model in the simulation is discrete and approximates to the real and referent systems which are of course continuous; there is no analytical solution for the referent system, hence the need for simulation.

Chapter 8   Urban Dynamics: Knowledge for Social Policy

1 For example, see: D. Bell (1961) *The End of Ideology* (New York: The Free Press). For further information and a critique of this position see: J. Habermas (1971) Technology and Science as 'Ideology', in *Towards a Rational Society* (London: Heinemann Educational Books Ltd.), 81–122; R. Boguslaw (1965) *The New Utopians* (Englewood Cliffs, New Jersey: Prentice-Hall Inc.). Habermas, for example, states: 'Marx, to be sure, viewed the problem of making history with will and consciousness as one of the *practical* mastery of previously ungoverned processes of social development. Others, however, have understood it as a *technical* problem. They want to bring society under control in the same way as nature by reconstructing it according to the pattern of self-regulated systems of purposive-rational action and adaptive behaviour.' (1971: 116–17).

2 The authors argue that there are several key similarities between *Urban Dynamics* and the outlook and policy conclusions of E. C. Banfield's (1970) *The Unheavenly City* (Boston: Little, Brown and Co.). Banfield's book is sociological in style, unlike Forrester's technical approach; however, Averch and Levine argue that the two books are notably conservative in their conclusions and that they share similar assumptions about lower-class people.

3 'For example, there has been considerable discussion in New York of limiting

population inflows. . . . An early approach suggested by Governor Nelson A. Rockefeller's office would mandate that big city immigrants who cannot find or afford adequate and safe housing would be denied welfare benefits and urged to return from whence they came. . . . Although there has been little or no mention of Forrester's Urban Dynamics research in these policy discussions, there does seem to be a growing feeling amongst a number of urban scholars and public policymakers that the urban crisis requires a limitation on underemployed's immigration to large cities' (Whithed, 1972: 170–3).

4   For examples of relevant texts see: L. E. Alfeld, A. K. Graham (1976) *Introduction to Urban Dynamics* (Cambridge, Mass.: MIT Press); J. W. Forrester (1968) *Principles of Systems* (Cambridge, Mass.: Wright-Allen Press Inc.); J. M. Lyneis (1980) *Corporate Planning and Policy Design* (Cambridge, Mass.: MIT Press); A. L. Pugh III (1976) *Dynamo User's Manual* (Cambridge, Mass.: MIT Press); J. Randers (ed.) (1980) *Elements of the System Dynamics Method* (Cambridge, Mass.: MIT Press); G. P. Richardson, A. L. Pugh III (1981) *Introduction to System Dynamics Modeling with Dynamo* (Cambridge, Mass.: MIT Press); E. B. Roberts (1978) *Managerial Applications of System Dynamics* (Cambridge, Mass.: MIT Press).

Bibliography

Adorno, T. W. (1974a) Theses Against Occultism, *Telos*, 19, 7–12.

Adorno, T. W. (1974b) The Stars Down to Earth: The Los Angeles Times Astrology Column, *Telos*, 19, 13–90.

Alfeld, L. E. and Graham, A. K. (1976) *Introduction to Urban Dynamics* (Cambridge, Mass.: MIT Press)

Alfeld, L. and Meadows, D. (1972) A Systems Approach to Urban Revival. In M. Mesarovic and A. Reisman (eds), *Systems Approach and the City* (Amsterdam: North-Holland Publishing Co.), 143–68.

Allaby, M. (1971) *The Eco-activists* (London: Charles Knight and Co. Ltd)

Ansoff, H. I. and Slevin, D. P. L. (1968) An appreciation of industrial dynamics, *Management Science*, 14(7), 383–97.

Averch, H. and Levine, R. A. (1971) Two Models of the Urban Crisis: An Analytical Essay on Banfield and Forrester, *Policy Sciences*, 2(2), 143–58.

Banfield, E. C. (1970) *The Unheavenly City* (Boston: Little, Brown and Co.)

Barkun, M. (1974) *Disaster and the Millennium* (New Haven, Conn.: Yale University Press)

Barnes, B. (1973) The Comparison of Belief-Systems: Anomaly Versus Falsehood. In R. Horton and R. Finnegan (eds), *Modes of Thought* (London: Faber and Faber), 182–98.

——(1974) *Scientific Knowledge and Sociological Theory* (London: Routledge and Kegan Paul Ltd.)

——(1977) *Interests and the Growth of Knowledge* London:(Routledge and Kegan Paul Ltd)

——(1981) On the 'Hows' and 'Whys' of Cultural Change (Response to Woolgar), *Social Studies of Science*, 11, 481–98.

——(1983) On the Conventional Character of Knowledge and Cognition. In K. D. Knorr-Cetina and M. Mulkay (eds), *Science Observed* (London: Sage Publications Inc.), 19–52.

Barnes, B. and Shapin, S. (1977) Where is the Edge of Objectivity?, *British Journal for the History and Philosophy of Science*, X, 61–7.

Belkin, J. (1972) *Urban Dynamics*: Applications as a Teaching Tool and as an Urban Game, *IEEE Transactions on Systems, Man, and Cybernetics*, SMC-2(2), 166–9.

Bell, D. (1961) *The End of Ideology* (New York: The Free Press)

Berlinski, D. J. (1970) Systems Analysis, *Urban Affairs Quarterly*, Sep. 104–26.

Bernstein, B. (1971) *Class, Codes and Control. Theoretical Studies Towards a Sociology of Language*, Volume 1 (London: Routledge and Kegan Paul Ltd)

Bloor, C. and Bloor, D. (1982) Twenty Industrial Scientists: A Preliminary Exercise. In M. Douglas (ed.), *Essays in the Sociology of Perception* (London: Routledge and Kegan Paul Ltd), 83–102.

Bloor, D. (1976) *Knowledge and Social Imagery* (London: Routledge and Kegan Paul Ltd)

——(1978) Polyhedra and the Abominations of Leviticus, *British Journal of the History of Science*, 11, 245–72.

——(1981) The Strengths of the Strong Programme, *Philosophy of the Social Sciences*, 11(2), 199–213.

——(1982) Durkheim and Mauss Revisited: classification and the sociology of knowledge, *Studies in the History and Philosophy of Science*, 13(4), 267–97.

Boguslaw, R. (1965) *The New Utopians* (Englewood Cliffs, N.J.: Prentice-Hall Inc.)

Boyd, R. (1972) World Dynamics: A Note, *Science*, 177 (11 Aug.), 516–19.

Bray, J. (1972a) A Model of Doom, *Nature*, 238 (14 Jun.), 112.

——(1972b) The Politics of the Environment, *Fabian Tract*, 412 (April).

Brewer, G. (1973) *Politicians, Bureaucrats and the Consultant* (New York: Basic Books)

Brewer, J. W. (1975) Backcasting, *Simulation*, 26 (March), 90.

Briggs, A. (1964) Drawing a New Map of Learning. In D. Daiches (ed.), *The Idea of a New University* (London: André Deutsch)

Britting, K. R. (1976) Backward Integration Tests of System Dynamics Models – a Useful Validation Test? In C. W. Churchman and R. O. Mason (eds), *World Modeling: A Dialogue* (Amsterdam: North-Holland Publishing Co.), 141–9.

Buckley, W. (1967) *Sociology and Modern Systems Theory* (Englewood Cliffs, N.J.: Prentice-Hall Inc.)

Burke, F. E. (1973) Ignorance about Limitations to Growth, *Nature*, 246 (23 Nov.), 226–30.

Burns, J. R. and Malone, D. W. (1974) Optimization Techniques Applied to the Forrester Model of the World, *IEEE Transactions on Systems, Man and Cybernetics*, SMC 4(2), 164–71.

Campbell, D. T. (1975) 'Degrees of Freedom' And The Case Study, *Comparative Political Studies*, 8(2) (July), 178–93.

Caneva, K. L. (1981) What Should We Do With the Monster? Electromagnetism and the Psychosociology of Knowledge. In E. Mendelsohn and Y. Elkana (eds), *Sciences and Cultures*, Sociology of Sciences, Volume V (Dordrecht: Reidel Publishing Co.), 101–31.

Castells, M. (1977) *The Urban Question* (London: Edward Arnold)

Checkland, P. (1982) *Systems Thinking, Systems Practice* (Chichester: J. Wiley and Sons)

Clark, J. A., Cole, H. S. D., Curnow, R. and Hopkins, M. (1975) *Global Simulation Models* (London: J. Wiley and Sons)

Cohn, N. (1970) *The Pursuit of the Millennium* (London: Paladin)

Cole, H. S. D., Freeman, C., Jahoda, M. and Pravitt, K. L. R. (eds) (1973) *Thinking About the Future* (London: Chatto & Windus/Sussex University Press)

Cole, H. S. D. and Curnow, R. C. (1973a) An evaluation of the world models. In H. S. D. Cole et al. (eds), *Thinking About the Future* (London: Chatto & Windus/Sussex University Press), 108–134.

Cole, H. S. D. and Curnow, R. C. (1973b) 'Backcasting' with the World Dynamics Models, *Nature*, 243 (11 May), 63–5.

Commoner, B. (1971) *The Closing Circle* (London: Jonathan Cape Ltd)

Conant, J. B. (1961) *Slums and Suburbs* (New York: McGraw-Hill)

Cotgrove, S. (1975) Environmentalism and Utopia, *The Sociological Review*, 24, 23–42.

Cotgrove, S. and Duff, A. (1980) Environmentalism, Middle-class Radicalism and Politics, *The Sociological Review*, 28(2), 333–51.

Crenson, M. A. (1971) *The Un-politics of Air Pollution* (Baltimore: Johns Hopkins Press)

Cuypers, J. G. M. (1973) World dynamics: Two Simplified Versions of Forresters's model, *Automatica*, 9, 399–401.

Dahrendorf, R. (1967) Out of Utopia: Toward a Re-orientation of Sociological Analysis. In N. J. Demerath and R. A. Peterson (eds), *System, Change and Conflict: a reader on contemporary sociological theory and the debate over functionalism* (New York: The Free Press)

Deutsch, S. E. (1971) Review Symposium, *American Journal of Sociology*, 36, 321–6.

Douglas, M. (1966) *Purity and Danger* (London: Routledge and Kegan Paul Ltd)

——(1973) *Natural Symbols* (Harmondsworth: Penguin Books Ltd)

——(1975) *Implicit Meanings* (London: Routledge and Kegan Paul Ltd)

——(1978) *Cultural Bias* (Royal Anthropological Institute Occasional Paper 35)

——(ed.) (1982) *Essays in the Sociology of Perception* (London: Routledge and Kegan Paul Ltd)

Douglas, M. and Wildavski, A. (1982) *Risk and Culture* (Berkeley: University of California Press)

Durkheim, E. (1964) *The Elementary Forms of the Religious Life* (London: Allen and Unwin Ltd)

Durkheim, E. and Mauss, M. (1963) *Primitive Classification* (London: Cohen and West)

Dynamics of Science (1982) Volumes I and II (Rijksuniversiteit Groningen/ Technische Hogeschoole Twente, The Netherlands)

Economist (The) (1972) 242 (11 Mar.), 20.

Elias, N. (1971a) Sociology of Knowledge: New Perspectives, Part One, *Sociology*, 5, 149–168.

——(1971b) Sociology of Knowledge: New Perspectives, Part Two, *Sociology*, 5, 355–70.

——(1978a) *What is Sociology?* (London: Hutchinson University Library)

——(1978b) *The Civilizing Process*. Volume One – *The History of Manners* (Oxford: Blackwell)

——(1982) *The Civilizing Process*. Volume Two – *State Formation and Civilization* (Oxford: Blackwell)

Enzensberger, H. M. (1974) A Critique of Political Ecology, *New Left Review*, 84, 3–31.

Erickson, S. A. and Pikul, R. A. (1976) Backcasting Global Models: A Resolution of the Controversy, *IEEE Transactions on Systems, Man and Cybernetics*, SMC 6(9), 648–50.

Evans-Pritchard, E. E. (1940) *The Nuer* (Oxford: Oxford University Press)

Feyerabend, P. B. (1975) Imre Lakatos, *British Journal for the Philosophy of Science*, 26, 1–18.

Fleck, L. (1979) *Genesis and Development of a Scientific Fact* (Chicago: University of Chicago Press)

Fleisher, A. (1971) Urban Dynamics, *Journal of the American Institute of Planners*, XXXVII(1), 53–4.

Forrester, J. W. (1961) *Industrial Dynamics* (Cambridge, Mass.: MIT Press)

——(1968) *Principles of Systems* (Cambridge, Mass.: Wright-Allen Press Inc.)

——(1969) *Urban Dynamics* (Cambridge, Mass.: MIT Press)

——(1971) *World Dynamics* (Cambridge, Mass.: MIT Press)

——(1973) The Fledgling Cheermonger, *Cambridge Review*, 2 (Feb.), 70–3.

——(1975a) Dynamics of Socio-Economic Systems, *Proceedings of the Sixth IFAC World Congress*, Part 3 (Boston, Mass., 24–30 Aug.), 1–8.

——(1975b) *Collected Papers of Jay W. Forrester* (Cambridge, Mass.: MIT Press)

——(1976a) Educational Implications of Responses to System Dynamics Models. In C. W. Churchman and R. O. Mason (eds), *World Modeling: A Dialogue* (Amsterdam: North-Holland Publishing Co.), 27–35.

——(1976b) Business Structure, Economic Cycles, and National Policy, *Futures* (June), 195–214.

——(1976c) The System Dynamics National Model: Understanding Socio-Economic Behavior and Policy Alternatives, *Technological Forecasting and Social Change*, 51–68.

——(1981) Innovation and Economic Change, *Futures*, (Aug.), 3, 23–31.

——(1982) Global Modelling Revisited *Futures*, (Apr.), 95–110.

Forrester, N. B. (1973) *The Life Cycle of Economic Development* (Cambridge, Mass.: Wright-Allen Press Inc.)

Foucault, M. (1972) *The Archaeology of Knowledge* (London: Tavistock Publications Ltd)

Freeman, C. (1971) Technical Assessment and Its Social Context *Studium Generale*, 24, 1038–50.

——(1973) Malthus with a Computer. In H.S.D. Cole et al. (eds), *Thinking About the Future* (London: Chatto & Windus/Sussex University Press), 5–13.

——(1974) The Luxury of Despair, *Futures*, (Dec.), 450–62.

Friedrichs, R. W. (1970) *A Sociology of Sociology* (New York: The Free Press)

Gaines, T. (1972) The Doomsday Debate, *Manufacturers Hanover Trust Economic Report* (March).

Galtung, J. (1973) 'The Limits to Growth' and Class Politics, *Journal of Peace Research*, 12, 101–14.

Gans, H. J. (1967) The Failure of Urban Renewal: A Critique and some Proposals. In J. Bellush, and M. Hausknetch (eds), *Urban Renewal: People, Politics and Planning* (New York: Anchor)

Gillette, R. (1972) The Limits to Growth: Hard Sell for a Computer View of Doomsday, *Science*, 175 (10 Mar.), 1088–92.

Goldsmith, E. (1970) Bringing Order to Chaos, *The Ecologist*, 1, 20–3.

——(1972) Scientific Myopia, *The Ecologist*, 2(4), 3.

——(1974) The Ecology of War, *The Ecologist*, 4(4), 124–35.

Goldsmith, E., Allen, R., Allaby, M., Davoll, J. and Lawrence, S. A. (1972) Blueprint for Survival, *The Ecologist*, 2(1), 1–43.

Golub, R. and Townsend, J. (1977) Malthus, Multinationals and the Club of Rome, *Social Studies of Science*, 7, 201–22.

Gouldner, A. W. (1971) *The Coming Crisis of Western Sociology* (London: Heinemann Educational Books Ltd)

——(1975) *For Sociology* (Harmondsworth: Penguin Books Ltd.)

Gourlay, A. R., McLean, M. and Shepherd, P. (1977) Identification and Analysis of the Subsystem Structure of Models, *Applied Mathematical Modelling*, 1 (June), 245–52.

Greenberger, M., Crenson, M. A. and Crissey, B. (1976) *Models in the Policy Process* (New York: Russell Sage Foundation)

Guedon, J. C. (1977) Michel Foucault: The Knowledge of Power and the Power of Knowledge, *Bulletin of the History of Medicine*, 51, 245–77.

Habermas, J. (1976) *Legitimation Crisis* (London: Heinemann Educational Books Ltd)

Habermas, J. (1971) Technology and Science as 'Ideology'. In *Towards a Rational Society* (London: Heinemann Educational Books Ltd), 81–122.

Hampton, J. (1982) Giving the Grid/Group Dimensions an Operational Definition. In M. Douglas (ed), *Essays in the Sociology of Perception* (London: Routledge and Kegan Paul Ltd), 64–82.

Hardin, G. (1968) The Tragedy of the Commons, *Science*, 162 (13 Dec.), 1243–48.

Hardin, G. (1972) We Live on a Spaceship, *Bulletin of the Atomic Scientist*, XXVIII(9) (Nov.), 23–5.

Harwood, J. (1979) Heredity, Environment, and the Legitimation of Social Policy. In B. Barnes and S. Shapin (eds), *Natural Order* (Beverly Hills, California: Sage Publications Inc.), 231–51.

Heilbroner, R. (1974) *An Inquiry into the Human Prospect* (New York: W. W. Norton)

Herrera, A. O., Scolnik, H. D., Chichilnisky, G., Gallopin, G. C., Hardoy, J. E., Mosovich, D., Oteiza, E., de Romero Brest, G. L., Suarez, C. E. and Talavera, L. (1976) *Catastrophe or New Society?* (Ottawa: International Development Research Centre)

Herzog, A. (1963) Report on a 'Think Factory', *New York Times Magazine*, (10 Nov.), 30–46.

Horton, R. (1971) African Traditional Thought and Western Science. In M. F. D. Young (ed), *Knowledge and Control: New Directions for the Sociology of Education* (London: Collier-Macmillan), 208–66.

Jahoda, M. (1973) Postscript on social change. In H. S. D. Cole et al. (eds), *Thinking About the Future* (London: Chatto & Windus/Sussex University Press), 209–15.

Jongh, D. C. J. de (1978) Structural parameter sensitivity of 'the limits to growth' World Model, *Applied Mathematical Modelling*, 2 (June), 77–80.

Kahn, H. and Wiener, J. J. (1967) *The Year 2000* (London: Macmillan Co.)

Kahn, H., Brown, W. and Martel, L. (1977) *The Next 200 Years* (London: Associated Business Programmes Ltd)

Kearney, M. (1975) World View Theory and Study, *Annual Review of Anthropology*, 4, 247–70.

King, A. (1974) The Club of Rome Today, *Simulation in the Service of Society*, 4(8), 1–7.

King, A. (1981) The Club of Rome and its Policy Impact. In W. M. Evan (ed), *Knowledge and Power in a Global Society* (Beverly Hills, Calif.: Sage Publications Inc.), 205–24.

King, M. D. (1971) Reason, Tradition and the Progressiveness of Science, *History and Theory*, 10(1), 3–32.

Knorr-Cetina, K. D. and Mulkay, M. (eds) (1983) *Science Observed* (London: Sage Publications Inc)

Krueckeberg, D. A. (1969) Urban Dynamics, *Journal of the American Institute of Planners*, XXXV(5), 353.

Kuhn, T. S. (1970) *The Structure of Scientific Revolutions*, Second edition. (Chicago: University of Chicago Press)

——(1976) Theory Change as Structure-Change: Comments on the Sneed Formalism, *Erkenntnis*, 10, 179–99.

——(1977) Logic of Discovery or Psychology of Research. In *The Essential Tension* (Chicago: University of Chicago Press), 266–92.

Ladd, Jr, E. C. and Lipset, S. M. (1972) Politics of Academic Natural Scientists and Engineers, *Science*, 176(4039) (9 June), 1091–1100.

——(1975) *The Divided Academy* (New York: McGraw-Hill)

Lakatos, I. (1970) Falsification and the Methodology of Scientific Research Programmes. In I. Lakatos and A. Musgrave (eds), *Criticism and the Growth of Knowledge* (Cambridge: Cambridge University Press), 91–195.

——(1976) *Proofs and Refutations* (Cambridge: Cambridge University Press)

Latour, B. (1983) Give Me a Laboratory and I will Raise the World. In K. D. Knorr-Cetina and M. Mulkay (eds), *Science Observed* (London: Sage Publications Inc.), 141–70.

Latour, B. and Woolgar, S. (1979) *Laboratory Life* (Beverly Hills, Calif.: Sage Publications Inc.)

Laudan, L. (1981) The Pseudo-Science of Science, *Philosophy of the Social Sciences*, 11(2), 173–98.

Lee, Jr, D. B. (1973) Requiem for large-scale models, *Journal of the American Institute of Planners*, May, 163–178.

Lewin, K. (1951) *Field Theory in Social Science* (New York: Harper and Row)

Lijphart, A. (1971) Comparative Politics and the Comparative Method, *The American Political Science Review*, 65 (Sept.), 682–93.

——(1975) The Comparable-cases Strategy in Comparative Research, *Comparative Political Studies*, 8(2), (July), 158–77.

Lilienfeld, R. (1975) Systems Theory as Ideology, *Social Research*, 42 (4), 637–60.

——(1978) *The Rise of Systems Theory: An Ideological Analysis* (New York: J. Wiley & Sons.)

Lipset, S. M. and Ladd, Jr, E. C. (1972) The Politics of American Sociologists, *American Journal of Sociology*, 78, 67–104.

Lockwood, D. (1956) Some Remarks on 'The Social System', *British Journal of Sociology*, VII, 134–46.

Lowe, P. and Worboys, M. (1978) Ecology and the End of Ideology, *Antipode*, 10(2), 12–21.

Lyneis, J. M. (1980) *Corporate Planning and Policy Design A System Dynamics Approach* (Cambridge, Mass.: MIT Press)

Malthus, R. (1830/1958) *Essay on the Principle of Population* (London: Dent)

Mannheim, K. (1936) *Ideology and Utopia* (London: Routledge and Kegan Paul Ltd)

——(1968) On the Interpretation of Weltanschauung. In *Essays in the Sociology of Knowledge* (London: Routledge and Kegan Paul Ltd), 33–83.

Marstrand, P. K. and Pavitt, K. L. R. (1973) The agricultural sub-system. In H. S. D. Cole et al. (eds), *Thinking About the Future* (London: Chatto & Windus/Sussex University Press), 56–65.

Marstrand, P. K. and Sinclair, T. C. (1973) The pollution sub-system. In H. S. D. Cole et al. (eds), *Thinking About the Future* (London: Chatto & Windus/Sussex University Press), 80–9.

Marx, K. (1979) Preface to a Contribution to a Critique of Political Economy. In T. B. Bottomore and M. Rubel (eds), *Karl Marx Selected Writings in Sociology and Social Philosophy* (Harmondsworth: Penguin Books Ltd)

Mass, N. (ed) (1974) *Readings in Urban Dynamics, Volume 1* (Cambridge, Mass.: Wright-Allen Press Inc.)

Mazzeo, J. A. (1978) *Varieties of Interpretation* (Notre Dame, Ind.: University of Notre Dame Press)

Meadows, D. L. (1971) *Project on the Predicament of Mankind* (Cambridge, Mass.: MIT Press)

Meadows, D. L. (1973) Introduction to the Project. In D. L. Meadows and D. H. Meadows (eds), *Toward Global Equilibrium* (Cambridge, Mass.: Wright-Allen Press Inc.), 31–45.

Meadows, D. H., Meadows, D. L., Randers, J. and Behrens III, W. W. (1972) *The Limits to Growth* (New York: Universe Books)

——(1973) A Response to Sussex, *Futures*, 5(1), (Feb.), 135–52.

Meadows, D. L., Behrens III, W. W., Meadows, D. H., Naill, R. F., Randers, J. and Zahn, E. K. O. (1974) *Dynamics of Growth in a Finite World* (Cambridge, Mass.: Wright-Allen Press Inc.)

Meier, R. L. (1951) The Origins of the Scientific Species, *Bulletin of the Atomic Scientists*, 7 (June), 169–73.

Mercer, J. and Hultquist, J. (1976) National Progress Toward Housing and Urban Renewal. In J. S. Adams (ed.), *Urban Policymaking and Metropolitan Dynamics* (Cambridge, Mass.: Ballinger), 101–62.

Meynell, H. (1977) On the Limits of the Sociology of Knowledge, *Social Studies of Science*, 7, 480–500.

Mills, C. W. (1970) *The Sociological Imagination* (Harmondsworth: Penguin Books Ltd)

Millstone, E. (1977) A Framework for the Sociology of Knowledge, *Social Studies of Science*, 7, 111–25.

MIT (1949) *Report of the Committee on Educaion Survey to the Faculty MIT* (Cambridge, Mass.: Technology Press)

Mitroff, I. and Turoff, M. (1973) Technological Forecasting and Assessment: Science and/or Mythology, *Technological Forecasting and Social Change*, 5, 113–34.

Mulkay, M. (1980) Sociology of Science in the West, *Current Sociology*, 28(3) (Winter), 1–184.

Mulkay, M., Potter, J. and Yearley, S. (1983) Why an Analysis of Scientific Discourse is Needed. In K. D. Knorr-Cetina and M. Mulkay (eds), *Science Observed* (London: Sage Publications Inc.), 171–203.

Nature (1972), 236 (10 Mar.), 47–9.

Neuhaus, R. (1971) *In Defense of People: Ecology and the Seduction of Radicalism* (New York: Macmillan)

Noble, F. (1977) *America by Design* (Oxford: Oxford University Press)

Nordhaus, W. D. (1973) World Dynamics: Measurement without Data, *Economic Journal*, 83(332), 1156–83.

Nunn, J. H. (1979) MIT: A University's Contribution to National Defense, *Journal of Military Affairs*, 43(3), 120–5.

Open University (1979) *Language and Social Class. E202 Schooling and Society, Unit 23, Block IV* (Milton Keynes: The Open University Press)

Ophuls, W. (1973) Leviathan or Oblivion?. In H. E. Daly (ed.), *Toward a Steady-State Economy* (San Francisco: W. H. Freeman & Co.), 215–30.

O'Riordan, T. (1976) *Environmentalism* (London: Pion Ltd)

Page, R. W. (1973) Non-renewable resources sub-system. In H. S. D. Cole et al. (eds), *Thinking About the Future* (London: Chatto & Windus/Sussex University Press), 33–42.

Parlett, M. (1969) Undergraduate Teaching Observed, *Nature*, 233 (13 Sept.), 1102–4.

Parsons, T. (1937) *The Structure of Social Action* (New York: McGraw-Hill)
——(1951) *The Social System* (London: Routledge and Kegan Paul Ltd)
——(1970) On Building Social System theory: A Personal History, *Daedalus*, 99, 826–81.

Peccei, A. (1969) *The Chasm Ahead* (London: Macmillan Co.)
——(1973) The New Threshold, *Simulation*, 20(6), 199–206.
——(1982) Global Modelling for Humanity, *Futures*, (April), 91–4.

Pimm, D. (1980) Why the History and Philosophy of Mathematics Should Not Be Rated X, *ICME-IV Congress* (Berkeley)

Popper, K. (1959) *The Logic of Scientific Discovery* (London: Hutchinson)

Pugh III, A. L. (1976) *Dynamo Users Manual* (Cambridge, Mass.: MIT Press)

Randers, J. (ed.) (1980) *Elements of the System Dynamics Method* (Cambridge, Mass.: MIT Press)

Rayner, S. (1982) The Perception of Time and Space in Egalitarian Sects: A Millenarian Cosmology. In M. Douglas (ed.), *Essays in the Sociology of Perception* (London: Routledge and Kegan Paul Ltd), 247–74.

Redmond, K. C. and Smith, T. M. (1980) *Project Whirlwind* (Bedford, Mass.: Digital Press)

Richardson, G. P. and Pugh III, A. L. (1981) *Introduction to System Dynamics Modeling with Dynamo* (Cambridge, Mass.: Wright-Allen Press Inc.)

Richardson, Jr, J.M. (1978) Global Modelling I, *Futures*, (Oct.), 386–404.

Riesman, D. (1980) *On Higher Education* (San Francisco: Jossey–Bass)

——(1966) Notes on New Universities: British and American, *Universities Quarterly*, 20, 128–46.

Roberts, E.B. (1978) *Managerial Applications of System Dynamics* (Cambridge, Mass.: MIT Press)

Rochberg, R. (1971) Some questionable assumptions in the model and method of urban dynamics. *Second Annual Pittsburgh Conference on Modelling and Simulation*, March 29–30 (University of Pittsburgh, Pennsylvania), 153–7.

Rosaldo, R. (1976/7) *American Journal of Sociology*, 82, 1152–6.

Rudwick, M. (1982) Cognitive Styles in Geology. In M. Douglas (ed.), *Essays in the Sociology of Perception* (London: Routledge and Kegan Paul Ltd.), 219–41.

Sahin, K. E. (1979) System Dynamics Models: Some Obscurities, *IEEE Transactions on Systems, Man and Cybernetics*, SMC-9(2), 91–3.

Sanbach, F. (1978) The rise and fall of the Limits to Growth debate, *Social Studies of Science*, 8, 495–520.

——(1980) *Ideology and Policy* (Oxford: Blackwell)

Schall, W. C. (1962) Industrial Dynamics Proves Out for One Firm, *Instrument Society of America Journal*, (Sept.).

Schroeder, W., Alfeld, L. and Sweezey, R. (1975) *Readings in Urban Dynamics, Volume 2* (Cambridge, Mass.: Wright-Allen Press Inc.)

Science, (1972) 175(4027) (17 Mar.), 1197.

Science Policy Research Unit (1967) *Annual Report 1967* (Brighton: University of Sussex)

——(1975) *Annual Report and Ten Year Review 1975* (Brighton: University of Sussex)

——(1976) *Annual Report 1976* (Brighton: University of Sussex)

——(1977) *Annual Report 1977* (Brighton: University of Sussex)

Shapin, S. (1979) Homo Phrenologicus: Anthropological Perspectives on an Historical Problem. In B. Barnes and S. Shapin (eds), *Natural Order* (Beverly Hills, Calif.: Sage Publications Inc.), 41–71.

——(1982) History of Science and its Sociological Reconstructions, *History of Science*, XX, 157–211.

Shepard, H. A. (1952) The Engineer and his Culture, *Explorations in Entrepreneurial History*, 41(May), Series 1, 211–19.

Siebker, M. and Kaya, T. (1974) Toward a Global Vision of Human Problems, *Technological Forecasting and Social Change*, 6, 231–60.

Sills, D. (1975) The Environmental Movement and its Critics, *Human Ecology*, 3(1), 1–41.

Simmons, H. (1973) System Dynamics and Technocracy. In H. S. D. Cole et al. (eds), *Thinking About the Future* (London: Chatto & Windus/Sussex University Press), 192–208.

Simonds, A. (1978) *Karl Mannheim's Sociology of Knowledge* (Oxford: Clarendon Press)

Singeltary, O. A. (ed.) (1968) *American Universities and Colleges* (Washington, D.C.: American Council on Education)

Smith, B. L. R. (1966) *The Rand Corporation* (Cambridge, Mass.: Harvard University Press)

Snyder, B. R. (1970) *The Hidden Curriculum* (Cambridge, Mass.: MIT Press)

Soderberg, C. R. (1965) The American Engineer. In K. S. Lynn (ed), *The Professions in America* (Boston: Houghton Mifflin Co.)

Solow, R. N. (1972) Notes on Doomsday Models, *Proceedings of the National Academy of Sciences U.S.A.*, 69(12), 3832–33.

Spurgeon, D. (1976) Modelling the World Again, *Nature*, 262, (22 July), 246–7.

Stegmuller, W. (1976) *The Structure and Dynamics of Theories* (New York: Springer-Verlag New York Inc.)

Stonebraker, M. (1972) A Simplification of Forrester's Model of an Urban Area, *IEEE Transactions on Systems, Man and Cybernetics*, SMC-2(4), 468–72.

Sullivan, W. M. (1976) Prometheus Rebound: the new Ecological Conservatism, *Philosophy Today*, 20, 243–56.

Surrey, A. J. and Bromley, A. J. (1973) Energy resources. In H. S. D. Cole et al. (eds), *Thinking About the Future* (London: Chatto & Windus/Sussex University Press), 90–107.

Swanson, G. E. (1971) Review Symposium, *American Sociological Review*, 36, 317–21.

Thompson, M. (1982) A three dimensional model. In M. Douglas (ed.) *Essays in the Sociology of Perception* (London: Routledge and Kegan Paul Ltd), 31–63.

Towards Survival (1972) Issue 4 (15 Oct.).

University of Sussex (1982) *23rd Annual Report 1981–1982* (Brighton: University of Sussex)

Urry, J. (1972) More Notes on Sociology's Coming Crisis, *British Journal of Sociology*, 23, 246–48.

Vries, G. de and Harbers, H. (1985) Attuning Science to Culture. In T. Shinn and R. Whitley (eds), *Expository Science: Forms and Functions of Popularisation. Sociology of the Sciences*, Volume IX (Dordrecht: Reidel Publishing Co.), 103–17.

Walsh, D. (1972) Functionalism and Systems Theory. In P. Filmer (ed.), *New Directions in Sociological Theory* (London: Collier & Macmillan), 57–74.

Whithed, M. H. (1972) Urban Dynamics and Public Policy, *IEEE Transactions on Systems, Man and Cybernetics*, SMC-2(2), 170–3.

Williams, R. M. (1960) *American Society* (New York: Knoff)

Woolgar, S. (1981) Interests and Explanation in the Social Study of Science, *Social Studies of Science*, 11, 365–94.

Wright, R. D. (1976) Backward Integration Tests of Dynamic Models. In C. W. Churchman and R. O. Mason (eds), *World Modeling: A Dialogue* (Amsterdam: North-Holland Publishing Co.), 129–40.

Wright, R. D. (1973) Retrodictive Tests of Dynamic Models, *Proceedings of the Summer Computer Simulation Conference*, July (Montreal), 1085–93.

Wuthnow, R., Davison Hunter, J., Bergesen, A., and Kurzweil, E. (1984) *Cultural Analysis* (London: Routledge and Kegan Paul Ltd)

Wylie, F. E. (1975) *MIT in Perspective* (Boston: Little, Brown & Co.)

Zerubavel, E. (1979) *Patterns of Time in Hospital Life* (Chicago: University of Chicago Press)

Index